CULTURE
and
PERSONALITY

CULTURE

and

PERSONALITY

Edited by

S. Stansfeld Sargent

Department of Psychology

Barnard College, Columbia University

and

Marian W. Smith

Department of Anthropology, Columbia University

Proceedings of an Interdisciplinary Conference
held under auspices of the Viking Fund
November 7 and 8, 1947

COOPER SQUARE PUBLISHERS, INC.

New York, N. Y. 1974

Originally Published 1949 by The Viking Fund
Reprinted by Permission of the
Wenner-Gren Foundation for Anthropological Research
Published 1974 by Cooper Square Publishers, Inc.
59 Fourth Avenue, New York, New York 10003
International Standard Book Number 0-8154-0488-3
Library of Congress Catalog Card Number 73-76142

PRINTED IN THE UNITED STATES OF AMERICA
by SENTRY PRESS, NEW YORK, N. Y. 10013

PREFACE FOR THE 25th ANNIVERSARY EDITION

Exactly twenty-five years ago Marian Smith and I were going over the manuscripts and recordings of the 1947 Conference on Culture and Personality sponsored by the Viking Fund (shortly to be known as the Wenner-Gren Foundation). To those who attended, it had been a most stimulating gathering, and the decision was made to publish the proceedings so they could be shared with a larger audience.

A paperback edition of 2000 copies was distributed by the Viking Fund to its anthropologist members and to other interested social scientists. The supply was soon exhausted, and a second printing was run. The next year Basic Books arranged to reprint it in hard covers, thus reaching several thousand more readers. But the volume has been out of print since about 1956.

The Viking Fund symposium was the first interdisciplinary conference of well-known contributors to the newly emerging area of culture and personality. The books of Margaret Mead, Ruth Benedict, Abram Kardiner, Erich Fromm and others were becoming increasingly popular. Ralph Linton had published in 1945 "The Cultural Background of Personality", and two important books of readings appeared in 1948: Kluckhohn and Murray's "Personality in Nature, Society and Culture" and Haring's "Personal Character and Cultural Milieu". The Viking Fund symposium played its part in this development, and was referred to and quoted in many volumes on cultural anthropology, social psychology, and psychology of personality during the fifties and early sixties.

Sullivan, Linton, Kluckhohn and co-editor Marian Smith have died, but many of the remaining participants have continued to contribute to this significant area where cultural anthropology, social psychology, sociology and psychiatry overlap. The interdependence of culture and personality is now accepted. Interest among social scientists has shifted somewhat and become more specialized. For example, many research articles deal with personality and subcultures like ethnicity or social class. In 1968 the Journal of Social Issues had a whole number on "Personality and Politics". Recently there appeared the *Journal of Cross-Cultural Psychology,* and *Transcultural Psychiatric Research Review,* both of which are international as well as interdisciplinary in character.

Such changes in focus or emphasis are normal and signify growth. But sometimes it is fruitful to pause, look back and re-experience a time of enthusiastic awakening such as occurred with culture and personality in the period following World War II. Thanks are due to the Wenner-Gren Foundation for giving permission, and to the Cooper Square Publishers for reprinting the proceedings of the Viking Fund Conference.

S. STANSFELD SARGENT,
Community Mental Health Center,
Oxnard, California

TABLE OF CONTENTS

FOREWORD

Since the 1920's scholars and scientists have become increasingly interested in the effects of cultural forces upon the personalities of individual members of the culture group. While the major contributions have been made by anthropologists, a growing number of sociologists, social psychologists and psychiatrists have turned their attention to the problem.

There is great potential value in the efforts of specialists from different fields focussing on a common goal. Certain difficulties, however, are likely to occur—difficulties of communication as well as of the more obvious differing approaches and interpretations. These must be recognized and dealt with if we are to avoid confusion and misunderstanding. In the study of culture and personality we face several such confusions. What do we mean by "culture" and by "personality"? What field-work procedures should be used in our investigations? Can quantitative methods, such as tests and experimentation, be utilized advantageously? How valid and useful are psychoanalytical interpretations? Projective techniques? Biographical methods? How important are subcultural factors, like family, community and class, within the broader cultural pattern? What are the possibilities for future cooperative research efforts?

These are a few of the questions growing out of interdisciplinary collaboration in the study of culture and personality. It seemed important for representatives from several fields to meet and discuss such matters, so a small committee of anthropologists and psychologists* planned the present conference, held in New York on November 7 and 8, 1947, and attended by over a hundred interested persons from the Middle Atlantic States and New England. The papers and discussions do not give conclusive answers to the more puzzling questions, but many issues are dealt with pro-

*Drs. Walter Dyk, George Herzog, Charles Wagley, Clairette Armstrong, and S. Stansfeld Sargent.

v

ductively, and an advance has been made toward further inter-disciplinary understanding and cooperation.

The anthropologists, psychologists, psychiatrists and sociologists who participated in the conference focussed their attention upon four main problem areas:

"Culture" and "Personality"—Defining Our Terms

Techniques for Studying Culture and Personality

Evaluation of Studies

Integration for Future Studies.

Each paper is given in full, with selections from the discussion which followed it.

The editors and the conference committee wish to thank the participants in the conference for their wholehearted cooperation. The meetings and publication of the proceedings were made possible by the generous sponsorship of the Viking Fund. Gratitude is expressed particularly to Dr. Paul Fejos, Director of Research of the Viking Fund, and to Dr. Ralph Linton, Editor of Viking Fund publications. Thanks go also to Virginia M. Sargent for transcribing the wire recordings of the conference, and for helping edit the manuscript.

CULTURE AND PERSONALITY — DEFINING OUR TERMS

ERICH FROMM

Psychoanalytic Characterology and Its Application to the Understanding of Culture

Psychoanalytic characterology dates back to Freud's paper on "Character and Anal-Eroticism", published in 1908. This paper marks the shift of attention from the neurotic *symptom* to the neurotic *character*. Freud and his fellow workers became increasingly aware of the fact that any symptom was embedded in a person's character; hence that in order to understand and to cure a symptom one has to understand the total character structure. They proceeded from the analysis of the symptom to the analysis of the character. They were led to this shift of emphasis not only by theoretical considerations, but also by the fact that many patients did not complain about isolated symptoms like a washing compulsion, hysterical vomiting, claustrophobia, etc., but about character difficulties which prevented them from attaining inner security and happiness.

Freud's theory of character was composed of two different sets of assumptions and observations. One was that Freud became more and more impressed by the dynamic nature of character traits. He saw that character traits were not mere habits of behavior acquired by early training and easily shed when new patterns of culture emerged, but that they were *relatively permanent passionate strivings*, the "*forces* by which man is motivated", as Balzac defined character.

He recognized behind the rationalizations which made it appear as if the character was nothing but an adequate reaction to external necessities, the rigidity and tenacity of the character trait even if under changed circumstances the character trait becomes useless or even harmful; furthermore he understood the gratification and pleasure which, often unconsciously, resulted from behavior in accordance with the character traits.

The second premise on which Freud's characterology was built

1

was the assumption that all conative, passionate strivings, besides those of self preservation, have their roots in sexual, libidinous desires.

These two assumptions, (1) the passionate nature of character traits and (2) the sexual nature of passion result in a theoretical difficulty: How can one explain something as manifold and varied as character traits by the *one* factor, libido?

Freud bridged this contradiction by an ingenious and brilliant construction. He proceeded from his broad concept of sexuality which comprised all physical sensations connected with pleasure (particularly the oral and anal libido) and explained various character traits as sublimation of (or reaction formation against) the various kinds of pre-genital libido. The libido was assumed to develop from primitive pre-genital forms to the mature genital orientation and the various character orientations were explained as outcome of those different phases of libido development.

Environmental factors were not neglected in Freud's concept but their effect was explained entirely in terms of the libido theory. Freud assumed that by the child's experiences with the significant persons in his early life his libido is influenced and moulded in certain ways; thus that the character development is determined by the *impact of environmental influences on the libido*. Clearly in this view early experiences, feeding, toilet training, the various forms of maternal care are considered the most significant data for the theory of character.

An increasing number of anthropologists and psychoanalysts recognized the significance of psychoanalytic characterology for the understanding of the problems of culture. If the character structure determines action, feelings and thoughts of an individual it must be a key factor for the understanding of cultural and social phenomena which are, after all, the products of so many individuals.

In this attempt to apply the findings of psychoanalysis to the problem of culture three main approaches can be distinguished:

1) The orthodox Freudian approach.
2) The modified Freudian approach.
3) The socio-psychological approach.

(1) The assumption underlying the orthodox Freudian approach was that social phenomena and cultural patterns are to be

2

explained as direct outcomes of certain libidinal trends. Thus, for instance, capitalism was explained as a result of anal eroticism or war as the result of the operation of the death instinct. The method used here was that of explanation by analogy. One tried to discover analogies between cultural phenomena and neurotic symptoms of a patient and then proceeded to explain the cultural phenomenon as being "caused" by the same libidinous factors by which the neurotic symptom had been explained.[1] While this method has receded in the background as far as psychoanalysts themselves are concerned it has been taken up recently by psychiatrists who do not belong to the psychoanalytic school. One of the outstanding examples of this recent development is R. Brickner's "Are the Germans paranoid?" where a method of crude analogizing united with insufficient knowledge of factual data is used to prove the paranoid character of German culture.

(2) The modified Freudian approach represented in A. Kardiner's work[2] differs from the orthodox approach by paying serious attention to the available anthropological and social data and by studying methods of child training and their impact on the development of personality. But in spite of these merits Kardiner's approach has over the naive orthodox approach they are similar in important respects. Kardiner believes that "the basic personality" is moulded by various methods of child training and in turn moulds the social patterns and institutions. By childhood training he understands the impact of parental influence on those primitive physiological functions which Freud called "erogenous zones". Hence methods of nursing, toilet training, etc., are the paramount data for the understanding of culture.

That Kardiner's theory is essentially based on Freud's libido concept becomes particularly clear in one of his key concepts, that of maternal care. He explains differences in basic personality, hence in culture, by differences in maternal care. But while weaning and sphincter control are mentioned among the main characteristics of maternal care the concept of *love* is not even men-

---

[1]Cf. E. Fromm, "Die Entstehung des Christusdogmas", Psychoanalytischer Verlag, Wien, 1930, where I discussed the fallacy of this method.

[2]A. Kardiner, "The Individual and Its Society", Columbia University Press, New York, 1940, and "The Psychological Frontiers of Society", Columbia University Press, New York, 1945.

3

tioned. On the other hand we find "constancy of attention" mentioned without reference to the totality of the mother-child relationship. Quite obviously the constant attention of the loving mother has an entirely different meaning and impact from the constant attention of a possessive and dominating mother.

Kardiner considers certain socio-economic factors as causative for the development of the basic personality but unfortunately this emphasis is more apparent than real. He mentions, e.g. that in Alor women have to work in the fields and therefore do not give good maternal care to their children. Here a socio-economic factor is introduced but it is viewed only in its, as it were, technical effect on maternal care—constancy of feeding and attention. In a theory which is centered around the quality of interpersonal relatedness the most relevant datum would be that of the mother's attitude toward the child, i.e. her love, warmth, acceptance and so on; obviously the expression of love and warmth is not seriously interfered with by the mother's working in the fields just as the expression of possessiveness is not interfered with by regular nursing and "constancy of attention".

(3) The socio-psychological approach which has been suggested in my own writings[3] centers around the concept of the "social character". By social character I refer to the nucleus of the character structure which is shared by most members of the same culture in contradistinction to the *individual character* in which people belonging to the same culture differ from each other. The concept of the social character is not a statistical concept in the sense that it is the sum total of character traits to be found in the majority of people in a given culture. It can be understood only in reference to the function of the social character which we shall now proceed to discuss.

Each society is structuralized and operates in certain ways which are necessitated by a number of objective conditions; such

[3]"Ueber Methode und Aufgabe einer analytischen Sozialpsychologie" (On method and aim of analytic social psychology), and "Die psychoanalytische Characterologie und ihre Bedeutung fuer die Sozialpsychologie" (Psychoanalytic Characterology and its significance for Social Psychology), in Ztschft. f. Sozialforschung, Hirschfeld, Leipzig, 1932; "Escape from Freedom", Rinehart & Co., New York, 1941; "Man for Himself", Rinehart & Co., New York, 1947.

conditions are the methods of production and distribution which in turn depend on raw material, industrial techniques, climate, etc., furthermore political and geographical factors and cultural traditions and influences to which society is exposed. There is no "society" in general but only specific social structures which operate in different and ascertainable ways. Although these social structures do change in the course of historical development, they are relatively fixed at any given historical period and society can exist only by operating within the framework of its particular structure. The members of the society and/or the various classes or status groups within it have to behave in such a way as to be able to function in the sense required by society. It is the function of the social character to shape the energies of the members of society in such a way that their behavior is not left to conscious decisions whether or not to follow the social pattern but that *people want to act as they have to act* and at the same time find gratification in acting according to the requirements of the culture. In other words, the social character has the function of molding human energy for the purpose of the functioning of a given society.[4]

Modern, industrial society, for instance, could not have attained its ends had it not harnessed the energy of free men for work in an unprecedented degree. He had to be moulded into a person who was eager to spend most of his energy for the purpose of work, who acquired discipline, particularly orderliness and punctuality, to a degree unknown in most other cultures. It would not have sufficed if each individual had to make up his mind consciously every day that he wanted to work, to be on time, etc., since any such conscious deliberation would have led to many more exceptions than the smooth functioning of society can afford. Threat and force would not have sufficed either as motive for work since the highly differentiated work in modern industrial society can only be the work of free men and not of forced labor. The *necessity* for work, for punctuality and orderliness had to be transformed into a *drive* for these qualities. This means that

---

[4]There are essential points in common between this concept and Ralph Linton's Concept of the "status personality".

society had to produce such a social character in which these strivings were inherent.

The *genesis* of the social character cannot be understood by referring to one single cause but by understanding the interaction of economic, ideological and sociological factors. Inasmuch as the political and economical factors are less easily changeable they have a certain predominance in this interplay. However, religious, political and philosophical ideas are not only projective systems. While they are rooted in the social character they in turn also determine the social character, and particularly systematize and stabilize it. Basic human needs rooted in the nature of man play also an active role in this interplay. While it is true that man can adapt himself to almost any condition, he is not a blank sheet of paper on which culture writes its text. Needs inherent in his nature like the striving for happiness, for harmony, for love, for freedom are dynamic factors in the historical process which when frustrated give rise to psychic reactions which in the long run tend to create conditions which are better suited for these basic human needs. As long as the objective conditions of the society and the culture remain stable, the social character has a predominately stabilizing function. If the external conditions change in such a way that they do not fit any more with the tradition and social character, a *lag* arises which often makes the character function as an element of disintegration instead of stabilization, as dynamite instead of a social mortar, as it were.

Provided this concept of the genesis and function of the social character is correct we are confronted with a puzzling problem. Is not the assumption that the character structure is molded by the role which the individual has to play in his culture contradicted by the assumption that a person's character is molded in his childhood? Can both views pretend to be true in view of the fact that the child in his early years of life has comparatively little contact with society as such? This question is not as difficult to answer as it may seem at first glance. We must differentiate between the factors which are responsible for the particular *contents* of the social character and the *methods* by which the social character is produced. The structure of society and the task of the individual in the social structure may be considered to be the cause of the social character. The family on the other hand may

6

be considered to be the *psychic agency of society*, the institution which has the function of transmitting the requirements of society to the growing child. The family fulfills this function in two ways. First, and this is the most important factor, by the influence the character of the parents has on the character formation of the growing child. Since the character of most parents is an expression of the social character, they transmit in this way the essential features of the socially desirable character structure to the child. The parents' love and happiness are communicated to the child just as their anxiety or hostility. In addition to the character of the parents the methods of childhood training which are customary in a culture also have the function to mould the character of the child in a socially desirable direction. But indeed there are various methods and techniques of child training which can fulfill the same end, and on the other hand there can be methods which seem to be identical and which nevertheless are different because of the character structure of those who practice these methods. By focusing on methods of child training we can never explain the social character. Methods of child training are significant only as a mechanism of transmission and they can be understood correctly only if we understand first what kinds of personalities are desirable and necessary in any given culture.

This application of psychoanalysis to culture is greatly furthered by a revision of Freud's libido theory. If character formation is caused by the impact of environment on the development of pre-genital sexuality then indeed the methods of childhood training are the prima causa of the social character. A theory however which sees the character molded by the kind of interpersonal relationship as it exists and must exist in a given social structure must be, to use H. S. Sullivan's term, a theory of *interpersonal relationship*.

Freud's concept of man was in accordance with nineteenth century materialism. He saw the individual as an isolated entity, endowed with certain drives rooted in his inner chemistry. The theory of interpersonal relationship is relational; it explains human personality in terms of the relatedness of the individual to people, to the world outside, and to himself.

Let us take Freud's concept of the anal character as an illustration. He assumes that the various traits he found together in the syndrome of the anal character were either sublimations of, or reaction formations to, the anal libido. Parsimony he explained as a sublimation of the pregenital wish to retain the stools; cleanliness as a reaction formation to the pleasure of playing with feces; orderliness, punctuality and obstinacy as traits having their roots in the early battle of the child against the mother, who demands surrender in the field of toilet training. While, in my opinion, the description of anal character as Freud and others gave it, is correct clinically, and indeed one of the greatest contributions in the field of characterology, the theoretical explanation is not tenable, unless we take it in a symbolic sense.

What Freud called the anal character can be understood as a particular kind of relatedness to the world. He is a person withdrawn, living in a fortified position, whose aim is to ward off all outside influences and to avoid letting anything from this entrenched position be carried into the outside world; on the contrary he wants as much as possible to be brought in from the outside and kept in this entrenched position, autarchically. For this character, isolation spells security; love and intimacy or closeness on the other hand spell danger. On the basis of this concept Freud's syndrome of the anal character is to be understood in the following way: Stinginess is an attempt to fortify this person's isolated position, to make it as strong as possible, and not to let anything go out of this entrenched position. Cleanliness is to be understood as in many religious rituals as an attempt to ward off contact with the outside world, which is felt to be dangerous and threatening. Orderliness, in Freud's sense of compulsive orderliness, is an attempt to put things in their place, to ward them off. Things, so to speak must not have a life of their own; they must be put in their place so that they cannot intrude upon or overwhelm the isolated position of this "orderly" personality.

What holds true for orderliness also holds true for punctuality. Punctuality is putting the world in its place in terms of time, while orderliness is putting it in its place in terms of space. Stubbornness is the expression of the same warding-off process in relation to people which punctuality or orderliness is in relation to things. It is the constant "no" against any person felt to intrude, and from the standpoint of this isolated position any suggestion, demand or even hope is felt as intrusion.

8

While we have the theoretical concepts which permit the study of the social character, we have hardly started to apply psychoanalytic characterology to the study of culture. I believe that the reasons for this situation are to be found in the fact that many social psychologists avoid studying the problems that really matter. One of the reasons for this attitude seems to be the fetish of the "Scientific Method". Social scientists have been greatly impressed by the success of exact science and try to imitate its method. Unfortunately their picture of scientific methods is more that of natural sciences which they learned in school twenty years ago than that of contemporary, most advanced types of science, particularly theoretical physics. Many social scientists believe that unless phenomena can be studied in a way which permits of exact and quantitative analysis they must not be studied at all. Instead of devising methods for the problems which are important, they rather devote their energy to less important problems in order to fit their concept of a scientific method. Our lack of knowledge, even of studies which tend to bring about such knowledge, is appalling indeed.

What, for instance, do we know about the happiness of people in our culture? True enough many people would answer in an opinion poll that they were happy because this is what a self-respecting citizen is supposed to feel. But the degree of real happiness or unhappiness is anybody's guess; yet this knowledge alone would answer the question whether our institutions fulfill the purpose they are devised for: the greatest happiness of the greatest number. Or what do we know about the degree to which ethical considerations and not plain fear of disapproval or punishment influence the behavior of modern man? From kindergarten to school and church, tremendous expenditures in energy and money are made to increase the weight of ethical motivation. Yet we hardly know anything about the success of these efforts beyond mere guesswork.

Or to take another illustration. What do we know of the degree and intensity of the destructive forces to be found in the average person in our culture? While it cannot be denied that our hopes for peaceful and democratic development depend largely on the assumption that the average man is not possessed by intense destructiveness nothing has been done to ascertain the facts. The

9

opinion that most people are basically very destructive is as unproven as the opinion that the opposite is true. Social scientists so far have done little to shed light on this crucial issue.

These problems of happiness, ethical motivation and destructiveness must be studied in the larger concept of the character structure prevailing in any given culture and in sub-groups of this culture. They must be part of extensive studies of the character structure typical of various nations, of their "national characters". It must be emphasized again that such studies must be not focused on childhood training but *on the structure of the society as a whole,* on the functions of the individual in this structure. They must understand childhood training in the context of the social structure, and particularly as one of the *key mechanisms of transmission of social necessities into character traits.* Social psychologists with a knowledge of depth psychology and of sociology and culture, must go into the field as anthropologists have done for many years and work out methods for such studies. This is not a task without great difficulties but they are not insurmountable. However, the difficulties will be overcome only if social scientists become convinced of the necessity of tackling these problems and of devising methods appropriate to the problems rather than to focus on problems which fit the traditional method.

DISCUSSION

DR. GREGORY BATESON: I noticed Dr. Fromm suggested that the shared elements in character are a nucleus, using a spatial metaphor, as though the shared elements could be presumed more profound than the elements which differ. I'd like to ask whether he intended that, and if so, what are we to understand by it?

DR. FROMM: I am very glad you raised this question. What I mean by shared elements is not a statistical concept. One figures out by some survey which elements of the character structure are the most common, and this is what I call social character. My concept of the shared elements means the functional aspect of character—the part of character structure which has developed to make culture or society proceed and operate. If most people in a society didn't share these common features, the society could hardly function. But the way I arrive at the concept of the shared feature is not by statistical means, but rather to understand social character in relation to its function, which is the survival and operation of society, both genetically and at any given historical period.

BATESON: I'm still not quite satisfied. For example, there are very superficial things, such as a tendency toward a certain grammatical form in speech, even a tendency toward a certain vocabulary, which is shared by very large portions of a population. A great many of these shared features are essential to the functioning of a society, in that they are part of the communications mechanism. So there appear to be a lot of superficial things which are shared, and generalized statements about these superficial things become something like statements about character structure. That is one side of my query.

The other side of my query would raise problems about which we know nothing; namely, those of temperament. There is the possibility that in order to tap the energies (I use the word with some hesitation) of specific individuals, there have to be built into those individuals certain structures not built into other individuals who do not have the same temperamental peculiarities.

FROMM: Well, as to the first point, I think the problem is comparatively simple. We would find, if we spoke of concrete incidents, that those superficial things you mention do not fall into the category of character. While there is, indeed, danger that one might classify them under character traits, a thorough character analysis would show that they are habits or customs, very important for social functioning, but not real "character traits". That is, they do not belong to that basic structure which has a motivating function as far as the individual is concerned.

As for the second point, I agree entirely that temperament is one of the most important things in human personality and that we know almost nothing about it; certainly not more than we knew two or three thousand years ago. Here is a very difficult problem, the relationship of temperament and character. Can one, for instance, assume that certain cultures developed their national character, and also prefer certain temperamental types, or that there is a greater affinity between certain temperaments and certain character structures? What happens to those whose temperament has little affinity to the character structure? How much is national character a matter of social character? How much is it a matter of temperament which has become predominant by a selective process? I am in the fortunate, or unfortunate, position of confessing my ignorance, which is softened by the fact that none of us knows too much about it.

DR. MUZAFER SHERIF: I should like to ask a methodological question. Where will we land if we keep on recasting the formulations of such a pioneer as Freud,—recasting them into symbolic terminology? Especially if the pioneer himself was very strict about his own formulations and didn't like any recasting of them?

DR. FROMM: Well, I think Kant was right when he once said we often understand an author better than the author understands himself. This is indeed part of the history of science—that a pioneer has a vision of a great system, and later generations discover that his statements were

11

limited, and need to be reinterpreted and enlarged. In fact, the history of science is a history of errors, isn't it? The difference is only that the great scientists make productive errors, and the small scientists make unproductive errors. I'm not afraid of where we land.

DR. JOSEPH BRAM: Does Dr. Fromm say that a society moulds a child's character according to its own necessities? I would like to take exception to the phrase "according to its own necessities" because that seems to imply an understanding of psychoanalytic procedures on the part of an average family in society. I think there is an educational purpose and an ideological awareness implied in this which is not warranted by our sociological knowledge.

DR. FROMM: I certainly do not attribute any profound wisdom to the average individual in regulating his child's life in terms of what is necessary for society. But I think we find the social process is rather complicated, and operates behind the back—or rather behind the conscious mind —of its participants. Indeed, it is a problem for social and cultural analysis to discover and understand why institutions are formed which are in line with the necessities of society, without assuming that somebody invented them or that parents are aware of their meaning for society. In other words, I believe the answer to your question can only be found in the analysis of the development and evolution of any given culture, and of the concomitant selection of institutions and ideologies, which lead to the predominance of certain institutions and certain character traits.

GARDNER MURPHY

The Relationships of Culture
and Personality

After trying to define the relations of culture to personality, it may be worth while to spend about half my time on the practical implications of these definitions in terms of the world emergency; and I was struck by the fact that Dr. Fromm pulled no punches in bringing out practical implications. I also was struck by the fact that almost every point he made was a point that my outline already told me I was to make. But instead of apologizing for that, I think the situation calls for an underscoring of the main problem. So I will go right ahead on that basis.

In the reciprocity of personality and culture I want first to develop the general implications of field theory, as it has spread through the sciences in recent decades. I will try also to show how true it is that research workers generally have converged on field theory in defining the reciprocal relations of personality and culture.

In Clark-Maxwell's study of electro-magnetism around 1875 it became clear that the atomistic approach to nature was running into bad weather; that a great many problems arose for which isolating and specifying component *parts* and their interrelations proved inadequate. Even if much attention is given the relations between parts and the contexts in which they appear, something goes wrong with assuming isolated or independently specifiable elements in the first place. The newer view, of course, came into the biological sciences early in this century. One thinks of embryological work by Spemann and Weiss; of Kurt Lewin's brilliant work showing the broader implications of psychological field theory, beginning in the twenties; of recent psychiatric definitions by Angyal, Sullivan and others. And one thinks of the many efforts that today appear in practical social situations, such as industry and education, to put the last-named conceptions to work.

Now what the conceptions seem to involve comes down to the central fact that we can define neither personality nor culture with-

13

out referring to the other term. A person's biological individuality, as we like to think of it for evolution, genetics, medicine, etc., leaves us in a hopeless fog. We would like to specify what the biological individuality is, prior to and independent of the influence of role in society. We find that in the prenatal period, the influences of nutrition and other factors must be considered. This holds true at birth and accumulates more and more thereafter, as the biological individuality asserts itself, even in bony structure, stature, predisposition to particular types of breakdown, etc.

Thinking of such studies as Stockard's much quoted experiments on the effect of alcohol over several generations, we find, without raising Lamarckian questions, that we simply can not decently describe biological individuality if we neglect environmental factors; and particularly in man, cultural factors. In so defining our problem we come to the view that each component in the biological system is itself a somewhat fluid, dynamically interacting component, just as the individual is an aspect of a cultural whole.

Gestalt psychologists similarly taught us the dangers of attempting to specify sharply defined independent physiological units, even at the level of biochemistry or the bioelectrical field of the retina. In experimental psychology today, where we use field theory to study the physiology of sense organs or nerves and muscles, the student of personality must recognize that as he gets to smaller and smaller units in the individual he finds field theory just as necessary as when he started with the total individuality related to a social context. He is also worried by the time factor which is usually involved in personality definitions. The personality as we used to see it was what you got out of a case history brought up to and focussed in the present. Personality was considered a sort of snapshot, as Bergson would have said. You might take motion pictures of the individual, cut slices through the living individual at several moments, yet consider it without much reference to gradual change through a long time span. But more and more we find that neglecting the individual's *perpetually changing* emphases gets us into insoluble problems. We can't predict anything, unless we can tell what a future environment will be. That is bad enough in itself. But we can't even understand the instability, confusion, inchoateness and lack of determination that ex-

14

ists in any given moment, unless we recognize frankly that personality expresses the current demands upon the individual. In other words, there is no "personality" at this moment, except in the sense of an interaction of individual and world.

We have, then, the notion of perpetually changing, recentering, reorienting activities in which the individual requires field interpretation. "Society" also proves to be a complicated system of interdependent events. The conception of society as an entity is not very useful in studying the individual who is immersed in institutions (language, kinship systems or anything else), even if technically the institutions could be detached from their complicated contexts—geographic, economic, historical, etc. Consequently we need roughly the same system of explanatory concepts in studying cultural phenomena and biological individuality.

Now one might say, "That's all right. It's arguing by analogy, and it pushes the analogy rather far, but let's accept it. Apparently culture and personality are subject to some of the same conceptual types of analysis. If so, however, why not content yourself with juxtaposing the two field problems and finding out how far one throws light on the other?" The trouble is that neither the definition of personality nor the definition of society can be carried far without considering in detail what this will do to the definition of the other. Defining personality rather fully in field terms, one finds out that more and more aspects of the cultural whole must be considered, and vice versa. If we want to study the influence of nutrition on the stature of Japanese children growing up in North America, we can keep the frame of reference relatively simple. If we get into the study of language, more factors come in. Studying the interrelations of temperament and of cultural coercions, we reach a point where practically the entire cultural picture must be studied to say anything meaningful about a person.

But we are traveling on a two-way street. We find the classical descriptions of culture, made before psychodynamic thinking arose, giving us good descriptions of basketry, pottery, linguistic forms, or what not. But ask what makes the thing tick—the factors responsible for relatively rapid change in one instance and relatively slow change in another—for heavy emotional loading in one situation, and a mild casual attitude toward the same phenomenon in another context; and we find we hold a fragment in our hands instead of a whole vessel. Just as we must specify the entire cultural situation which is confronted before we can say much about human personality, we must specify the personal factors, including interpersonal relations, and the phenomena of leadership, before we can describe the culture. It makes one wonder whether the academic separation of psychology from the cultural sciences can be maintained.

The final difficulty, I think, is the impossibility of specifying either phenomenon without specifying at the same time how mutual *selection* goes on between culture and person; we must specify which aspect of each, at the given moment, is drawn into the functional area of the other. We can not define a problem in temperament, even from the most rigidly biological point of view, without determining how culture selects from a given individual certain kinds of temperamental expression; how it draws from him, almost in the manner of a vacuum cleaner, his latent personal attributes. In the same way, we can not effectively specify how the individual grows without specifying how he sucks in this or that aspect of the cultural total. Even as a nicely defined academic task, it seems to me that one can no longer talk about personality *and* culture. I incline to think that despite changes in semantics and orientation, it will turn out that we are talking about two aspects of one phenomenon, calling for new names and new definitions of research needs.

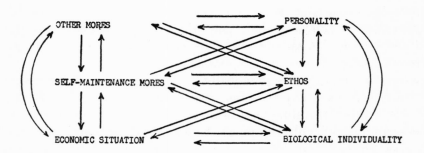

I will try to summarize this field approach by using six interdependent variables. Of course more than that are involved. In the lower left-hand corner appears the "economic situation". The situation does not strictly determine the nature of the mores of self-maintenance. The presence of salt water, sea weed, fish, etc., does not tell us how people will fish and how they will share with one another the fish they catch. Between the economic situation— forestry, mining, agriculture, etc. — and the self-maintenance mores there are two-way streets. If one dislikes economic inter- pretations and wishes to put some other system of activity at the bottom of the chart, it will do no harm, so far as the conceptual scheme is concerned; the important thing is the conception of inter- dependence. But even with the chart as it stands, other institutions are seen to determine in some measure the economic situation.

At the right-hand side of the chart, one finds what might be called biological individuality—the raw stuff that makes the indi- vidual. From this biological individuality is partly derived the ethos or feeling tone toward life. I am taking liberties here with Gregory Bateson's formulations, and using ethos to mean simply the affectively toned perspective which the biological individual maintains toward his life situation. Proceeding to the upper right hand corner of the chart I hope to show the dependence of person- ality upon biological individuality and ethos, and also upon self- maintenance mores and other mores.

Personality can not be ripped out of this total except by a type of surgery that will kill the patient. Personality is embedded in this kind of matrix, and cannot live without it. And personality reacts in turn upon all of these aspects of its context; it is a func- tioning system of events, modifying the events that surround it. This chart is not a particularly good one. Such charts are all bad; and I suppose this is as bad as the others. But it is well to keep in mind the hopeless interconnectedness of the variables we work with.

But our primary research problem has to do with the specific ways in which personality grows and develops within this matrix. In recent decades information has become available regarding at least five types of social factors in personality formation.

(1) Freud noticed the first of these long before academic psy- chologists did. He called it cathexis (Besetzung; literally "invest- ment"). Cathexis is similar to McDougall's *sentiment-formation* or the French *canalization*. It means the progressive narrowing of one's demands, until in time one needs to satisfy a given drive in a specific way. The food-wants of newborn individuals all over

17

the world are probably much alike and certainly very diffuse. But before long they demand food they have become accustomed to. In the same way other objects that satisfy human cravings become more and more specific. The individual invests the precious object with tremendous value and is relatively dissatisfied with other goal-objects which originally might have been satisfactory, and which in other cultures *are* satisfactory. A primary thing which culture does to us is to canalize us or develop cathexes in particular directions, until we want a particular type of music, or food or any other institutional satisfaction.

(2) A second process in personality-moulding is *symbolization;* the development of appropriate responses to standard signals. The conditioned response is a clue to the symbolization process by which a given word, flag, slogan, gesture or facial expression comes to arouse fairly dependable and recurrent forms of response from members of a cultural group.

(3) The third is perhaps less obvious, but it has recently been much stressed. It is *perceptual structuring.* We owe here a great deal to Sherif, who has reminded us of the tremendous power the social group possesses to define the anchorage points and modes of articulation of perceptual totals, so that we come to see things as others do. In growing up, one's way of experiencing the world becomes crystallized just as is one's pattern of motor response. One may naively say, "I will lean over backwards, put away my biases, and see things dispassionately and objectively." But we have a very limited conscious understanding of the social standardization of perception; we cannot by an act of will discover and make allowance for such perceptual habits; they are centered in our make-up as personalities. Such processes may be grouped together under the term *autism,* defined as the movement of cognitive process (whether perception, learning, recall, recognition, imagination or thought), in the direction of drive satisfaction. We have, then, a direct relation between cathexis and autism. The perceptual structure appears to develop as a learned reaction, just as motor structures develop as learned reactions on the basis of satisfactions achieved in the process. Learning is subject to the principle that satisfaction and frustration tend in general to reinforce and inhibit response patterns, and likewise to the Gestalt principle that alteration in structure involves dynamic reorganiza-

18

tion, shift and balance rather than the piecemeal addition or removal of separate parts.

(4) Fourth, we must stress that society constantly emphasizes one's own body. We may call the body, as experienced by the infant, the first core of the self. One's system of verbal symbols, one's personal philosophy, and one's social attributes are not visualized as bodies in space, yet become central to this precious object which we carry around with us, put to sleep, wake up and for which we are generally responsible. This self-object connects with society in other ways. It must carry out roles in doing the tasks assigned by society. Fortunately most roles are assigned before the self is old enough to reject them. Thus one device which Dr. Fromm pointed out is taken care of relatively early, since one is born into particular kinds of roles. Roles follow from sex, age, neighborhood, who the parents are, what jobs they hold, etc.

In this connection I think of Ralph Linton's studies showing that we are not just born "into a culture" but into a specifiable social group in which overlapping or intersecting roles can be specified. One becomes an individual in whom certain roles are conjoined. The self is perceived in accordance with a dynamic brought out by three principles earlier sketched: cathexis, symbolization and wishful or autistic response. All enter into one's perception of oneself. As a result, one strenuously defends this precious object and enhances it in competing with those against whom one is thrown. Among cultural groups enormous differences appear in the sharpness with which the self is perceived, in the degree to which perception of the self becomes a competitive task, and in the degree to which self-enhancement falls within one's own control, rather than being left to the activity of others on one's own behalf.

It is no longer possible to study the self as though there were first a self, then a society. Self-awareness is possible only as an example of our general principle of reciprocity of individual and culture. One can speak of the self meaningfully only if one stresses both individual development and at the same time the influence of the perception of other persons, especially the parents, as conveying a sense of what selfhood is and as affording suitable objects for identification.

(5) Finally, personality must be considered in terms of the

modes of *integration, conflict* or *escape* which occur when one discovers that several drives must be satisfied at once, so that satisfaction of one alters the situation in which satisfaction of the others may be expected. We find, in ordering our lives, whether we hook up things in series or in parallel, that drive problems can not be solved piecemeal any more than perceptual problems can be. This means that if society is to exist at all the individual must find some way to build his wants into an integral pattern. (Perhaps many societies have done this ineptly and have therefore disappeared.) Personality is largely the mode of selection from cultural opportunities that makes possible the integrated satisfaction of the various drives. Failing this, temporary or permanent conflict appears.

This is an attempt to write a coda to what Dr. Fromm said a few minutes ago about shifts from a biological to a social orientation. From the present point of view the question of conflict is rooted right here in the question of the form in which the integration of drives is permitted the individual. It is not just a question of how an individual makes his peace with a society which demands something of him. Society does not simply determine the separate ways of satisfying separate drives; it determines to a considerable degree how they may be integrated, the conditions under which they may not be integrated; and therefore the conditions under which conflict must appear. In certain cases it provides methods of escape from the conflict, so that the more unbearable conflicts are sometimes invisible, or are visible only in certain persons.

I add this point about integration and conflict because I am unhappy about the customary arbitrary division between psychology and psychiatry; the general feeling that psychology deals with normal persons in culture, and psychiatry with persons laden with so serious a load that they can't make a go of life. Psychology has learned enormously more from psychiatry than it has learned from anything else up to the present. Psychiatry could learn something from psychology if psychologists would come out of their academic seclusion. Fortunately, they are doing this to some degree.

Now in applying our biosocial approach, as shown in the chart presented earlier, contemporary psychological literature seems to me to present a misconception that is worth mentioning, in the hope that the difficulty may be discussed and clarified. The point came out in a paper done by Stofflet under Klineberg's direction; his investigation of delinquency and crime pointed to some phenomena of great theoretical importance. This was one of the studies in which the crime rate for a social group is followed through several generations. The data, appearing shortly after the Wickersham report, were not altogether new. The point was made that the homicide rate of a particular group was low among the first generation European immigrants, high in the second generation, low again in the third. It was clear that members of the second generation were actually *exposed* to stimuli leading to crime much more often than were members of the first and third groups, so that the question arose whether this change in crime rate was internal to the personality at all, or whether it was a response to something external—something, let us say, like the frequency with which members of a given group are struck by lightning. The second generation would suffer more from lightning-strokes if they went out more frequently into the fields during thunderstorms.

The issue came up again recently, I was interested to see, in the film which you may have seen entitled "This Is Robert." Here a normal and adequate little boy is seen to be full of aggressive responses, some of them obviously a kickback against a rather clumsy upbringing, a response to severe pressures to which he had been exposed. Students have asked me rather eagerly whether Robert's aggressiveness did not indicate that he was normal and well adjusted, since a boy incapable of aggression in the situations in which Robert was caught would be a withdrawn, timid, frightened little bunny, unable to cope with life. Robert's violence, which some persons had interpreted as evidence that he was "sick," was cited by others as evidence that he was supremely competent to meet the situation. The difficulty which I want to bring to focus by referring to Stofflet's study and to the film of Robert is that in discussing personalities we often fail to specify the *situation* in which they appear.

From the present viewpoint personality is an interaction of organism and culture, and the situation is consequently part of the personality. Are we willing to see this through? In Stofflet's study of the crime rate, one might say: "This approach is very

21

arbitrary, because we cannot lift those people out of the second generation and put them in the first generation where they were not exposed to crime." This is really an admission, however, that personality is definable only when we can define the situation which it confronts. At this point it may be asked: "Then is anything left for personality? You are studying social interactions, or interpersonal relations; but is there a place for a person in his own right?" To this I can only reply that the interpersonal relations depend on the individuals, but that the individuals also depend in the relations.

These issues were fought through years ago by W. I. Thomas, and by Hartshorne, May and others. The term "situation," or "situationism," will occur to some of you as an attempt to solve this problem. An ingenious solution was offered by Eugene Lerner, who found that some nursery school children adapted almost instantly to any demand, while others went on being themselves no matter what you did to them. He referred to these two groups as *chameleons* and *beavers*. Chameleons adapt immediately to situations; beavers go on ruggedly gnawing through their trees regardless of what happens. In these terms you might then say that a situationist emphasizes the chameleons, or the chameleon-aspect of all of us, and that the biologically-minded psychologists prefer to emphasize the beavers, or the beaverish aspect of all of us. But no real social problem exists in which biological individuality is held constant; and even if we create an artificially uniform environment (like Blatz's environment for the Dionne quints), the thing will collapse because, as Larry Frank pointed out, the Dionnes' nurses, being human, will handle the little girls in five different ways.

Now I've tried to give you my prejudices. They fall under the general head just indicated. I don't think there is a problem of personality as such. We encounter a problem of fields, in which we always have a bi-polar relation of organism and environment. This prejudice, I hope, is subject to fundamental revision if it proves inconsistent or useless in making predictions. Perhaps facts have been overlooked. But it seems to me harmful to continue the clinical psychologist's and psychiatrist's belief that there is such a thing as a sick personality which comes for help. On the other hand so-called situational therapy is often "hit or miss," because one runs into deep-seated individual differences in the way in which situations are grasped and used. More fundamental redefinition, I think, is called for.

II

If it's true that we are forced more and more into wider social definitions of personality, why do we so often overlook the functional social groupings of individuals? It's easy to classify people by skin color, sex or age; it's relatively easy to classify them by the number of dollars they earn in a year. Very little grouping of human beings is done in terms of the roles they reveal in their own immediate social world. Take for example the various leadership relations. It's very late in the present crisis-period to study the phenomena of leadership and initiative—the question how an oligarchy arises and ultimately controls society, leads it into new institutional forms. Yet such a study of leadership is absolutely at the heart of the human family's problem of existence in the mid-twentieth century. Perhaps it will turn out that others have thought through these problems. To me they still are very foggy. And we do not seem to be asking the crucial questions. One might think that when one comes to a conference on personality and culture under the aegis of the Viking Fund, people would at once demand: "What, if anything, can be learned in a hurry, while there still is a chance, about democratic types of leadership that might be effective both nationally and internationally? Is the personality-and-culture problem definable in such a way that we can focus research on getting sounder and deeper democratic leadership?"

One reason why I am biased toward my definition lies in a rather desperate feeling that we must begin studying interpersonal relations in terms of those functional groups that make the difference whether our society survives or goes under; whether some aspects of our society survive and others die; whether anything can be done by social scientists to show us how the leadership process can become more thoughtfully and humanely defined and studied.

Yet take the next hundred case studies that you look through in the next few weeks. How many deal with people near the power-centers of society? How many throw light directly on our leadership? Don't they deal mostly with disturbed people, who are so mutilated psychologically that they have to be treated as amputees, or as people who might lose a leg if they were not promptly taken care of medically? Is enough attention given, with our resources of manpower, time, money and so on, to the really crucial personality-and-culture problems, to problems of types of leadership and followership of which our society is capable? I stress problems at the middle level; we probably can not get many of the top people, but we can get a good many representative middle-level people on whom top leadership depends for general guidance, orientation and administrative work, if not policy making. This is more a social-science problem than a psychological problem, as the fields now exist; but all the techniques of existing psychology need to converge on it, if we are to do the job that needs to be done.

I wonder why the problems of initiative, the seizure and delegation of power, of lines of communication through the oligarchy in power, have been almost entirely neglected by psychologists and social scientists. The Communist Party of the USSR does not neglect such problems. It is acutely aware of middle leadership, which is not solely a problem of direct control by the Kremlin nor of spontaneous activity on the part of Tom, Dick and Harry. It is an implementation problem in selecting and guiding middle-level leaders. The processes of continuous selection, drilling, party work, supervision, orientation and gearing people together has been, for a long time, a matter of competent middle-level leadership. It seems odd that we Americans know so little about those involved in our own leadership, in view of the fact that development of a democratic orientation demands that our own community make use of grass-roots long-range participation by people of every type and class. Why is so little done to clarify community leadership, to study the people who become leaders, how they exercise control, and how the power structure is maintained? Perhaps when Bob Lynd gives us his book on power structure, we'll get some orientation on that. Perhaps now material exists that I do not know about; I should be glad to be challenged. Are there good materials on leadership and power? It seems odd to me that people working on personality-and-culture are so per-

24

sistently concerned with remote or esoteric problems—however appealing, fascinating, rich, bizarre such problems are—rather than with those at the heart of the present world predicament.

Now for the questions of social orientation raised by Dr. Fromm. I want to ask three questions about world peace as they concern research upon personality and culture. If world order as we understand it is to be maintained, there must be some degree of mutual respect between the Soviet Union and the western peoples. However their political philosophies differ, there must be some rapprochement; at least, an agreement in defining areas in which collaboration is feasible. This means that a social science research group, like ourselves, must be continually concerned with the question: how can we understand Russian temperamental attributes, under the peculiar conditions of Russian history before, during and after the Russian revolution? How can we understand the orientation towards Marxism that developed with Lenin and others during the Russian revolution? How can we grasp *their* autisms through our *own* autisms? In particular, how can we understand their leadership, so as to use intelligently every gesture, however slight, toward world understanding? If, as some say, the Russian leaders are determined on war as the only way to achieve world revolution, and their decision is regarded by them as irrevocable, how can we persuade them to take a *new* orientation? While human beings remain human beings, there is some chance for flexibility. Indeed, if they have determined on any one course rather than another—I don't know whether they have or not, and I don't know anyone else who knows—the psychological problem is to study Russian leaders. Are we students of personality and culture at work in studying the Russians? If not, why not?

Ruth Benedict has shown us how to study the Japanese under difficult and complicated conditions. Russians are at least as available as were the Japanese when she did her work. Rensis Likert, in his presidential address to the Society for the Psychological Study of Social Issues, defined some additional ways of studying Russian character, utilizing a series of new devices, including Benedict's techniques and others. People coming from the Soviet Union could be studied by a combination of public opinion research and depth interview. Many methods to get supplementary data could be worked out with the day-by-day communications materials: film, radio, press, etc.

We can rationalize our way out of this by making it supremely difficult. Or we can say: "Well, fundamental economic policies determine behavior. We don't need to study individuals." This is just a way of focussing on one part of the chart which we sketched out earlier, and blinding our eyes to the rest.

I take a second illustration: why not a really adequate study of Chinese character? We talk about the Soviet Union and the United States. There's India, too, and China—half the members of the human race. The Chinese are waking up to many issues to which they were earlier insensitive, just as we are waking up to many issues to which they were awake long before we as a nation existed. It's becoming "one world," whether one likes it or not. We have facilities to study Chinese character. Some Chinese psychologists are already working on the problem. Dr. Kardiner has attacked the problem in terms of one approach; there is a rich possibility to administer all sorts of other techniques for study of the life history in China as compared with the western world. There are projective approaches, psychoanalysis and related procedures, group-work methods, experimental work with individuals and with groups. We should get a systematic study of Chinese character within the next ten years. It is a realizable goal and it might make a huge difference in world-scale orientation toward world-mindedness.

I see I have prepared for an anti-climax. If the Russians and Chinese can be studied, why can't Americans? Our rather precious concern for individuals makes interesting case histories; Americans get gastric ulcers, allergies, and what not, and hundreds of thousands of dollars are spent on the cures. That's good, and I'm glad it's spent. But why not think of the people who will make the difference between survival or collapse of what we know as civilization—the top and middle leaders? Why not orient our personality-and-culture investigations to problems of power organization—particularly at the middle level—and its relation to the broader matrix of interpersonal backgrounds? We have worked long to develop the machinery; now we need to focus on areas of crucial social importance.

Middle level leaders in business, in the labor movement and

in politics should be studied just as systematically as the University of Michigan graduate students who go through hours of personality study before being taken into the clinical program. I am told that these students will be carried through five years to see what clinical psychology does to them as they study and participate in it, to see which ones it automatically leaves out, which ones it makes into better human beings, or worse human beings, or whatever may be the evaluation by Lowell Kelly and the other people doing it. Why couldn't we use Crutchfield's idea: to integrate public opinion research with attitude and personality research in the United States so as to get a deeper conception of American character than the momentary cross-sections ordinarily obtained from public opinion material? Ultimately the two great streams—psychiatry and clinical psychology on the one hand, public opinion analysis on the other—might converge into a slowly-moving torrent, a continuing study of the American character. It would express itself now in disease, now in public opinion (if they are distinguishable), now in interactions or pressures from which new leadership types emerge.

But in this kind of research no goals can be achieved if we set up personality as the thing to study. If on the other hand we decide that "personality-and-culture," more or less fused as in binocular vision, is really the thing to study, we have a chance of getting it done while there is still life.

DISCUSSION

PROF. RUTH BENEDICT: I would like to speak to the last point that Dr. Murphy made, in terms of my experience in training students to study personality and culture. That includes not only training students, but also training myself. People in anthropology learn to study personality and culture largely through the experience of culture shock. The problem of training Americans to study personality and culture within the United States is a very specific and highly difficult one. Persons who are in mixed cultural positions also often find it difficult to isolate the cultural points which are more easily grasped by the trained anthropologist. I think both difficulties can be surmounted but I wanted to point them out particularly in relation to the study of American culture and personality.

DR. HORTENSE POWDERMAKER: I would agree with Dr. Benedict that there are difficulties in working in our own civilization, but I would like also to point out that work in primitive societies has difficulties too. This is particularly true for problems of personality and culture, when one does not know the language or when work is limited to a relatively short period of time. It seems to me that there are advantages and disadvantages in both types of study; neither one is easy. But no scientific research, I think, is easy. In working in our own society we do not have to face the problem of language; we know the history. In fact, we know a great deal before we start. In our society we can also segmentalize research. I quite agree that we have to get the whole, but I think we can get it only by studying the different parts and then, perhaps, by getting at some of the relationships.

I am particularly interested in the problem of mass communication. It seems to me that if we are going to study the middle ground mentioned by Dr. Murphy we should also study the institutions which affect the large majority of people, among which are the radio, motion picture, pulp magazines, and advertising.

The anthropologist has stepped out of his own society; he has a degree of objectivity; and he has been trained in not taking things for granted. This last is perhaps the most valuable part of his training. If the anthropologist could turn to the study of his own culture it would give most promising returns.

DR. MURPHY: I want to underscore simply the point that we are not likely to get the dynamics of the shift of various persons into positions of power unless we put it high on our priority list. The study of mass communication is important and, when it is combined with techniques for understanding how these communications are accepted, autistically distorted, elaborated, or used by the individual, it is of the utmost value. But I still think there is a prominent place needed for study of motions toward the positions of control: what kinds of people get to own newspapers? Particular kinds of influences lead one person rather than another to exert controlling influences *within* the whole sphere of public communication. Unless one regards the whole situation as rigidly determined by factors which are extra-psychological, a very prominent place remains for the study of the duration and flow of processes which lead these forms of social communication to draw into their network certain kinds of persons, and of the reciprocal return effects which certain kinds of people have as power centers on the other component aspects of society.

DR. POWDERMAKER: Wouldn't you say that in addition to studying the power centers you have also to study the people who give the power and who follow the leadership?

DR. MURPHY: Yes, you have to consider the whole field, for reasons which I have indicated earlier. Yet I am inclined to think that, although we are neglecting all three levels, our neglect of the middle level is the most unforgivable. We need to study the processes by which the people are drawn into middle level positions of leadership—who they are, what acts on them, and how they in turn react. Of course, if we can get the top leaders too, so much the better.

DR. GREGORY BATESON: I think it will be important for later discussion to put data somewhere on that diagram of Dr. Murphy's. Let us suppose that there is a great field outside the diagram where things actually happen. Of that, a certain amount gets into the diagram, that is, into the scientist's notebook. A lot of items are recorded. Now, the things in the diagram are abstractions built by us from the data. An institution is not there at all except in so far as the natives themselves analyze the data on their own society, and give the institution a name or recognize it in some way. Thus, "institution" is used in two senses: one in which the natives recognize it, and one in which the anthropologist has created it out of data bundled into lumps after his own making. These field relations, rather than being casual, are logical interrelations between deductions *we* make from data which *we* collect.

DR. MURPHY: I am sure Dr. Bateson is deliberately throwing a bombshell into our camp in order to mix us up. A man chips stone according to a neolithic technique and thus learns something that palaeolithic people did not know. This will have certain consequences in the ways tools work whether neolithic man called himself a neolithic man or not. If a man has several wives, various things are going to happen that would not happen if he only had one wife, whether he calls it polygamy or not.

I don't think that Dr. Bateson meant that the process of bundling data is all that the social scientist does. He bows down to facts exactly as astronomers do and perhaps the area of controversy is where the facts get fuzzy. But there *is* a hard core of fact. We are likely to forget that an enormous amount is dictated by the data themselves, regardless of any bundling process. In psychology the situation is very similar. Psychologists can discover that certain people, let us say, cannot see some of the colors that other people see, and any elementary experiment with Holmgren yarns will prove it. Of course, psychologists argue about classification. But the *fact* of color weakness is too patent to be overlooked. You cannot imagine a group of people trained at all in the study of psychophysiology missing such a thing. We do miss an awful lot of things, but certainly there is in any discipline that we call science an enormous amount of material, some of which comes under the head of institutions, which is tough, hard, unavoidable, and factual.

Dr. Bateson made two points: (1) that certain things get into the notebook, and (2) that the things that get into the notebook aren't facts, but rather conceptualizations.

DR. BATESON: No, no. The point is that one is influenced in choosing one's facts. But I assume you can get facts. Out of those facts you get those broad things which I have made, which we all have made . . .

DR. MURPHY: But it's the business of any science to develop to a point where its task is more and more one of prediction and control, and where more and more engineering follows, so that it arrives at the plastic or whatever other practical result it may want to reach. The degree of subjectivity which you describe is characteristic of the infancy of a science, and if you mean to say that psychology and anthropology are in this infantile condition, I would agree with you. But I would add that we are rapidly freeing ourselves of these swaddling clothes. Perhaps our main emphasis ought to be on the techniques by which we can accomplish this.

DAVID BIDNEY

Towards a Psychocultural Definition
of the Concept of Personality[1]

As the first topic we are supposed to discuss at this Conference on Culture and Personality is entitled *"Culture" and "Personality"—Defining Our Terms*, I intend to follow the unusual procedure of actually discussing the concept of culture and its significance for an understanding of the concept of personality. I am assuming that, unless our basic concepts are rigorously defined at the outset, there is hardly any point in going ahead with any practical program of research.

1. *The Concept of Culture and Its Significance for the Study of Personality*

One of the outstanding characteristics of contemporary cultural anthropology is its serious concern with· the study of the personality of the individuals participating in a given culture. Whereas anthropologists of a previous generation were primarily concerned with an impersonal factual survey of the traits of a given culture and paid little attention to the subjective or inner life of the carriers of the culture, the latest tendency is to reverse this trend and to put the major emphasis upon the influence of given cultural institutions and patterns on the personality and character of their adherents.

One reason for this change in perspective on the part of cultural anthropologists, it would appear, is to be found in their altered view of the cultural process itself. The older anthropologists tended to view culture in general as an impersonal, "superorganic" tradition and environment comprising the aggregate of

[1]This paper represents an expansion of the one presented by the writer at the Conference on Culture and Personality on Nov. 7, 1947. Some material not then available has been included. The research involved in the writing of this paper is part of a larger project on theoretical anthropology being sponsored by the Viking Fund.

material and ideal achievements of historical, human society. They assumed, furthermore, more or less explicitly, that culture comprised a distinct, conceptual level of reality, a discrete order of purely cultural phenomena which develop according to laws of their own. Culture was said to be a process *sui generis* requiring no reference to other orders of phenomena for an explanation of its origin and stages of development. Hence a sharp boundary was drawn between the sphere of culture on the one hand, and that of organic biology or psychology on the other. The study of personality was thought to pertain to the domain of psychology and psychiatry but was considered as beyond the province of the cultural anthropologist. Otherwise, it was thought, there was grave danger that culture, which constituted the highest level of the orders of natural phenomena, might be "reduced" to the level of psychology, and the purity of cultural phenomena corrupted by uniting orders of events which by nature and science ought to remain separated.

On the other hand, there has been a persistent, though minor, tendency to regard culture realistically as referring to acquired forms of technique, behavior, feeling and thought of individuals within society. From this point of view, culture is essentially a subjective or personal attribute of individuals, since it is a state or quality acquired by, and attributed to, individuals participating in a given cultural configuration and specific cultural institutions. Cultural forms are said to be abstractions from cultural behavior and experience and as such have no concrete reality apart from the individuals who have produced them. On this basis, the cultural anthropologist may be interested in all forms of human expression insofar as they have been affected by cultural influence. There can be no sharp line of demarcation between the sphere of culture on the one hand, and that of organic and psychological phenomena on the other. Culture is an attribute of human behavior and is therefore to be studied as an integral part of human behavior, and not *as if* it were a dynamic entity capable of acting and developing apart from the organisms which express themselves through it.

Logically, it should be noted, there need be no conflict between the realistic, individualistic approach and the idealistic, superorganic approach provided it is realized that we are dealing with different levels of abstraction.[2] Actual or concrete culture is primarily that state or modification of the behavior and thought of individuals within society which is the direct result of the process of education and of participation in the life of a community. Abstract or ideal culture is an impersonal or superorganic aggregate or configuration of forms of experience transmitted by human society and embodied in the sum total of human artifacts, socifacts (institutions) and mentifacts (ideas and ideals) produced by human effort. In actual or concrete culture the major emphasis is upon the real cultural processes manifested in the life and experience of individuals within society; in abstract culture the emphasis is upon the cultural forms and achievements apart from the human agents who produced them. Obviously, one need not quarrel from the point of view of methodology with the attempt to study the sequence of forms or patterns of cultural products or achievements while taking for granted the human agents involved. One becomes involved in what I have termed *the culturalistic fallacy*[3] only when these cultural abstractions are reified or hypostatized so that culture is regarded as a process *sui generis* subject to its own natural laws of development. It is the mistaking of an epistemological abstraction for a concrete reality and of an abstract form for a concrete process which constitutes the culturalistic fallacy. But obviously there is no fallacy involved in the abstraction of cultural forms as such for the purpose of separate analysis. One may be said to commit the culturalistic fallacy only insofar as he confuses the abstract and the concrete in attributing to epistemological cultural abstractions an efficient causality and dynamic power which only pertain to concrete human agents.

2. *The Concept of the Superorganic*

It is important to bear in mind in this connection that the concept of the cultural superorganic may be, and has been, conceived

[2]See D. Bidney, *Human Nature and the Cultural Process*, American Anthropologist 49, 1947.
[3]See D. Bidney, *On the Concept of Culture and Some Cultural Fallacies*. American Anthropologist, 46, 1944.

in at least three distinct senses.[4] First, as originally used by Herbert Spencer, the term superorganic refers to the cumulative aggregate of human achievements which constitute the artificial, hereditary environment of man. Second, culture is said to be superorganic in the sense that man's psychological capacity for cultural invention and symbolization enables him to develop new cultural forms without any corresponding change in his organic or mental structure. In other words, culture is superorganic in the psychological sense that human mental functions which under-lie cultural expressions are to some degree independent of man's organic structure, since cultures vary while the organism remains constant. Thirdly, there is the concept of the superorganic as originally formulated by Kroeber and lately taken up by L. A. White[5] according to which cultural phenomena are regarded as being "superpsychic" in the sense of requiring no reference to the psychological nature of man. Cultural phenomena are said to constitute an independent level of reality which is intelligible in itself and which it is the special task of the "culturologist" to investigate.

It is gratifying to note at this point that Kroeber has lately modified his original idealistic view of the superorganic and that in the revised edition of his *Anthropology* he now employs the term in the second sense as referring to man's psychological ca-

---

[4]Ibid; see also D. Bidney, *The Problem of Social and Cultural Evolution: A Reply to A. R. Radcliffe-Brown.* American Anthropologist, 49, 1947.

[5]L. A. White, *Culturological vs. Psychological Interpretations of Human Behavior.* American Sociological Review, 12, 1947, pp. 686-698. While White follows Kroeber in regarding cultural phenomena as superpsychic, his metaphysical or meta-cultural presupposition is the antithesis of Kroeber's. White's concept of the Superorganic is material-istic and shows the predominant influence of Lewis H. Morgan's *Ancient Society* whose general scheme of evolutionary cultural development he accepts. On the other hand, Kroeber's concept of the Superorganic is essentially idealistic and positivistic. Kroeber, however, is also empirical in his approach, refusing to posit any *a priori* theory of the dynamics of cultural development. White, by contrast, is dogmatic and, like the Marxists and historical materialists in general, assumes that "the motive force of culture is technological." See L. A. White, *Kroeber's "Configurations of Culture Growth"*, American Anthropologist, 48, 1946, pp. 78-93.

pacity for cultural invention and communication. Thus he writes:

"In one sense culture is both superindividual and superorganic. But it is necessary to know what is meant by these terms so as not to misunderstand their implications. 'Superorganic' does not mean nonorganic, or free of organic influence and causation; nor does it mean that culture is an entity independent of organic life in the sense that some theologians might assert that there is a soul which is or can become independent of the living body. 'Superorganic' means simply that when we consider culture we are dealing with something that is organic but which must also be viewed as something more than organic if it is to be fully intelligible to us. In the same way when we say that plants and animals are 'organic' we do not thereby try to place them outside the laws of matter and energy in general. We only affirm that fully to understand organic beings and how they behave, we have to recognize certain kinds of phenomena or properties—such as the powers of reproduction, assimilation, irritability—as added to those which we encounter in inorganic substances. Just so, there are certain properties of culture—such as transmissibility, high variability, cumulativeness, value standards, influence on individuals—which it is difficult to explain, or to see much significance in, strictly in terms of the organic composition of personalities or individuals. These properties or qualities of culture evidently attach not to the organic individual man as such, but to the actions and the behavior products of societies of men—that is, to culture. In short, culture is superorganic and superindividual in that, although carried, participated in, and produced by organic individuals, it is acquired; and it is acquired by learning. What is learned is the existent culture."[6]

This passage is historically significant, especially in view of the author's great influence upon American anthropologists and sociologists, in that it shows that Kroeber no longer identifies the superorganic with the superpsychic as he did in the earlier edition of his *Anthropology* and in subsequent papers, but rather holds, in agreement with the present writer, that there need be no conflict between the organic and superorganic views of culture provided

[6]A. L. Kroeber, *Anthropology*, Revised Ed.. New York, 1948, pp. 253-254; see also pp. 574-577 for references to personality and culture.

culture is not regarded as an entity or process *sui generis*. As evidence of his conciliatory attitude, Kroeber has accordingly added a chapter on *Cultural Psychology* to the revised version of his *Anthropology* which takes up the problem of "Personality in Culture." While he still retains some reservations and maintains "a certain caution" in face of the alleged danger of "intellectual reductionism" which may reduce cultural to psychological phenomena, he is nevertheless now prepared to concede that "Anthropology is now in a position to call such a halt and review the tie-up with psychology."

The contrast between the superpsychic and the psychological conceptions of the superorganic may be pointed up by reference to Pitirim A. Sorokin's analysis in his recent work on *Society, Culture and Personality*.

According to Sorokin[7]: "The superorganic is equivalent to mind in all its clearly developed manifestations. Superorganic phenomena embrace language; science and philosophy; religion; the fine arts (painting, sculpture, architecture, music, literature, and drama); law and ethics; mores and manners; technological inventions and processes from the simplest tools to the most intricate machinery; road-making; building construction; the cultivation of fields and gardens; the domestication and training of animals, etc.; and social organizations. These are all superorganic phenomena because they are the articulations of mind in various forms; none of them arise mainly in response to blind reflexes or instincts."

In a footnote to the above passage he continues: "The best definition of the superorganic is given by E. De Roberty. He rightly indicates that the transition from the inorganic to the organic and then to the superorganic is gradual. Vital phenomena have rudimentary mental processes like irritability, sensation, feeling, emotion, and association of images. But no species except man has the highest forms of mind represented by four main classes of social thought: (a) abstract concepts and laws of scientific thought; (b) generalizations of philosophy and religion; (c) symbolic thought of the fine arts; and (d) rational applied

[7]P. A. Sorokin, *Society, Culture and Personality*. New York and London, 1947, pp. 3-4.

thought, in all disciplines from technology, agronomy, and medicine, up to ethics, social planning, and engineering. This superorganic thought is the "stuff" of sociocultural phenomena. Concrete historical events and sociocultural phenomena always represent a mixture of physical, biological and superorganic phenomena. See E. De Roberty, *Nouveau Programme de Sociologie* (Paris, 1904). Social scientists who state that social phenomena are in their nature psychological or mental say, in a less distinct form, the same thing. This means that practically all representatives of the psychological and sociologistic schools in sociology (and they make up the main streams of social thought) are in implicit or explicit agreement with the thesis of this work . . . See also A. L. Kroeber, 'The Superorganic'."[8]

Sorokin, it appears, employs the concept of the superorganic as referring to those distinctively human mental functions involved in abstract symbolic thought, and distinguishes this human superorganic thought from the organic thought which is the product of blind reflexes or instincts. Thus he is inclined to accept the position that sociocultural phenomena are in their essential nature psychological or mental and finds it difficult to draw any sharp boundary line between psychological and sociologistic studies.[9] It is of interest to note in this connection that Sorokin appears to be unaware in referring to Kroeber's paper on "The Superorganic" that the latter was committed to a superpsychic view of the superorganic.

Nevertheless, Sorokin does not appear very happy about his identification of the superorganic with the mental and later differentiates between "the psychological school" and the "sociologistic or sociocultural school."[10] The former is said to take some psychological element as an independent variable and to trace its effects in sociocultural life with a view to establishing a causal connection between the psychological and the social aspects of cultural life. The sociocultural school, on the other hand, is said to study sociocultural phenomena in all their essential aspects.

[8]A. L. Kroeber, *The Superorganic*, American Anthropologist, 19, 1917, pp. 163-213.
[9]P. A. Sorokin, op. cit., p. 25.
[10]P. A. Sorokin, op. cit., pp. 25-26.

"Consequently," he maintains, "only this school gives us real sociology in the strict sense of the term. The other school surveyed —namely, cosmosociology, biosociology, and psychosociology— are but peripheral and derivative disciplines." In fact, Sorokin explicitly takes the position that sociocultural phenomena are more significant than psychological ones for an understanding of human personality. Thus he states:

"Consequently, sociocultural phenomena do not require explanation from the standpoint of the psychological properties of their members, quite the reverse; psychological characteristics need to be elucidated from the standpoint of the properties of the sociocultural interaction into whose matrix they are embedded. Without a knowledge of the society and culture into which a given individual was born and reared none of his personality traits— beliefs, ideas, convictions, tastes, likes and dislikes—can be understood; his whole mentality, his manners and mores, his ways of conduct and life, are entirely incomprehensible. Not only his whole psychosocial personality but many of his biological properties are molded and conditioned by the sociocultural universe in which he is reared."[11]

Sorokin's dilemma, it would appear, has been brought about by the fact that he is employing the concept of the superorganic in two distinct senses. On the one hand, he has identified the superorganic with the mental in its higher forms of expression and is thus committed to the position that human culture and personality are to be explained in terms of psychological, symbolic thought or mental processes. On the other hand, he reverts to the older sociological position that sociocultural phenomena are unique and primary, and that the latter are to be differentiated from the psychological processes which underlie them. This implies that sociocultural phenomena are superorganic in the sense that they are superpsychic. Hence Sorokin maintains that sociocultural phenomena are to be conceived and explained through themselves alone and do not require psychological data for their explanation; on the contrary, sociological data serve to render intelligible the psychological characteristics of the personality of the individuals who are subjected to their influence.

[11]Ibid., p. 27.

Sorokin's position is instructive precisely because it serves to render explicit the underlying issue in contemporary sociological and anthropological culture theory which has given rise to conflicting approaches to the problem of human personality. In actual practice, an eclectic compromise has been reached, many social scientists accepting the superpsychic view of sociocultural phenomena while themselves engaging in, or promoting, studies of personality which imply or presuppose an antithetical, psychological interpretation of the concept of the superorganic.

3. The Polarity of Cultural Phenomena

The opposition to the study of personality on the part of the adherents of the superorganic, superpsychic view of culture is owing in large measure to their extreme view of the autonomy of cultural phenomena. Historically this opposition is understandable, since the superorganic view of culture was originally formulated (by Kroeber in particular) in opposition to the extreme claims of organicists who failed to differentiate cultural phenomena from biological, psychological and social phenomena and attempted to derive cultural phenomena directly from the latter. But instead of maintaining simply that cultural phenomena involve a new element of historical experience which, while it presupposes biological, psychological and societal conditions, is not entirely explicable in terms of the latter, the superorganicists went to the opposite extreme in claiming that culture constitutes a new level of reality which is to be conceived through itself alone. Any attempt to correlate psychological or psychiatrical data with cultural processes was, therefore, regarded with suspicion as undermining the autonomy of cultural anthropology or as a reduction of culture to psychology.

By way of reconciling the historically antithetical organic and superorganic approaches to the study of human culture, I have elsewhere,[12] and particularly in my paper on *Human Nature and the Cultural Process*,[13] submitted the view of the polarity of cultural phenomena. Briefly put, my thesis is that culture in general

[12]*On the Concept of Cultural Crisis*, American Anthropologist, 48, 1946.
[13]American Anthropologist, 49, 1947.

may be understood as the dynamic process and product of the self-cultivation of human nature as well as of the natural, geographical environment, and involves the development of selected potentialities of nature for the attainment of individual and social ends of communal life. Culture is essentially a polar concept in the sense that it is unintelligible apart from a reference to nature. The polarity or complementarity of nature and culture implies that while there is some degree of independence or autonomy of natural and cultural phenomena, there is also an essential interdependence or mutual dependence. The cultural process requires, as its indispensable conditions, a determinate human nature and natural environment that are subject to transformation by man himself.

The polarity of nature and culture implies furthermore that natural and cultural selection are disparate processes. Cultural selection is normative and ultimately involves the active choice of the human agents of a given culture system. Natural selection alone does not explain either the great diversity of cultural forms of expression or the adherence to given forms of culture by certain societies notwithstanding the biological cost. Creative, normative cultural selection is often at variance with, or opposed to, natural, biological selection. The attempt on the part of the organic as well as superorganic determinists to reduce the cultural process to an automatic process of natural selection disregards the essentially human and unpredictable element in the cultural process, namely, the normative choice of distinctively human cultural values.

In sum, all cultural phenomena are composed of two disparate elements, namely, the element of nature conceived in physical, biological, psychological or social terms, and the element of human creativity and choice. There are purely natural phenomena but there are no purely cultural phenomena which are conceived through themselves alone. All cultural phenomena are natural phenomena as modified through human effort and interaction.

4. *Human Nature, the Person and Personality*

The cultural anthropologist, as distinct from the psychologist, is concerned with the cultural expression of human nature. He is indebted to the psychologist for data as to the psychological conditions and processes underlying cultural forms or modes of expression and attempts to correlate these cultural phenomena with given psychological processes. A knowledge of psychology enables him to understand the universal patterns and motivations of cultural phenomena and to appreciate the distinctive, special role of historical experience and tradition in relation to a given society.

As Durkheim has noted,[14] there are two egos in every individual, namely, a psychobiological ego with which he is endowed by nature and a sociocultural ego which he acquires through participation in a given society and culture system. These two egos are in a constant state of tension and never quite harmonize. By encouraging the development of some human potentialities and impulses, the cultural process makes for an actual increase in individual liberty and power of activity, and thereby enables man individually and collectively to engage in a multitude of enterprises which he would otherwise be unable to pursue. On the other hand, the cultural process is also a restraining discipline which checks or suppresses the individual's impulses in the interests of society. There is, therefore, in all cultures some degree of tension between the individual and his society, between the egoistic impulses one would fain indulge and the altruistic ideals one is more or less compelled to obey. Hence arises the problem of the "fitness" of a given culture for its adherents on the one hand, and of the adjustment of its adherents to a given culture, on the other.

Actual historical cultures differ markedly from one another in the selection of possible forms of activity and organization, and every society therefore has the defects corresponding to its self-imposed virtues. This cultural selection is manifested by the ideal type of person which the members of a given society prefer relative to the ages of life and the sex of the individual. Each ideal type, at a given stage of development, calls for the expression of some human potentialities and the suppression or restraint of others.

Insofar as an individual (or aggregate of individuals) carries out a given culture role or ideal he may be said to be a person

[14]In *Le dualisme de la nature humaine* (Scientia, 15, pp. 206-221) as quoted by Sorokin in his *Society, Culture and Personality*, p. 346.

(*persona*). A person is simply one who performs a given function in the cultural life of a given society. Apart from sociocultural life there are organisms or psychobiological egos but no persons.[15] Personality, in brief, is an attribute which human nature acquires through participation in a given culture; it is the product of sociocultural participation and recognition. A person, in sum, may be described as the product and agent of the sociocultural process.

It is implied in the foregoing propositions, that human nature is logically and genetically prior to personality. Personality is an attribute which man acquires historically through participation in sociocultural life; human nature is a pre-cultural or meta-cultural notion in the sense that it is postulated as the condition of the cultural process and is therefore not to be explained in terms of the latter. Otherwise, if one attempts to explain human nature in terms of culture, as La Piere and Farnsworth have done in their *Social Psychology*,[16] one commits the culturalistic fallacy of reducing nature to culture.[17] If, as the culturologists maintain, it is fallacious to reduce cultural phenomena to psychology, it is equally fallacious to reduce psychology to cultural processes. Personality is a cultural attribute of human nature but is not identical with the latter.

5. *Some Psychological Definitions of Personality in Contemporary Personality and Culture Studies*

Although contemporary cultural anthropologists are keenly aware of the influence of culture on the formation of personality, they are still inclined to define personality in purely psychological terms. They tend to imply that the concept of personality is primarily a psychological notion but that one must take into consid-

[15]See also A. Angyal's *Foundations for a Science of Personality*. New York, 1941. p. 199. According to Angyal "The factor of acculturation makes a person out of a human organism."

[16]R. T. LaPiere & P. R. Farnsworth, *Social Psychology* (2nd ed.). New York, 1942.

[17]For a more detailed discussion of this point, see the writer's paper, "Human Nature and the Cultural Process," *American Anthropologist*, 49, 1947.

eration the cultural background of personality in order to provide
an adequate analysis of the structure and functions of given personality types.

Thus we find that Ralph Linton in his *Cultural Background of
Personality* writes:

"For the purpose of the present discussion, personality will be
taken to mean: 'The organized aggregate of psychological processes and states pertaining to the individual.' This definition includes the common element in most of the definitions now current.
At the same time it excludes many orders of phenomena which have
been included in one or another of these definitions. Thus it rules
out the overt behavior resulting from the operation of these processes and states, although it is only from such behavior that their
nature and even existence can be deduced. It also excludes from
consideration the effects of this behavior upon the individual's
environment, even that part of it which consists of other individuals. Lastly, it excludes from the personality concept the physical
structure of the individual and his physiological processes. This
final limitation will appear too drastic to many students of personality, but it has a pragmatic, if not a logical, justification. We
know so little about the physiological accompaniments of psychological phenomena that attempts to deal with the latter in physiological terms still lead to more confusion than clarification."[18]

Linton's definition of personality is essentially psychological
and idealistic, and bears a close similarity to the structuralistic,
mentalistic psychology of Titchener and Wundt. By excluding
from his concept of personality overt behavior and the effects
of this behavior on others, as well as the physical structure and
physiological processes of the individual, he is left with the intro-
spected or inferred covert responses and value-attitudes. It is of
interest to the student of cultural anthropology to remark in this
connection that while Linton has modified his former idealistic
concept of culture and now adopts a realistic approach which
includes overt behavior, he still retains an idealistic, mentalistic
position as regards the concept of personality.

Similarly John Gillin states in his text *The Ways of Men:*

[18]R. Linton, *Cultural Background of Personality.* New York, 1945, p.
84.

"We shall regard a personality, for present purposes, as an internal organization of emotions, attitudes, idea patterns, and tendencies to overt action. This internal organization is empirically manifested in a continuity which may be called the 'style of life'."[19]

Gillin's definition of personality is essentially identical with that of Linton since the former explicitly agrees that personality is an "internal organization" of psychological states and tendencies to action. Nevertheless, Gillin later explains that "The difference between an *individual* and a *person* is that the latter is an individual who has been socialized, who has absorbed and organized internally to some extent the tenets of his culture so that he is recognized by other individuals as a personal integration, the cultural components of which, at least, are commonly understood in the group."[20] This statement implies that a person is essentially a cultural product and hence may not be conceived in purely psychological terms as may an individual. In actual fact, however, Gillin, like Linton, provides a psychological definition of an individual while claiming to present a definition of personality.

Kluckhohn and Mowrer also provide a psychological definition of personality but unlike Linton, they adopt the approach of social behaviorism and define personality in terms of "social stimulus value." In their paper on *"Culture and Personality": A Conceptual Scheme* they explain:

"We follow May in assuming that the parameters of a personality may be defined by a human organism's effects upon others. All attempts to describe an individual 'as he really is' must be regarded as extra-scientific unless they are firmly based upon the regularities in the stimulus value which this individual has *for others*. The only way an observer can 'know' other personalities is by noting and making inferences of their *social stimulus value* —whether in casual social relationships, in controlled interviews, or as manifested in more refined experimental situations such as those provided by the various projective techniques. A subject's own statement of his needs, motives, etc., will normally constitute an important part of the data but can never be taken at their face

[19]J. Gillin, *The Ways of Men.* New York, 1948, p. 573.
[20]Ibid, p. 577.

44

value without critical evaluation—they must always be interpreted in terms of the reactions of one or more observers. The definition of personality as social stimulus value seems to us one which will permit relatively objective operations."[21]

As contrasted with the Watsonian behavioristic approach wherein personality is defined as "the sum total of habit systems," Mark May shifts the emphasis from the individual's response or reactions to the stimulus value or effects of his behavior upon others.[22] The nature of one's personality is said to be determined by how one is responded to, by how one is treated, so to speak, rather than by one's own response or self-estimation. In accepting May's position, Kluckhohn and Mowrer have thus adopted a social, behavioristic approach which is the antithesis of the introspective, subjective approach of Linton who explicitly excludes overt behavior and its effects upon others from his definition of personality. It is of interest, furthermore, to note here that whereas Kluckhohn's concept of culture is idealistic inasmuch as he holds culture to be "a mental construct," his definition of personality is objective and behavioristic. For Linton, on the other hand, the situation is reversed since he now accepts a realistic view of culture but still retains an idealistic concept of personality.

In another publication on *Dynamic Theory of Personality* written a little earlier, Kluckhohn and Mowrer reject the position that personality is to be defined as identical with social stimulus value. Thus they write:

"Although we thus recognize the two-fold meaning of the term, we shall employ 'personality' in this chapter to refer to the individual as an organized, adjusting, behaving entity, not to the way in which this individual may influence other individuals (or things). We acknowledge that before any 'personality' can become an object of scientific study, that individual must indeed *have* 'social stimulus value' i.e., other human beings must be able to observe and make coherent statements about him; but this is not to say that this 'social stimulus value' *is* the individual's per-

[21]C. Kluckhohn and O. H. Mowrer, *"Culture and Personality": A Conceptual Scheme*, American Anthropologist, 46, 1944, pp. 1-29.
[22]See M. A. May, *The Foundations of Personality*, Ch. 4 of "Psychology at Work," (P. S. Achilles, ed.), 1932, pp. 82-83.

sonality. The order of effects which an object of scientific study has upon the observing scientist is very different from the type of effects, namely, the rewards and punishments, which are instrumental in determining both an individual's 'reputation' with others and his own habit structure. It is, we believe, in the latter sense that clinicians most often use the term personality; and this definition is also most consistent with our emphasis on learning; for what an individual is or becomes is determined, not primarily by the way in which his actions reward or punish others, but by the way in which these actions directly or indirectly affect the individual himself."[23]

Here the authors acknowledge that while an individual as a person does indeed have social stimulus value, the latter is not to be identified with his personality because the order of effects varies so greatly. Instead they prefer to employ the term personality in the clinicians' sense as referring to an individual's habit structure acquired through the process of learning.

In a footnote to the above publication, Kluckhohn and Mowrer refer to the disparity in their concepts of personality. They remark:

"Elsewhere an attempt has been made to explore and elaborate the concept of personality as 'social stimulus value.' In adopting a different conception for the purposes of this chapter, we make no judgment as to which is ultimately 'right,' i.e., most generally useful. Such a judgment would demand an analysis of the nature of *observation of* vs. *participation in* social events and of the factor of reciprocity in relation to all social roles which would take us far beyond the scope of this chapter."[24]

Again, in another footnote to their paper on *"Culture and Personality": A Conceptual Scheme* they explain:

"Second, we are addressing ourselves to two different sets of questions in our two publications. In this article the interest centers upon classificatory abstractions and upon the query: how do we attain our knowledge of personality? The other paper has a point of view which might be designated as 'clinical'; the central

[23]In J. McV. Hunt, ed., *Personality and the Behavior Disorders.* New York, 1944, vol. 1, pp. 77-78.
[24]Ibid, p. 78.

46

question is more nearly: what *is* personality? Here personality is seen largely from the standpoint of the reactor; there we try to see personality as it may be imputed to the actor. Perhaps a philosopher might say that the point of view of this paper approaches the 'epistemological,' that of the other the 'ontological.' The history of science permits two inductions: 1. it is useful to behave experimentally with respect to conceptual schemes without necessarily claiming 'truth' for one to the exclusion of another. 2. a conceptual scheme may be appropriate for analyzing one group of problems, utterly inappropriate for treating the same set of data with a view to a different group of equally legitimate questions."[25]

These candid comments are significant in that they explicitly raise the problem of the validity of scientific definitions. In general, it would appear that Kluckhohn and Mowrer as well as Linton take the position that a scientific definition is to be evaluated by its pragmatic utility in a given context of research. "Truth" as regards definitions is taken as the equivalent of general utility for a given purpose and hence it is claimed that the scientist is not bound to accept any one definition as *the* "true" or "right" one.

As against this pragmatic position it may be pointed out that a real or scientific definition is supposed to define the universal or logical essence of an object—that in virtue of which a thing is what it is. A scientifically valid and adequate definition, as distinct from a purely conventional or arbitrary one, is one that delimits the nature of an object *as a whole* and does not identify the properties which pertain to a part only with the object as a whole. A scientific definition, in sum, is one that may be *epistemologically* verified in every instance of the object's presence, and that has *ontological* import as well in the sense that it defines the essence or principle of being of its object, so that granted the actual presence of a given form or set of properties the object in question is also present. Thus the attempt made on the part of Kluckhohn and Mowrer to differentiate between an epistemological and an ontological definition appears to be invalid, since a valid definition has both epistemological and ontological import

[25]Kluckhohn and Mowrer, American Anthropologist, 46, 1944.

at one and the same time.

Furthermore, while it may be granted that a scientific definition is one that may be pragmatically verified and leads to specific practical consequences, as pragmatists since Charles Peirce and William James have maintained, the fact remains that unless a definition provides a universal, logically coherent concept, there is no way of determining whether one is dealing with one and the same type of object. That is to say, an adequate, scientific definition is one that provides a coherent, universal logical concept which, in practice, may be verified by the consequences to which it leads. The primary factor, however, is the universal, logical concept. Otherwise, if one accepts the pragmatic criterion as primary, then he becomes involved in an arbitrary pluralism and nominalism so that it becomes impossible to obtain any common measure of agreement as to what a thing is or how it is to be conceived. Thus one and the same pragmatic investigator finds himself providing many definitions of the same object, each of which he claims is pragmatically justified in a given context. The situation becomes truly scandalous when two or more "scientific" pragmatists provide conflicting definitions, as in the case of Linton's and Kluckhohn's definitions of personality, and find that they have no common measure of "truth" and "rightness" beyond their own preferences. The only way out of this impasse, it would appear, is for scholars to acknowledge that an adequate and scientific definition is one that provides a logically coherent as well as practically verifiable concept—one which connotes the essential properties of an object and at the same time denotes the practical epistemological means of its own verification.[26]

6. *Person and Personality as Polaristic, Psychocultural Concepts*

The implicit assumption underlying the attempts of contemporary cultural anthropologists to provide psychological definitions of personality is the notion that there is a duality of personality *and* culture, each of which is intelligible in itself, and that it is

[26]For a more detailed discussion of this problem, see N. S. Timasheff: *Definitions in the Social Sciences*, American Journal of Sociology, 53, 1947, 201-209.

the task of the ethnologist to demonstrate their interrelation in given sociocultural systems. This explains why anthropologists such as Linton, Gillin and Kluckhohn, while fully cognizant of the role of culture in the formation of personality, nevertheless proceed in their formal definitions of personality to exclude culture entirely.

As against this basic current assumption, my thesis is that the concept of personality is *a priori* a psychocultural notion. It is not merely that there is a cultural element or aspect to personality, as Margaret Mead,[27] for instance, has maintained, but that the concept of personality connotes logically and esssentially a polaristic, psychocultural entity. Hence it does not make sense to provide a purely psychological definition of personality, since psychology tells us nothing about the special attitude and mode of activity of a person in a given sociocultural context.

By way of concise and systematic formulation, I wish to submit the following definitions of person and personality together with some inferential comments:

1. *A person may be defined as the socially recognized subject or agent of psychocultural interaction.*

A person may be either an individual or a corporation such as the state. Any one who performs a given cultural role in society involving duties and rights is a person.

2. *A personality is a determinate psychocultural action and reaction pattern, whether overt or covert, which is typical or characteristic of an individual (or organization of individuals) in the performance of his sociocultural role at a given stage of development.*

Personality is an attribute of persons; it is a property which is the product of sociocultural participation and recognition. Personality refers to the form or structure of a person and hence implies the prior existence of a person. Only persons are the agents or patients of the cultural process.[28]

[27]Margaret Mead, *The Cultural Approach to Personality* in P. L. Harriman, ed., "New Dictionary of Psychology," New York, 1947.

[28] Compare Gardner Murphy's views in his *Personality*. New York, 1947, pp. 7-8. Murphy fails to distinguish between *a person* who is a concrete entity capable of initiating sociocultural activity and *a person-*

Personality is something historically acquired by an individual in the course of sociocultural life in society and hence requires social recognition. A person depends for his very existence upon the sociocultural recognition he receives. Hence there can be no persons apart from human society.

A person is a polaristic entity in the sense that he comprises two distinct elements, namely, the element of human nature and that of culture. As noted earlier (section 4) human nature and personality are not to be identified since human nature is pre-cultural or meta-cultural. The polarity of personality is manifested by the fact of tension between the individual and his society which gives rise to deviants or non-conformists who fail to conform to the modal personality type.

Furthermore, since the personality of an individual changes with his cultural role as well as his psychosomatic constitution as he passes through the ages of life, any one individual may be said to have a plurality of personalities at a given time or in a sequence of time. There may be a plurality of persons in one individual and many individuals may unite to form a single corporate person, such as the state, with a distinct personality over and above the personalities of its participant members.

The uniqueness of any given person is a product of the special constitutional, social and cultural factors which have combined to make him what he is. Every personality may be said to have its special as well as its general aspects which it shares with other personality structures. In general, it would appear, the psychologists have tended to stress the uniqueness of the person, while the cultural anthropologists have drawn attention to the common elements or traits, to the "basic personality structure" or "modal personality" which the individual shares with the other members of his cultural community. Either approach taken by itself is an abstraction since the concrete person manifests both particular or special as well as general or universal personality traits. For general purposes, however, such as the evaluation of a person's

ality which is a conceptual abstraction of the attributes of a given person. Personality is said to refer to an individual, a structured whole and to a structured organism-environment field.

political rights, the uniqueness of personality may be ignored and the "equality" of all persons before the law proclaimed. All men are not born equal, but persons may be treated and recognized as equals.

It is important to distinguish in this connection between the general, *ideal personality structure* and the *real personality structure*. The ideal personality structure is a product of the cultural ideals one has acquired and professes. The real personality structure is an inference from the observable behavior or practices of the average member of a given sociocultural group and only partially corresponds to the social ideals professed. A major source of prejudice and misunderstanding may be traced to the tendency to evaluate the "social character" of one's own ethnic group in terms of the ideal personality structure and to form "stereotypes" of alien ethnic groups, especially minority groups in one's midst, which are based on partial observation of the behavior of a few individuals, and hence do not correspond to actual social facts and norms.

As a member of a particular group or class, an individual also acquires a class or "status" personality which may be in conflict with the class or status personality of other groups. One of the fundamental issues of contemporary political thought and practice is whether the individual as a citizen may participate in a common or communal personality whose interests transcend those of his class personality, whether the state as a person is to govern in the common interests of all classes or whether it must necessarily govern in the interests of some one class. To my mind that is the basic issue as between democracy and totalitarianism (whether of the left or right) from the perspective of personality and culture.

Finally, with the progress of cultural ideals and cultural diffusion there is gradually emerging the notion of a fundamental, universal culture for humanity as a whole. Insofar as men come to regard themselves as citizens of a common cultural world they may also acquire a cosmopolitan or universal personality and recognize universal human rights. At present the concept of a universal ideal personality is far from realization but it is nevertheless significant as a norm and objective which the social scientists of the world may help mankind attain in the future. The recent Universal Declaration of Human Rights approved by a committee of the United Nations is a step forward in this direction.

DISCUSSION

DR. RALPH LINTON: When a philosopher accuses anyone of being pragmatic he ought to smile as he says it! The value of a definition always is relative to a particular matter in hand. I have no quarrel with Dr. Kluckhohn's definition and I think he has little quarrel with mine. It's a little like one of us defining a bomb in terms of the amount of damage it does and the other by the amount of explosive charge it contains. It depends on what you're trying to do. Other than the pragmatic test, the test of utility, I don't know what tests to apply. Has the idealist some form of absolute truth that can be arrived at in a definition?

DR. BIDNEY: I do think that a scientific definition of any phenomenon aims at taking into consideration all available data.

DR. LINTON: But that ceases to be a definition, and becomes a treatise.

DR. BIDNEY: No, it does not. It's simply that if there is such thing as greater or less adequacy of a definition.

DR. LINTON: Adequacy for what?

DR. BIDNEY: There are two criteria for a definition; let me put it this way. I am not denying that the pragmatic test is significant; I am saying that it is not enough, because then one becomes involved in a hopeless relativity. In addition, there is the logical test of coherency and adequacy for all perspectives. That is, for a complete understanding of a phenomenon, pragmatism is not enough.

DR. ASHLEY-MONTAGU: We are here engaged at the beginning of a problem that requires definition. A definition can be meaningful only at the end rather than at the start of an inquiry.

DR. CLYDE KLUCKHOHN: I agree with Linton and with Ashley-Montagu. At the present stage of this inquiry it seems useful to behave experimentally—by trial and error, if you like—with respect to conceptual schemes. Mowrer and I, in another paper published about the same time, in "Personality and the Behavior Disorders," unashamedly and with full awareness, used another definition. And I may say that in the volume Henry Murray and I have in press, we have still another definition of personality! With the evidence in hand we can't tell on logical grounds what definition is (a) most useful, and (b) most logically consistent, though I agree with Dr. Bidney that both of those criteria are relevant in the long run. I also tend to agree with Dr. Bidney when he ticks Dr. Linton and me off for not having culture somewhere rearing its pleasant head in our definitions of personality. This came to me as something of a shock; I'm afraid it's true.

DR. GARDNER MURPHY: I am in agreement with Dr. Bidney's presentation. Just two things call for comment—perhaps semantic issues. First he noted that in my definition of personality, several emphases were made which would apply to other things in nature that are not personality. The matter of being field-determined, or of being an aspect of a complex multi-dimensional whole, might be said to be true of biological reactions or physico-chemical reactions generally. I not only don't object to that accusation, but would say that it is very important to get a definition of personality which is completely naturalistic and at the same time gives full weight to cultural factors. But I would say that the field issue applies to a certain *genus* of events; that particular kind of field-definition which applies to human personality is a *species* or even a *variety*. It's a more narrowly contained group. I personally would agree with Katz's use of the term, defined long ago in connection with the personalities of animals. Anyone who knows pets realizes that all the phenomena we talk about, including reciprocity, mutual selection, control by complex interpersonal factors, hold at least for higher animals as they do for man. I don't want to get into an argument about whether the term culture should be stretched, but as far as the interpersonal phenomena are concerned, under the head of temperamental molding and all that, that applies to animal personality. And so I don't think it would get us anywhere and would greatly confuse the issue to introduce the word human. What I tried to do in speaking of organism-environment selection was to emphasize that I thought the problem was broader than the problem of culture. With human beings in a cultural setting the same basic issues are involved as with living organisms generally in relation to their environment.

Now in relation to the terms "person" and "personality"; unfortunately we're living in a community which uses these terms in all sorts of different senses. I indicated three uses of the term personality which are found rather generally in existing literature. I tried to make the point that the first two uses, while frequently found, are not in general suitable to most psychological problems, although there are problems for which they are useful. But for most problems with which you and I are concerned it is the third definition which essentially agrees with Dr. Bidney's definition, and with which I concur.

DR. JOSEPH BRAM: When Dr. Bidney tells us that social scientists use the same word personality to refer to different phenomena, I don't think we should quarrel with him. It happens to be true. So we should say "personality as understood by Ralph Linton," or "as understood by Mowrer and Kluckhohn," or as understood by someone else.

DR. BIDNEY: I'd like to comment on this point of using the same term for different phenomena. Anyone who has listened to the detailed and illuminating talk by Dr. Murphy about the inseparability of personality and culture has been provided with an analysis of what the preceding speaker regards as objectively true in some sense. A definition of personality, to be adequate, must indicate precisely this predominance of culture. It must indicate that, *a priori,* your definition of personality must be in terms of culture. Once one has granted the predominance of culture, it must be utilized in the definition. So it is not just a matter of "as you like it," or of different perspectives; there is a certain objective situation which has to be taken into consideration.

Dr. BERNARD STERN: You seem to assume that there are sociologists and anthropologists who formally separate the cultural-historical pattern from the personalities who convey and participate in this pattern. Actually, in introductory textbooks and in recent journals, the role of personality and of persons in conveying the cultural tradition is adequately taken care of. In fact, the issue of the American Anthropologist which followed directly after Dr. Kroeber's article on the superorganic, contained an article by Professor Sapir on the hazards involved in treating the superorganic in this formalistic sense.

I think the danger lies not in the cultural fallacy but in the personality fallacy. And your later remarks stressed that very point—that in dealing with the participants in culture and being so concerned with the personality role, we forget the historical continuities and the structural parts of culture and the objective traditions of culture which go on irrespective of the generations, and of the individual and group which participates and shares in the culture at any specific time.

Dr. BIDNEY: I think attention has been paid to the study of personality in social science literature, but on the other hand you have considerable stress on the superorganic theory of culture which would preclude that sort of study. Among anthropologists, by and large, the concept of the cultural superorganic has until now maintained its predominant position. My latest paper in the "American Anthropologist" on *Human Nature and the Cultural Process* attempts to show how those two aspects can be reconciled.

Dr. A. H. KROEBER: We have this curious situation: a man, primarily a philosopher, gives a definition of personality which, stripped down, makes it an expression, a product, of culture. And in the main, Dr. Murphy accepts it, emphasizing the role of culture in the formation of personality; whereas we have two definitions of personality by anthropologists which leave culture out! That may be an accident or an oversight. But each side seems to be deferring to the other, which strikes me as a healthy situation.

Dr. LINTON: If personality is entirely a reflection of culture, does Dr. Kluckhohn have a different personality when he is living among the Navaho, a culture different from the one from which presumably his personality was derived?

DR. BIDNEY: I did not say that personality is *entirely* a matter of culture. I said it is *primarily* to be conceived in cultural terms, but I do not exclude psychobiological aspects. In that sense, Dr. Kluckhohn among the Navaho would be carrying with him action and reaction patterns adopted in this particular culture which he would not shed so easily.

MRS. KLUCKHOHN: He acts very differently though when he's down there!

DR. POWDERMAKER: Part of Dr. Bidney's difficulty arises from selecting one or two sentences as representing the point of view of Dr. Linton, Kluckhohn, etc., in regard to personality or culture. In Dr. Linton's book, "The Cultural Background of Personality," he includes the cultural factors. The same is true of Dr. Kluckhohn's article which gives, as I remember, 16 boxes representing 16 influences on personality. I don't like a method which takes a person's point of view from one sentence.

DR. BIDNEY: I am fully cognizant that Dr. Linton and Dr. Kluckhohn are aware of the role of culture in personality. All I say is that any anthropologist who is as fully aware as they are of the role of culture in personality should take account of it in his definition, since definitions are supposed to be comprehensive and reflect an objective situation. To point up the disparity between their formal definitions and the general context of their analysis is not to distort or misrepresent their position.

DR. FRANK: This situation has been met with before. When two or more disciplines find that their focus of attention begins to overlap, then something takes place. With biochemistry, biology and chemistry had to refashion some of their concepts. The same thing happened with biophysics. When psychiatry and internal medicine began to realize that they overlapped, we got psychosomatic medicine. Aren't we faced with much the same situation? Maybe we'll have to find some new terminologies and a new conceptual framework. This term "psychocultural" that some of us are using may represent a rather clumsy attempt at bringing together culture and personality. This difficulty will be resolved by a synthesis and not by saying "my way is better than another."

TECHNIQUES FOR STUDYING CULTURE AND PERSONALITY

ABRAM KARDINER

Psychodynamics and the Social Sciences

Psychodynamics is now upwards of half a century old. It has had its testing in the labors of hundreds of independent workers, the world over. The conclusions and techniques of psychodynamics have more recently been subjected to a great deal of experimental verification. There is hardly a psychology today that has not been influenced by it. A large proportion of the problems now being worked over by all psychologies was created by it. It is not too soon therefore to appraise its merits, and to discard the spurious uses that have been made of it. Among the latter was the effort to subvert the conclusions of psychodynamics as a justification for a philosophy of hedonism, or a justification of the position that frustration produces aggression and if man suppresses his aggressions, he will blow up—or the like. We cannot allow these vulgarizations to detract from the real achievements of psychodynamics. This discipline has enriched man's knowledge of himself; it introduced the genetic and dynamic points of view; it showed how integrative processes operate to create such end products as the neurotic trait or the character trait and demonstrated the possibility that some of these reactions are reversible.

This is achievement indeed. But this achievement still rests on a tentative basis because the maneuvers and conclusions of psychodynamics, having no universal precise language like mathematics, could not be expressed in quantitative terms—to which the natural sciences owe so much of their authority. They could only be expressed in terms of identifiable constellations arranged in terms of sequence or other relationships. Beginning with an end product like a symptom or character trait, Freud studied the trait genetically. That is, every end product was shown to have certain identifiable antecedents, some of which could be tracked down to infancy. If these antecedents were not the same as the end product, what accounted for the change? Some intrapsychic maneuvers were responsible for the change. These intrapsychic maneuvers were the dynamic changes. This portion of Freud's observations belong to the *data*. However, no series of data can be of much use unless they are strung along some frame of reference. And this is where the great difficulties arise.

Freud settled on a certain frame of reference, after trying several others. He began with the assumption that the maneuvers he described in his dynamics were *defensive* in intent, protective in function. This assumption would in itself hardly ever be challenged. But something more was necessary, for the assumption had to be implemented with more operational concepts whose workability could be demonstrated on the observed data. Some allowances must be made for the fact that Freud was improvising his operational concepts as he went along and hence did not have any foreknowledge of how effective any group of operational concepts would be twenty years hence. It is no wonder, therefore, that he yielded to the operational system that gave the most satisfactory immediate results—not knowing what incompatibilities might ultimately arise.

And so it happened that he settled on an operational scheme based upon the interference with *instinct* gratification. The die was cast for two reasons: first that many neuroses are the natural consequence of that part of western mores which interfere with normal sexual maturation; and secondly because of sexual "instinct" had a rich representability in the imagery of dreams and symptoms. Hence Freud had an excellent opportunity to demonstrate dynamics by showing successive changes in instinct gratification. (See Fig. 1.)

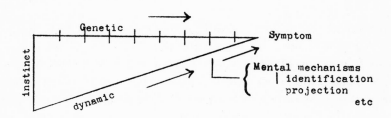

This operational scheme is commonly known as the libido theory. A great many students of human nature, who ought to know better, cannot tell *data* from *operational scheme* or *frame of reference,* and are constantly mistaking one for the other. Most of the confusion in contemporary psychology which deals with data of direct experience and behavior is caused by the failure to differentiate data from frame of reference. Thus it comes about that most of the discoveries of Freud, as data and their relations (e.g. temporal, causal, or dynamic sequence), are completely accepted and even taken for granted, but the frame of reference is altered, and on this basis the claim is made for a new *psychology*. This is not only false, but dishonest as well. Having dabbled a good deal with frames of reference, I have only a limited respect for them. They are implements with which to manipulate facts; but no one who accepts the basic discoveries of Freud and translates them into a new frame of reference has any claim to a new discovery.

This battle over frames of reference is much over-estimated, and is creating endless confusion over nonessentials. It is the penalty of having to describe psychological events in terms of sequence and structure and not in quantity.

The libido theory had a good deal of operational effectiveness, up to a point. Freud recognized this and tried many times to alter it, but without much success. This was only one of the difficulties of the libido theory. Another source was the assumptions which Freud entertained in connection with its use. These assumptions all came from the theory of evolution or rather that aspect of it that was promoted by Haeckel. Recapitulation was the slogan of the German evolutionists. From the theory of evolution sprang the concept of fixed stages of human development which were identified in the genetic picture of man. What stage of man's phylogenetic evolutionary march did such and such a stage of development mean? This was always the answer sought.

This assumption was not merely a gratuitous ornament of an operational scheme; it was an integral part and it assisted in the interpretation of the significance of clinical facts. For instance, in one place Freud asks what catastrophe the human species went through that was recapitulated in the latency period of the growing child. Thus the "stages of development" were marked off according to the primacy of certain erogenous zones. There was a narcissistic, phallic, anal and sadistic Oedipal, latency, genital phase.

61

Whatever the merits of this aspect of the libido theory, it created difficulty in the interpretation of facts encountered in the comparative study of culture. Freud's own efforts in this direction were limited in scope. He sought only to establish the analogy between primitive ritual and the obsessional neurotic, etc. Moreover, Freud was reading all the evolutionary anthropologists who, if anything, encouraged his point of view. Thus a pseudo-problem was created: what was due to phylogeny and what to experience? This issue could not be settled on the merits of any theoretical considerations. It could only be settled in the laboratory of comparative social psychology.

For this purpose psychodynamics had already evolved a consistent operational scheme. Leaving out some of the assumptions of the libido theory, it was a good scheme for tracking down the origin of certain traits of man, not as fixed stages of development,

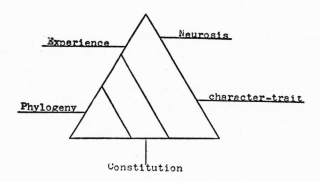

but as reactions of innate predispositions to environmental pressures. Once this new hypothesis was accepted as a working plan, a wide range of comparative research was opened up. Anthropology had already refined the concept of culture to a degree that one could begin to compare the institutions of different cultures, and trace the effect these institutionalized practises have when they are genetically integrated. This study of the effects of certain practises on the growing individual gives an adequate basis for predicting what kind of a human being will be the product of these cumulative influences. This was called *Basic Personality*, which means ego structure.

The influences whose effects are thus tracked down in the personality structure are all institutionalized practises. They include maternal care, induction of affectivity, initial disciplines, permissive or restricted behavior in any phase of adaptation, sexual permissions or restraints, activities of parents, etc., through the life cycle. Crucial and decisive factors which influence the personality can occur in any phase of the life cycle. Childhood is decisive only if the influences are of a constricting character.

Thus the concept *basic personality* is merely an inventory of characteristics. In itself it not only has no operational value, for this is supplied by psychodynamics, but it has been known since Herodotus. Psychodynamics did not discover basic personality. Intuitively it has long since been known. But what psychodynamics did do was to supply a specific bill of particulars as to what practises are responsible for what traits, or what combination of influences yield what end results in personality configurations. To track these down requires an expert knowledge of psychodynamics. The real achievement of psychodynamics was to demonstrate that this basic personality is not an idiosyncratic conglomeration of traits, but is a direct function of the institutions by which it is moulded. In addition, psychodynamics demonstrated that the relationship of formative institutions to personality formation does not end with the personality itself; but this personality then goes on to create characteristic secondary phenomena. The following scheme shows the relationship:

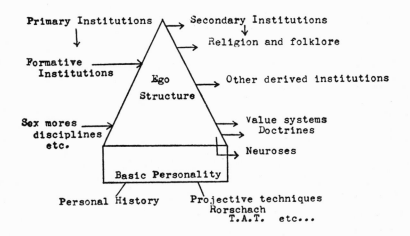

It is apparent from this scheme that the study of personality in a given culture is therefore central. But not as an isolated phenomenon, but as a nodal point in the study of culture itself. I might observe parenthetically that recent efforts to pursue this line of research concentrate much effort to describe basic personality without regard to the connection of personality to the institutional practises from which it is derived, or the secondary derivatives which spring from it. Also there have been wholesale efforts to describe the "national character" by making an inventory of so-called traits which are supposed to be characteristic of national groups. The errors in these attempts are uniform: they are descriptive, have no dynamic connections, and are very misleading. No effort is made to differentiate between basic traits and local idiosyncracies, no distinction between learned and integrative systems, between superficial and in many cases transient vogues and basic traits. But the most serious objection to these attempts is that no use can be made of them. Just as at one time the attitude in anthropology was that one people do one thing and another people another. Now it reads some people behave one way and some another. This is gratuitous information of no use to the social sciences and assuredly no implement in the hands of the social engineers. It tells us nothing about the dynamics of social processes.

Another equally foolish debate has arisen over the proper name for common group characteristics. This comes under the head of slogan invention, and has no bearing on the basic problem, which is one of social dynamics and not of catch phrases.

Another tendency in connection with this type of research is to gather data which seem to satisfy the requirements of the synthesis, but which on close examination fail to live up to the specifications. There are personality studies which do not supply the crucial information; tests which do not jibe with personality studies, and conclusions which have nothing to do with any of the material presented. In other instances two collaborators will join in a common effort, but have no agreement; hence no valid conclusions can be drawn from material, the parts of which are based on different frames of reference. Naturally, no valid conclusions can be drawn from such material because most authors do not publish their original protocols, but an edited version. It is this editorial selection which is a function of the frame of reference. In many instances no psychodynamic frame of reference can be detected. A work which shows such confusion is a pitiful waste of opportunity. For the need is urgent, and the task workable, to describe forty or fifty basic patterns of social organization, and to test the limits of the hypothesis outlined above.

In other words, one cannot separate the study of personality from the circumstances in which it arises or from the secondary or expressive activities and needs which such a personality has. The entire scheme is one finely interarticulated unit.

Whereas the scheme as a whole has, to a measure, been fairly well established, some parts of it are subject to a more complete verification than others. The basic personality can be checked directly. One can investigate the personalities themselves by a process of sampling. One can study 12-20 individuals in any given culture. Here, of course, a sharp distinction must be drawn between the *basic personality* and the *specific character* of the individual. The first tells you how an Eskimo differs from an Okinawan; the second tells you how one Eskimo differs from another Eskimo. All character variations move within the ambit of the same basic personality.

It is in connection with both basic personality and individual character variations that the projective tests, notably the Rorschach, are of great value. The work of Oberholzer on the Alorese is a confirmation of the technique and in part a vindication of the principles in back of the technique. His analysis is divided into a part which deals with those traits common to all Alorese, and another to the specific characters of the individuals. Those traits common to all are the basic personality.

There is no absolute way to prove the validity of the technique. What is offered in the way of confirming the personality configurations is no absolute proof. All one can do is to get more and more evidence. That tends to confirm or contradict. When such discrepancies occur, it is an invitation to reexamine the original evidence. In short, the Rorschach can check the results of the projective anlysis, or offer new suggestions about what to look for.

So far the personality constellations alone can be checked by

65

some direct evidence. The other two facets, the formative institutions and the derived institutions, can only be checked by cross-cultural surveys. This is extremely difficult to prove, because no two cultures are alike, and what one learns from one culture is translatable into another only to a limited extent.

The first facet—the formative institutions—leads inevitably to the question why one culture seeks one type of solution to a social difficulty, and another culture a solution of entirely different character. One cannot avoid being teleological in a question like this. Purpose is obviously involved. Yet evidence points strongly to the probability that purpose is defined after experience and not before. What means is suited for what end may become apparent after some accidental experience which works toward a desired end and not *a priori*. "Social planning" is not characteristic of man—not as far as human relations go—in contrast to his behavior to the outer world. Sex mores is a case in point. Why do some cultures interdict sexual activity in childhood and others not? The only visible consequence of completely free expression of the sexual drive would be an uncontrollable increase in population. Conceptions of kinship can only be based on several restrictions and claims on either cooperation of some kind or vested interests. Is it an important correlation that some cultures that have permissive attitudes toward sexual activity of children limit population by female infanticide?

These questions are difficult to answer without a history of the culture. For the greater part, such histories are forever lost, and cannot be reconstructed. The reason for this is that certain types of mores can outlive any original purpose for which they were designed, the reasons forgotten, but nevertheless persist indefinitely. Who could reconstruct the original purpose of our own mores relative to the sexual activities of childhood? No one knows anything about it; the people who transmit these mores do not know why they do so, except that it has always been that way.

This problem of origins and purposes is not crucial to the research here described. It makes no difference why a group of mores arose; its effects on personality formation can be accurately traced. One can always work with these mores as one of the fixed conditions of a vast social experiment.

The other facet, the derived institutions, is at once the most difficult and interesting aspect of this type of research. If we look down the right hand column on Figure 3, we note an array of social manifestations which seem to have very little in common. What indeed have the kind of neuroses found in a culture to do with their religion and folklore? They all have an expressive function; they are all tension relievers. Suppose we take a single illustration, show how a basic institution, through its effects on personality, influences all secondary systems:

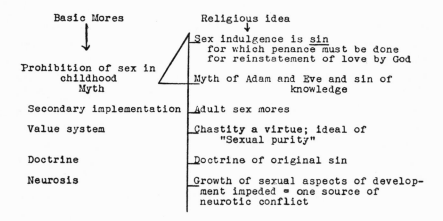

We can see from the events recorded that if this one condition in the basic training of the child, restriction of sexual activity, were *not* present, the other derivative issues would never arise.

Let us consider this series from the bottom up. The neurosis is a very remarkable phenomenon. From the parochial standpoint of medical practise, it is just a disease. It is much more than that. It is an indicator that some essential need tension is being denied outlet—but not to the extent that the individual is being crushed. It is an indication of a tolerable squeeze, one to which man can make some accommodation. Neurotic manifestations are therefore bound to differ in different cultures. It is no accident, therefore, that Linton reports a common neurosis among Marquesan women —feigned pregnancy—which is rare in Western society. From a comparison of our culture with Marquesan we cannot expect the same neurosis in both. Disturbances of potency abound in Western

67

culture, but are not to be expected in Marquesan. This could only take place there under very atypical circumstances—quite outside the cultural mould.

We can expect no Adam and Eve myth in Marquesas; no doctrine of original sin, no idea of penitence and forgiveness, no ideal of chastity as a virtue or ideal.

This scheme does not encourage any idea of any unanchored relativity in mores or ethics. It does not encourage the belief that the human being can tolerate any pressure put on him in any arbitrary way by cultural mores. Let it be remembered that all those cultures we have a chance to study have survived; we do not know how many thousands of cultures have perished because of the incompatibilities in the culture which led to mutual destruction. Such a fate should not surprise us—Rome went down for this reason, even though it survived for over a millenium.

Many questions arise in connection with this frame of reference. The most important is, does it work? Haven't we just made a lucky strike by picking out a particular system of basic mores in which all these secondary effects are so easily traceable? Maybe so. It may be a freak. This can only be verified by more intensive study.

A second question is, how are these basic mores, like permissive sexual attitudes to children, determined? From those cultures studied we can conclude that sex mores are never arbitrary; they are in all cases related to basic problems in adaptation, but conditioned by one biological fact—that sexual maturity precedes social maturity. Hence there is always some need for sexual restriction.

A third question concerns the contingency of projective systems on mores and not on differences in temperament. Temperament only decides basic attitudes within the fixed system determined by the basic personality.

The question of *fixed human* nature as against a *complete relativism* raises a spurious issue. The psychodynamic study of culture shows certain points in human nature that are fixed by culture and remain so for long periods of time. They remain fixed as long as the basic institutions from which these traits originate remain unchanged. When the basic institution changes, the rest of the derived system changes also, because the personality structure changes in accordance with the altered experience. Why does it need such unusual circumstances to produce change in these basic mores? Because man is not aware of their effects. It took psychodynamics to show that in Western society the neurosis originates in the effects of certain sex and disciplinary mores on the biologically fixed parts of human nature.

Man can only react to unfavorable social arrangements if he knows they exist. One cannot compare the fight against harmful sex mores with the fight against arbitrary power to exploit—like slavery. In the latter domain, man has waged a progressive and successful fight; in the case of basic mores he has not. The social roots of neurosis were not known until Freud, and even he obscured the insight by assuming that more of human nature was phylogenetically fixed than seems to be the case, as demonstrated by the study of the effects of different mores on the personality structure of man.

But here again we have a quantitative and a qualitative problem. Certain kinds of social obstacles man cannot fight against because he doesn't know where the obstacle is. The other is one of quantity—how much strain a given social obstacle creates for men.

The frame of reference described above is not proven. It is merely suggested by those cultures I had the opportunity to study with the collaboration of Drs. Linton, DuBois, West, and others. The older and more complex a culture, the more difficult to track down this simple scheme. Here, as for example in Western society, one runs across traditional evaluations of mores on the basis of ethical and philosophical systems. One gets into still more trouble if one tries to reconcile the findings of psychodynamics with these traditional points of view. This is an exceedingly difficult task, the usefulness of which is very dubious. It is, moreover, the kind of problem that does not occur to the student of comparative culture. In primitive societies one has ethics and value systems also, but there are no systems of thought about them. Hence the task of relating them to basic mores is much simpler. It is only the students of Western society who become weighted down with these problems of reconciling the findings of psychodynamics with traditional philosophical views.

It will take a great deal of labor to demonstrate the usefulness of the operational scheme here described. Those who do not know psychodynamics cannot use it effectively. This statement is not an effort to corner the market for psychiatrists. It merely says that those who use this technique should at least have a working knowledge of human nature according to some definite frame of reference. Published work in this last five years indicates an effort to use it. Therefore, why not use it effectively and not amateurishly? There is a sound reason for this caution. Vast sums of money will be spent on research of this kind which, if not carefully checked and double checked, will be inconclusive and will have to be done over again some day anyhow. There is altogether too much haste and eagerness to put defective material to use, sometimes without any awareness of the errors, sometimes with. We are thus saying that the conditions for applying this technique are exacting. The data must be complete if the conclusions are to be soundly based and capable of demonstration.

The chief innovation that psychodynamics has introduced into the implements of the social sciences is that it makes the human individual again the prime object in the study of social phenomena. There are no primary and secondary institutions in nature; that is the way institutions can be grouped if we take man as the chief focus. The uses of psychodynamics will differ according to the subject matter we choose. The technique yields different results on anthropological data than it does when applied to a segment of our contemporary culture. If we were to study the American negro in his efforts at adaptation we might arrive at a basic negro personality. As an inventory of traits we would not be inclined to set high value on it; but as a correlation of personality distortion under the impact of environmental pressures, its value is likely to prove very high.

The negro has, by common consent, a serious disturbance in his self-esteem. But this information is not enough; even though it is correct. What we need to know in addition is the effects of this disturbance of self-esteem on the remaining personality functions. We need to know what compensatory efforts are set in motion, whether these efforts have any chance of realization, and what

70

happens when these latter, in turn, are blocked. The end products of these blocked compensatory efforts differ in different individuals. In some the outcome is suppressed rage, diminution of general affectivity, and depression. In others the outcome is a complete denial of all these trends and a substitution of abandoned hedonism and a living from moment to moment. The social significance of these two types of resolution of a basic self-esteem difficulty differs widely. At all events, no precise form of social action can be contrived unless we know where the social disturbance comes from and what effects are created in the human unit which makes society.

In other words, psychodynamics has furnished us with a precise instrument for tracking down social pressures. Hence it becomes a powerful implement in the critique of social configurations whether it is used as an all over survey, as in anthropology, or to explore limited segments of a complex society like our own.

DISCUSSION

DR. ERNST KRIS: I wonder whether Dr. Kardiner would agree to a point of view slightly different from his own, not in substance but in approach. If we look upon psychoanalytic propositions from the point of view of verification, we undoubtedly gain the impression that many of those which describe dynamic conditions in the field of present experience are more easily verified than those which make assumptions on relationships of past to present experiences. Verification in the field of Dr. Kardiner's work seems to me to lie in this: if we vary the environmental conditions under which systematic observation is carried on, we should expect to find to what extent the propositions developed in one area of experience are applicable in another. In this process, we may have to modify some of our constructs. We could say: what is true in one civilization, stated as a proposition, may or may not be true in another. In other words, we aim to study variance.

Secondly, I would like to have Dr. Kardiner's reaction to this point. It seems established that experiences of the human being are not all of the same importance. The same experience taking place under certain predisposing conditions will have a different effect from what it would have if it took place under other conditions. This is very largely true of the relationship of gross processes to the dynamic processes of child development. Much of what we today consider knowledge about the development of man is simply related to certain constructs on gross assumptions, in which we take into consideration experiences likely to happen at a given age with the specific biological demand of that age. We would like to ask: Are the ideas which we have formed about the sequence of development variable or invariable, and to what degree? What of some of Freud's assumptions? Is his assumption which is called the latency period itself correlated to cultural changes?

Perhaps I may mention a third field in which the problem of variably and invariably valid propositions could be studied, and that is the comparative study of psychiatric conditions, specifically of psychoses. I remember that C. G. Seligman felt that in no other field could concrete insight into that very problem of variant and invariant conditions be achieved with greater probability. Perhaps that verification so essential in science could be gained by systematic observation under varying cultural conditions, as a means of checking and correcting our propositions.

DR. KARDINER: I can't take exception to anything Dr. Kris said. The only thing I can do is to try to comment. What is true in one culture is not true in another. If you get only the genetic picture of the individual, the particular disciplines and influences to which he is subjected, you can not reconstruct his personality. What sources did I have, therefore, to find what was important in one culture and in another? I had to use the systems shown in my diagrams to give me the clues, because I figured that if a thing operated in one place, it was bound to be an influence in another. Now sometimes these influences are invisible. For example, in Alor a trend was absent—which gave me the idea that something happened. I refer to the absence of constructive interests. Why do these people live in shabby houses? Why do they tolerate dilapidation the way they do? This is so different from western society. This gave me a clue to something. The folklore gave me a great many clues. I can not predict from any picture what is going to happen because there are too many variations, and you always are at the mercy of the ethnographer's data. You also are at the mercy of the particular operational scheme with which you are working. That has its drawbacks too. When you practice psychodynamics for 27 years you acquire not only a great deal of knowledge, but a great many blind spots.

Now with regard to the third question: what affects an individual under one set of conditions and not under another in reference to the latency period? Certainly one cannot imagine that a latency period would exist in a society like the Marquesas, and we don't know how to interpret this latency period if we find it. I believe that the endogenous psychoses are a universal phenomenon, but with differences in content. When I find a psychotic in Alor, and I have seen several, I can't put them into any of the categories that I know. I can't call them manic-depressive. I can't call them schizophrenic or catatonic. I don't know what they are. They behave more like psychopaths in our society, rather than schizophrenics. In regard to neuroses, there is great speculation. And the specificity is most remarkable. Hysteria and obsessional neurosis and the paranoid states in our society take stereotyped forms that are easy to recognize. This is an indication that the personality flows into certain grooves, not only because of the particular conflict situations that are brought to bear on a person in the process of growth, but because of things that happen afterwards. The Freudians so frequently found symptoms of sexual origin, because that happens to be one of the particular places in western society where we squeeze the individual. You don't expect this kind of neurosis in the Marquesas, but you can find feigned pregnancy with great frequency there as a means of avoiding the hardships that accompany the life of a woman.

DR. JOSEPH BRAM: I understand we can use projective systems for the reconstruction of a culture only if these projective systems were known to have originated with the group under investigation. Now we know that most religious systems, ideologies and doctrines are of a historically diffuse nature. A faith like Islam comprises 500 different societies. The same is true of many other world religions. To what extent can we trace the personality of participants in these religions if they are not responsible for the origination of the system as such?

DR. KARDINER: Well, that question is altogether too easy. You know what happens to a religion when it diffuses. It never preserves its pristine quality. It is always modified. And it is always modified in the direction that happens to suit a particular personality. One of the clearest cases on record is the case of Alor. They have the usual stereotyped family gods and all the rest. You can't evaluate their religion on the basis of form, but rather on the basis of how they practice it. They practice it *with neglect*. They don't give a hang about it. It means nothing to them because they expect nothing from their deity, just as they expect nothing from their parents. So it's not the form that counts; it's the actual way in which it is practiced.

CLYDE KLUCKHOHN

Needed Refinements
in the Biographical Approach[1]

In some quarters during the past decade there has flourished uncritical enthusiasm over life histories. There has been a great overestimation of the place of the hastily gathered document set in only a general cultural context.

The personal document requires many safeguards of objectivity in the collecting and analysis of data, techniques of presentation, and rigorous, explicit interpretation. At best the life-long retrospective biography is an imperfect alternative to the contemporaneous, on-going life history, controlled by current observations and the current testimony of others. If, from a single culture, retrospective autobiographies, contemporaneous life histories, and episodic documents were collected by a number of observers of both sexes from a representative sample of the society, the gains to the study of culture and personality could be enormous. Commensurate energy and skill would, of course, also have to be expended upon annotation, analysis and interpretation. Multiple techniques, carried out by multiple observers and analysts, are the key to the problem of "subjectivity".

Until recently, biographical materials collected by anthropologists[2] have represented in most cases somewhat incidental by-products of field work oriented to an over-all description of a culture. Where life history documents have been taken at all they

[1]In part, this paper represents a re-grouping and re-working of materials presented in *The Personal Document in Anthropological Science* (Bulletin 53, Social Science Research Council, 1945). The writer expresses his thanks to the Council for permission to re-publish these sentences.

[2]Most of what will be said will be applicable in principle to other fields. But for valuable suggestions as to sociological, historical and psychological work, see: H. Blumer, *An Appraisal of Thomas and Znaniecki's The Polish Peasant in Europe and America* (Critiques of Research in the Social Sciences: I. New York, 1939). R. Angell, "A Critical Review of the

have been seen as a means to this end of ethnography. The majority of the published results are sketchy and too limited to objective events and description of customs. They do not give even the shadow of a life—merely the partially outlined skeleton, for the subject's reactions to these happenings has seldom been sought. Annotation has been limited and almost entirely restricted to cultural points. Hence we have, for the most part, merely interesting curiosities, enlivening material for teaching anthropological courses. A few ethnographic footnotes have been gleaned from them; a pitifully few theoretical questions have been asked. Internal contradictions have been dismissed as due to "inconsistency" in the informant rather than analyzed in personality terms. But if one end of a piece of paper reacts to sulphuric acid in one way and the other end to hydrochloric acid in another, this does not prove that the paper is inconsistent.

With the growth of interest in culture and personality and the development of field approaches, a few individuals have pioneered in establishing biographical research as a major objective of anthropological field work in its own right. During the past ten years four substantial biographies have appeared.[3] Du Bois has published brief autobiographies of four men and four women from a single culture with the individual's dreams and associations, with Rorschachs, and with interpretations by a Rorschach expert and by a psychiatrist.[4] Opler has almost ready for publication an extremely rich and long autobiography which will be intensively

---

Development of the Personal Document Method in Sociology" in *The Use of Personal Documents in History, Anthropology and Sociology*, New York, 1945. L. Gottschalk, "The Historian and the Historical Document", in *The Use of Personal Documents in History, Anthropology and Sociology*, New York, 1945. G. Allport, *The Use of Personal Documents in Psychological Science*, New York, 1942.

[3]W. Dyk, *Son of Old Man Hat*, a Navaho autobiography recorded by Walter Dyk, with an introduction by Edward Sapir. New York, 1938; *W. Dyk, A Navaho Autobiography*, Viking Fund Publications in Anthropology, No. 8. New York, 1947.

C. S. Ford, *Smoke from Their Fires*, New Haven, 1941. L. W. Simmons, *Sun Chief, the Autobiography of a Hopi Indian*, New Haven, 1942.

[4]C. Du Bois, "Some Psychological Objectives and Techniques in Ethnography", *Journal of Social Psychology*, 1937, 8, 285-301.

analyzed in both cultural and psychological dimensions. Much carefully designed field work is completed or under way. For example, John Adair and Evon Vogt have collected autobiographies from a large number of Zuni and Navaho veterans respectively and from an equal number of men in the same age group who did not leave their communities for the armed services. A clinical psychologist, Burt Kaplan, obtained Rorschachs and Thematic Apperception Tests from the same individuals.

In other words, a few anthropologists are no longer content to treat biographical work as a somewhat romantic diversion. The utility for cultural studies is generally accepted. It has been shown that life histories are not only helpful in establishing the range of conformity to patterns but also in indicating broad resemblances between groups of cultures.[5] Still, most anthropologists do not show too much imagination in getting biographical materials. They continue to follow a flat and colorlessly standardized pattern. This is, in some measure, because the prestige rewards within the anthropological profession are based upon the production of ethnographies or of scrupulous monographs on accepted topics such as kinship, basketry, and the like. Unless the biographical approach receives a comparable recognition, only an occasional field worker will treat this area seriously. Actually, somewhat different personality types and somewhat different professional training are required for first-class work in the ethnographic and culture and personality fields. The gentle techniques that promote a free flow of spontaneous reminiscence are often incompatible with getting the specific details and the cross-checking of data required in good ethnographic work.

Refinements are required in two main areas of biographical research. The first is that of library research, the second that of the design and carrying out of field studies. With some honorable exceptions, American anthropologists are notorious among social scientists for their neglect of library research. Future field work could be much more specifically pointed if intensive analyses of present materials were made and published. For the Navaho, for instance, personal narratives of at least a hundred individuals are

[5]A. L. Kroeber, "A Southwestern Personality Type", *Southwestern Journal of Anthropology*, 1947, 3, 108-113.

now available. They were collected by seven different field work-ers[6] and the age of the subjects ranges from grade school children into old age. The variation in length and quality is great, but at least eight of the documents are extremely substantial. One of the most pressing needs of contemporary anthropology is extensive, sustained, and high-quality library research upon collections of this sort. Unless a greater proportion of available source materials is collated and synthesized, field research will suffer materially, for the right questions will not be asked.

Library research must get abreast of field research if investigations in the personal document field are not to be dismissed by future historians of science as "much-advertised in some decades of the twentieth century, often pretentious, but essentially unscientific in content, form, and utility." Among other things, the studies of reliability which psychologists have carried out on personal documents are wanting in anthropology. A special phrasing of the problem might be to discover the varying reliabilities of groups of judges who: a) knew the culture of the subject first-hand; b) had done no field work but had studied the relevant literature intensively; and c) had no specialized preparation in anthropology but training in social or clinical psychology. Other analyses should consider systematically different subjects' accounts of the same events, the varying selectivity or consistent emphasis in documents obtained from different subjects by the same field worker, the effects of a given culture on the systematic distortion of verbal material, etc. Standardized techniques for content analysis also need to be developed.[7]

[6]W. Dyk, *op. cit.*, A. Leighton and D. Leighton, Chapter VIII "Navaho Lives" pp. 95-134 in *The Navaho Door*, Cambridge, Mass., 1944. (Also unpublished manuscripts). D. Leighton and C. Kluckhohn, *Children of the People*, Cambridge, Mass., 1947. C. Kluckhohn and D. Leighton, *The Navaho*, Cambridge, Mass., 1947. C. Kluckhohn, "A Navaho Personal Document", *Southwestern Journal of Anthropology*, 1945, 1, 260-283. E. Sapir and H. Hoijer, *Navaho Texts*, Iowa City, 1942. Wetherill, Louisa Wade, *Around Hogan Fires* (unpublished life story of Wolfkiller, a Navaho headman). O'Brien, Aileen, *Sandoval's Autobiography* (unpublished). Vogt, Evon (see *supra*).

[7]J. Dollard and O. H. Mowrer, "A Method of Measuring Tension in Written Documents", *The Journal of Abnormal and Social Psychology*, 1947, 42.

On the basis of theoretical and factual information already at hand, a number of suggestions for field work may be made. The anthropologist who is to specialize in getting autobiographic or introspective statements needs training supplementary to that offered in the conventional anthropological curriculum. If he can obtain a didactic psychoanalysis, well and good. At the very least he should have some supervised practice in clinical and social psychology. Conversely, the clinical psychologist or psychiatrist must not expect to step directly from the clinic to the field with only a casual acquaintance with anthropology through reading. Ideally, he should begin his field work in an apprentice relationship to an experienced anthropologist. This would be less necessary if anthropologists had taken more pains to discuss their techniques in print. One may comb the literature and find only a few discussions of any length, although tantalizing *obiter dicta* occur here and there. Were each report on field work to include consideration of the concrete situations encountered and how they were met, a corpus of general principles for entering a society, selecting informants and intepreters, motivating informants or revelants, handling interpreters and linguistic problems, note-taking, and interviewing might be developed. Thus anthropological skills could become less esoteric and more communicable.

The scientific significance of a biography varies directly with the amount and variety of supplementary information collected on the subject and with the care with which context of utterance (as well as content) is recorded. What the individual does or does not do or say *now*—how, where, and in whose presence—gives some basis for interpreting historical data in organized hindsight fashion. What the individual says repeatedly or reveals only under special circumstances or pressure becomes a richly valuable clue.

Balanced information is enormously important. Time-sampling observations and behavior-sampling observations should supplement the record. Much to be desired are photographic studies, both cine and still, of subjects. They should be both posed and unposed and should show the informant's characteristic motor habits, mannerisms, and posture in a variety of situations. These will be taken, of course, after the subject's confidence has been gained and after his daily occupations and habits have been observed. Of some utility would be a photographic record (by a second observer) during the course of a day's interviewing on the life history. Were they not so expensive, talking moving pictures (if subject and interviewer behaved naturally before the camera) would be an ideal means of checking and re-studying the interview situation after leaving the field. Wire recorders supply a practical and reasonably inexpensive means of securing a complete and permanent record of the verbal part of the interview. Any technique which means "turning off the intellect and turning on a machine" is useful because it provides a way of controlling to some slight degree the personal equation of the observer by having first-hand data analyzed independently by others.

Night and day dreams and records of normal conversations will give one kind of perspective to the subject's depiction of himself in the life history interviews. Another kind of perspective must be secured by seeking other informants. As a minimum, there may be suggested: interviews (formal or informal, but preferably both) with persons of both sexes in the generation older than the informant (where possible), in his own generation, and in the generation younger. These interviews should give a cross-sectional picture of the informant as regarded by the members of his own society. Also worthwhile would be accounts by several different eyewitnesses of sample events described in some detail by the subject. A useful addition would be the reactions of whites or of members of alien tribes who know the individual.

Besides interview and observations, the supplementary material should include, wherever possible, a physical examination and projective tests upon the subject. These also are probably best obtained when the full life record is already safely in hand. The physical examination should be as thorough as circumstances and facilities permit; analyses of blood and urine and basal metabolisms should be made if at all possible. Any existent hospital records should be carefully copied. There should be interviews with the subject and with the members of his family to establish as full and accurate a health history as possible and to establish whether there are any pathological predispositions in the genetic strain. Any kind of reliable testimony as to the relative energy potential of the subject at various points in his life history should be obtained and collated. Where possible, photographs in standard positions in the nude or near nude should be secured so that the Sheldon somatotype may later be determined. In short, a strenuous effort must be made to assemble any and every type of useful data upon the constitution of the individual. Perhaps the greatest single hindrance to a full-bodied interpretation of existing documents upon "primitives" is the lack of other than slight and subjective material on biological factors.

The projective tests used will depend on the subject's age, the culture, and the field worker's training in test-administration. Perhaps the two which most recommend themselves for general use are the Rorschach and the Thematic Apperception Test (with pictures adapted to the general culture area in question). If these tests were administered as a routine matter to all life history subjects, the possibilities for comparative analysis would soon be very rich. Much can be said for having the interpretation of the Rorschachs done "blind" by an expert who has never seen the informant or the tribe—even in those few cases where the field worker is himself qualified to interpret as well as to administer the Rorschach test. The use of a so-called "culture free" intelligence test is worth while where time permits, although present evidence does not suggest that the value of these is very great.

Projective techniques, however, can now be regarded as almost indispensable to fineness of interpretation at the personological level. Especially for those fairly well adjusted in their society, the communal and role components of the personality tend to constitute disguises. Just as the outer body screens the viscera from view and clothing the genitals, so the "public" facets of personality shield the private personality from the curious and conformity-demanding world of other persons. This self-protection becomes so habitual that it is not likely to be relaxed fully even when the person deals with an investigator who is an outsider—and when an interpreter is present the subject is still, after all, reacting in an intimate social setting.

Usually, too, many motivations are excluded from the individual's own consciousness. Nor is even the most sustained and most sensitive observation of the individual in interaction a com-

81

pletely adequate corrective. The person who has painfully achieved some sort of integration and who knows what is expected of him in a particular social situation will produce those responses with only a slight idiosyncratic coloring. That is why the uniformities provided by the communal and role components can—at least in the case of "normal" individuals—be penetrated only by the *combination* of the long-continued and intensive interviews and the oblique procedures of the projective tests. Often only projective techniques will bring out what the individual does not want to tell about himself and what he himself does not know. Such clues are sometimes the surest guides in estimating the extent to which the subject has "created the past" in telling his story. For, as Colson has noted, "Things which the informant cannot say about the present because it is so close and engrossingly personal can be said in the context of the past in the belief that they do not betray the present. It is always one's own present personality that one seeks especially to guard." But the consciously defensive or self-protective behaviors are only part of the picture. Many individuals, for example, are really quite unaware of their fears even if constantly under their domination. The Rorschach tests seem especially useful in revealing what the subject does not know about himself, in getting beneath the cultural screen.

In addition to improved training and techniques and more intensive and systematic efforts to obtain data which will give controls upon the main document, greater variation should be introduced in types of biographical materials secured. Present materials are top-heavy in the direction of retrospective, sequential records. If, when the recital of his life up to the present has been completed, the interviewer would persuade the subject to share his random phantasies and free associations about the immediate and more distant future, a new purchase on his personality would be secured. Moreover, where follow-up field work is possible, most interesting and entirely new (to anthropology) investigations could be carried out. How far was the subject realistic in predicting his own future? To what extent did "chance" interfere with the actualization of trends which appeared as reasonable to the observer as to the participant? How did the subject react to unfulfilled anticipations?

With trifling exceptions, all anthropologists seem to have assumed that a life history had to be an all or none affair. Either the story went from birth to the time of the interview or it was worthless. Actually, dealing with small units (single episodes of personality) would seem to offer great possibilities over and above the appeal to limitations of time. To be sure, comprehension of an episode would require the outlines of the past as seen by the subject, but these can be obtained quite rapidly. With any kind of personal document the advantages of overlapping accounts are tremendous for the scientist. But even in the most favorable cases field workers cannot hope for more than a few full-length biographies. Hence the attraction of getting a considerable number of persons of both sexes and of varying statuses to describe very intensively certain episodes of their lives which converged. If a period were chosen when some momentous event occurred (famine, war, or the like), which affected all, the documents could reasonably be expected to supply almost limitless sorts of illumination.

Besides these *episodic* life histories, *topical* life histories should be useful. This was, in effect, the method of Gilbert Wilson. Such an approach has also more recently been developed by sociologists: Blumer in his study of the moving picture, Angell in analyzing the effect of the depression upon families, Shaw in analyzing the development of the criminal and delinquent behavior. Here the interest is not in dealing with either culture or personality in its entirety (showing relation of parts to the whole) but in selecting one "social problem" or one facet of the personality and in making that central to the life history. The anthropologist might, for instance, follow the subject's participation in ceremonial life from childhood to old age with an eye to the changing tribal culture.

Then, there is what may be called the contemporaneous life history—another variant of the personal document which has yet to make its appearance in the literature of anthropology. We too often forget that the retrospective life history sees the past entirely from the vantage point of a present very distant from those past events. Let, on the other hand, the interviewer work with the subject only on, say, two separated days when he has not been working with the anthropologist and make his comments upon them. The field worker has himself seen these events or portions of them, or he can at very least get almost current accounts of them from others. This places in a quite different light many problems of interpretation. This current and on-going biography, made up partly of actions observed by the anthropologist or by other tribesmen, partly of the subject's own account of these events and his reactions to them, would be the perfect type of life history if the record could be maintained for a sufficiently long period and if it could be carried out without too much disturbance to the normal order of the subject's life.

Anthropologists have clung too closely to the conception of the life record in strictly chronological terms. This is reflected in the manner in which they have presented their materials and probably channeled the interviewing too. For certain types of cultural studies this chronological interest and arrangement has some justifications, but, in many cultures which conceive time so very differently from what Western culture regards as "natural", too much pressure on the subject to specify absolute dates or even sequences must mean that all his recollections or comments are forced through a very artificial screen. And for personality-in-culture interests a much more fluid type of interviewing is desirable. Du Bois' stated objectives may be recommended to other anthropologists: ". . . to get at the predominating emotional and social preoccupations of the subject and to secure inferentially the dynamics of such preoccupations."

If episodic or topical biographical data are sought, a truly meaningful research design can be created. Depending on theoretical interest, one may choose husband-wife, parent-child, sibling-sibling, generational-generational or other pairs or any combination of these. A more intricate matrix might be laid out that would permit genuine control of certain variables, so that information on one major theoretical question might be factored out. Where time allows, the same principles could, of course, be applied to the longer documents.

In any case the selection of revelants must no longer remain so haphazard. If the investigator spends a preliminary period working on the language, he will have had an opportunity to see, meet, and hear about a sizable number of potential subjects. On the ground of need to become accustomed to different voices and "accents" he will indeed have worked with a variety of natives and had an opportunity to discriminate those with whom his rapport most easily and naturally is good. He can also have, in the guise of seemingly casual conversations, acquired considerable information on the social status, availability, articulateness, of many persons.

Naturally, his selection will be limited and channeled by the particular problems he has chosen. These should, of course, have been clearly thought through in advance. Previous studies leave much to be desired in this regard. In many cases, there are indications that the subject or subjects were hardly "selected" at all. The ethnographer's interpreter or the old man who hung around the agency or anyone else who happened to be at hand was used, with little attention to representativeness or to bearing upon other problems. When the gathering of life histories has been rather incidental, this procedure was perhaps justifiable. If, however, the personal documents are taken seriously as major research objectives, the selection hardly dares be so casual.

Is the research interest primarily ethnological? Then the problem of representativeness becomes central. Depending upon the amount of time available and upon other factors, the anthropologist must decide whether one or two very extensive life histories will best serve his purposes or whether a series of shorter documents will more fully cover the ground. Sometimes one man and one woman might constitute a good choice. But in what sense are they to be "representative"? Are they to be leaders or admired types or are they to be representative in the sense of modal or average, The chronological factor also is always relevant. Is the aim primarily to recover as much as possible of the aboriginal culture or to reconstruct the past history of the tribe as far back as possible. If so, the old must be sought—with consideration of such matters as cultural participation, health, senility, memory. For some objectives an acculturated informant is preferable—not only because of the possibility of eliminating an interpreter but also because an informant can see his own life and culture more clearly because of experience with a contrasting culture.

Where a series of, say, four to eight autobiographies is thought the preferable alternative, elementary considerations of sampling come to the fore. Sex, economic position, occupational specialization, and other diversities of position and experience must be taken into account. In any case where more than one biography is to be obtained there are great advantages in choosing subjects where there will be considerable overlap in the events recounted. This will make possible some control on reliability as well as a purchase on the central interests, anxieties, and distortions of a personality.

Obviously, these are only some of the questions relevant to the selection of subjects for ethnological study. The important thing is that such questions should be explicit in the consciousness of the field worker and later revealed by him to his readers. There have been too many instances where it was not at all clear whether the subject was selected and presented as a "typical" member of his group or as a ceremonial practitioner or as an aberrant type. Too often, it seems likely, other students have seized upon material as primarily culturally implicative when in fact it mainly represented personal idiosyncrasy. This has resulted from the circumstances that the subject was not really chosen but "just happened" and that the recorder did not specify the subject's position with respect to the curves of culturally tolerated variation. Of course, one must pick one's fruit where one finds it, and no sensible person who has done much field work would wish to underestimate the role of luck in coming by good informants. But there is such a thing as shutting the door on possible good fortune by not being in the right places or with the right people. And the field worker has an inadequate basis for knowing whether he has been lucky or not unless he knows where a prospective informant fits into the social structure.

Is the interest primarily "psychological"? In this event, subjects may properly be selected for their very nonrepresentativeness: because they are deviants, because they have had most unusual life careers, because they have manifested behaviors regarded as neurotic by our culture or by theirs. This type of interest is also legitimate, but, again, it should be conscious and stated. Also, it should be emphasized that studies of deviants are of little use if there are not comparable studies for non-deviants.

In general, as Murray points out, the worker with "sociological" training and interests "can get a quicker understanding of a personality by ascertaining his affiliates and rejectates than by inquiring into other matters." The psychologist, on the other hand, "can learn more about the group from the subject than he can learn about the subject from the group."

When—as is the case with a mounting number of investigations —the questions asked are both "cultural" and "psychological," there are many inviting possibilities for designing the experiment. A series of male-female pairs in different age grades might throw great light on the process of acculturation: tempo, resistances, motivations, attitudes. Or, the study might be focused on the related problems of innovation and leadership through recording autobiographies of persons who were known to have brought in radical changes or to have fostered or opposed their adoption. Life history techniques can profitably be linked with investigations of the acquisition of the culture by children or of the socialization process generally. Where longitudinal studies of socialization are being carried on, a sequence of brief autobiographies of older children—repeated at intervals of a year or longer—suggests itself as an attractive undertaking. Equally promising would be biographies or autobiographies of the parents or other relatives of children being intensively studied by observation and experiment. In general, it may be maintained that subjects closely linked to other individuals upon whom detailed information is available should always be selected where possible.

To be sure, these and other criteria cannot be rigorously applied in every society. Much depends on the size of the group, linguistic availability, culturally enjoined intransigeance toward whites, and other variables. They are admittedly counsels of perfection. It is insisted only that an honest attempt be made to choose informants with some sense of problem rather than following a line of least resistance or needlessly allowing fortuitous circumstances to shape the choice.

Finally, a special type of field work which seems one of the prime desiderata of the immediate future is a series of experiments, as carefully controlled as possible. By reasoning alone we cannot hope to solve certain problems or to estimate with any approach to accuracy how much gain or loss results from the adoption of various approaches or techniques.

A few suggestions will be given, but a number of others could equally well be tried. Suppose two different recorders obtain accounts of the early life (or any other segment of the life cycle) from the same informant. This experiment, like the others, would have to be very carefully worked out to be of any value. Each recorder would need to work long enough with the subject to get beyond the initial stages of rapport establishment. It would be essential that the second recorder should not work with the subject so soon after the first as to find the informant either bored with the material or inclined to spout forth mechanically what he had recently dug from his memory. On the other hand, if the interval were too long, there might be the risk that the subject's life situation had so altered that he would see the past from an altogether different perspective. There are admittedly all sorts of perils that what would be revealed in the test would not be difference in reaction to recorders but alterations in other aspects of the context situation. Granting that no completely satisfactory standardization is possible, sufficient enterprise could work out an adequate approximation in concrete cases. If, for example, two subjects were interviewed and in one case one recorder worked first with the subject while in the other case the second recorder worked first, the variations resulting from this factor could be eliminated to some degree.

Similarly, this first experiment could be further refined and controlled by having both recorders later obtain an incident or two out of the same life period from the subject under different conditions. In this way there would be an additional check upon the amount of variation due to alteration in recorders and the amount traceable to alterations in other phases of the informant's situation. Comparable studies of the reliability and validity of the content of expressive interviews from twenty or more different revelants are badly needed. It isn't just a question of what A said. It is also a question of what B, C, . . . X saw and/or of what b, c, . . . x heard.

Next, the effects of language factors need experimental examination. Let a part of a life history be recorded (simultaneously, if an interpreter were being used) in the informant's and in the observer's language and then let them be checked for differences, gross or subtle. Another useful experiment would be to obtain the same incident from the same informant but with different interpreters. Finally, in cases where either the subject or the recorder had some pretensions to bilinguality, it might be instructive to obtain the identical episode with and without the intervention of the interpreters.

Such experiments have had a tiny role in past anthropology, but, if the discipline's standards are to be raised, they seem a necessary step. Until anthropologists *can* deal rigorously with the "subjective factors" in the lives of "primitives" their work will be flat and insubstantial. Unless they can learn to delineate the emotional structure of societies, serious persons who wish to learn about the life of human beings in groups will properly continue to turn to literature rather than to science for enlightenment. The "subjective factor" in the lives of human groups is a problem of crucial importance. But it must be remembered that data are never, in themselves, subjective or objective. What may be more objective or less objective is the manner of dealing with them. The anthropological mode must become more objective both in gathering and analyzing data. This will be much facilitated by a number of needful experiments. Anthropology, in general, stands on the threshold of an epoch when the coarseness and crudeness of its work requires the refinement which can only be brought by a partially experimental approach.

DISCUSSION

DR. HORTENSE POWDERMAKER: Cultures vary greatly in the expression of affect. In some they are expressed easily; in others, not. Sometimes we tend to think there is a lack of feelings because we have difficulty getting expressions of them. There is the additional problem of getting at intimate feelings through an interpreter—a process necessary in many cultures. Also, how does one overcome the difficulty of working with a people not accustomed to verbalizing about their feelings? We don't have that situation in our own society.

DR. KLUCKHOHN: I agree with the person who said that when one works through an interpreter it is like an exchange of telegrams between two persons in distant cities. I would suggest, as Margaret Mead has done, that learning a language or not learning it are not the *only* alternatives. There is such a thing as using a language without learning it. I feel strongly the need to learn the language of those among whom one does intensive field work, but I think even a small amount of the language can help. At a crucial place in the discussion a few adjectives and qualitative expressions that draw out can loose a flood tide on the subject, which the interpreter then translates. Another dodge is to have certain projective tests like TAT ready to give at the moment in a person's life history which you believe is crucially significant for him.

DR. SULLIVAN: A striking thing about every institutional psychiatrist's experience is that the beginning student is put to getting the patient's history. It's amazing how valid the beginning student's efforts in this direction are, unless they're too bad for words. I don't mean to suggest that the field worker is in the position of the young psychiatrist, because I can't imagine an anthropological student being turned loose on the unsuspecting populace with as little training in critical judgment as is the average medico who goes into psychiatry. But what we finally succeed in beating into our more promising students is that they take histories with the following in mind: Can they imagine what it would be like to undergo the events they have heard about? To be where the informant claims he was? That is, do they have a sense of its being possible really to follow what he says? If they don't, they should say they don't understand! When they can not follow, they should ask questions. It's that simple. This also calls for competence in language—a remarkable sense of the nuances of communication—as well as the ability to imagine living what the informant reports. I surmise these might be extended to field work, but I realize there are staggering differences, arising from extremely different cultural values.

Let me ask another thing: how often in your discussions with representatives of different, if not less elaborated, societies are *you* considered to be a human being—a puzzling, interesting object of curiosity for your informants? I can hear a great deal about the Alor or something else, but if I don't hear anything about how a *particular* Alor dealt with a *particular* investigator I wonder what I am hearing about. Have you the techniques, and do you notice the nuances that indicate the intervention of purely personal considerations in what are presumed to be generally valid inquiries?

DR. KLUCKHOHN: I am grateful to Dr. Sullivan for bringing out two things actually in my outline which I didn't touch on explicitly: namely, the interpreter and the interviewer. Some of us have found it extraordinarily valuable to use an interpreter actually as an informant. A main criticism of existing life history studies in anthropology is that so little is specified about the relationship between investigator and subject. If we are going to be objective about interpersonal relations we must be prepared to be honest, even if we give away something about ourselves.

Dr. Abram Kardiner: The most discouraging thing I ever heard about history taking and personality studies I heard from Freud himself. A friend of mine expressed to Freud one day a great disappointment with another friend who did something unexpected. When he complained to Freud he said, "Well, I guess you don't know anything about anybody until you analyze them." Freud replied, "And what do you know then?"

Life history taking is always, as Dr. Sullivan quite correctly implied, a terrible imposition on any human being because it always is a private matter. Our social facade and our private lives are different. One of the things Dr. Kluckhohn didn't quite take up is, what kind of incentive do you give an individual to tell his life history? In the practice of psychiatry, the poor patient is bludgeoned into telling secret facts about himself because there is a promise of relief. He is seduced into telling these things. Now what inducement do you give a primitive man to tell his story? I suspect you have to pay him. But that is an inducement to give peripheral facts. Among the Alorese, the ethnographer was instructed particularly to take down reactions to the abnormal, and other materials not in answer to direct questioning. The analyst can instruct the ethnographer to use what can be called the dragnet method, to recall everything whether he considers it relevant or not. When you take life histories of primitive people you had better settle, not for a life history, but for a cross section of the day to day adaptation of the individual over a stretch of two or three months. What you get then is a sampling. I think Dr. Kluckhohn said it should be repeated every year, but we must have some consideration for the time at the ethnographer's disposal.

Dr. Kluckhohn: I think one finds in non-literate cultures as well as in our own that the easiest people to get as informants for life-history documents are persons who, in general, are the least representative—maladjusted in some sense, neglected in their culture—the old, the crippled, the lame, the halt and the blind in every sense—who are glad to have someone to whom they can talk.

If one is able to get someone who seems representative, the motivation other than pay (and I agree with Dr. Kardiner that pay itself is not adequate) which I have found most useful are these: First, structuring the situation so there is an element of swapping experience. In some cultures at least, it helps to make the man or woman you're working with feel you're not putting him on a pin. You can say, "Well, that's kind of like what happened to me when I was a kid. My mother died too, and I hated the guts of my stepmother too. The way we went at it was this, etc." I found again and again that that brings things up.

Another thing, which is a two-edged sword and must be used with caution, but which, at least in American Indian cultures, I found useful, is that very often this is the first time in an Indian's life, psychologically

91

speaking, that he has a white man where he wants him. Just as sometimes patients in analysis will pick on the analyst and try to choke him or her, so it is at the verbal level with informants. More than once I have found that someone difficult to get for life history purposes, because he was a busy and successful member of the community—a singer, or leader, for example—gets considerable reward out of this. He has a chance to slap you verbally in the face, and in slapping you he is really slapping all the whites who have slapped him around ever since he was a child.

GEORGE HERZOG

Linguistic Approaches to Culture and Personality

The preceding discussions have brought to our mind again how infinitely subtle the verbal expression of man is in his relations to others. We also know all too well that man spends, certainly in a culture like ours, perhaps half his waking energy in talking and expressing himself. While we have no data on how true this may be generally we know that the most clearly organized way man becomes aware of himself, of his culture and his social institutions, is through the language he speaks. It stands to reason, then, that we have a rich, subtle, elaborate tool that man uses in his culture, without which his personality would fold up, probably, anywhere unless he found perhaps a moderately acceptable substitute.

We know all the generalities. Now we can ask ourselves: What can the study of language do as we approach the questions that lie between and connect the studies of culture or society and of personality? Up to that point we must say we know only too little and we face rather complex problems. We have thought for a long time about the best way to visualize the problems involved, and the best methodological safeguards against fumbling.

Culture and personality represent the joint interests of social scientists, psychologists and psychiatrists. Now a linguist, a third type of human being, of tradition, enters the picture.

Recently we have had spectacular technical and conceptual development in linguistics in this country. On the other hand, the interest of technicians has been limited largely to the phases of language where one can operate with a type of conception similar to that found in, say, geometry or crystallography. But when we come to broader aspects of language, such as semantics, this linguistic brilliance of the technician doesn't do us much good. On the other side of the picture we have the social scientist, let's say an anthropologist, with an interest in linguistics. He is not attracted by the atmosphere emanating from this highly technical linguistic crystallography which operates in a vacuum without much regard to cultural or even psychological reality. Hence the anthropologist doesn't have a very sympathetic response to the linguist, doesn't find him very useful, and in general doesn't find the territory of language very attractive.

I think it worthwhile for our purposes if I offer not so much a general theoretical scheme of procedure, as some illustrations of what we can do with comparatively modest resources as field workers in non-literate societies, so the true anthropologist is the one primarily involved in what I suggest.

I might make one more general comment about some impressive results we have gained in recent years in this country studying certain phases of language expression. In the study of political, editorial and radio material, we can find spectacular results based to some extent on statistically verifiable procedures. Counts of various symbols give us interesting results. This type of procedure could be applied in different fashion to text materials already available from non-literate cultures.

Those who have studied mass communication, mass media, often find to their sorrow that these techniques haven't yet taught much about certain important things. You can count, for instance, the number of times a certain type of word occurs in a certain kind of communication. However, a psychiatrist doesn't count the number of times a patient mentions certain kinds of words; yet he quickly notes the relative frequency with which they occur. In person-to-person communication, in writing and printing, there are innumerable devices used for emphasis and for special effect, devices that have special personal or general cultural significance. These are matters about which we are concerned when we try to discuss style in literature and the arts. Sapir was especially interested in developing linguistic techniques. He was interested not only in structure as such, but believed you can also, perhaps, learn something about subtle arrangements and psychological significance which we call style.

In the following, then, I shall not attempt a systematic presentation of what may be done or what has been done in this borderline field. I shall suggest some procedures and points of departure, which seem promising and fruitful, and then look for group norms and their effect on the individual. I shall use materials from primitive or pre-literate societies, and shall keep in mind conditions that prevail when we work in a comparative or cross-cultural perspective.

The examples I use are comparatively simple. Compared to the high level of methodological awareness and severity used in the preceding discussions, any examples may look gross or even shaky. That is partly because we must admit much ignorance and poverty in this approach to culture and personality. We must keep in mind the limitations of practical situations where the field worker seldom is a technician or a linguist sophisticated from the cultural or psychological point of view.

First I will give examples touching on the phonetics of self content of language, commenting especially on lisping and baby talk. Then I will give examples involving vocabulary as the most immediately meaningful phase of language. Because the grammatical and the phonetic systems of every language are so basic, standardized and largely unconscious or subconscious, the individual becomes most easily visible when he is extremely deviant, when his management of this system breaks down. This may occur with extreme personality disturbance or disorganization. For example, the manifestations of aphasia or schizophrenia in language performance have been traced in considerable detail and clarity.

But we might think of much milder deviations that are more instructive, perhaps, in the cultural perspective. A good example is lisping. You are all acquainted with the varying pronunciations of adult sound norms among children. Among grownups it has a curious symbolic significance that differs at least according to sex.

Using central Europe about a generation ago, I can say that men considered it attractive for a girl or a woman to have a slight lisp, especially if she was attractive to start with. It was dangerous for a homely woman to lisp; that was a crude affectation. Lisping by a man was suspicious. A man was suspected of effeminacy if he did this. Significantly, after the onset of middle age people tended to give up lisping, men especially. With women it may have lingered on to old age.

In this country I have the impression that lisping by women

has been on the decrease in the last couple of decades; it is fading out. I do not believe any of our movie actresses lisp, at least the well known ones. As for men, I want to quote one of my students who said very severely: "If a man lisps, he is effeminate or even a pervert." With lisping, then, we have a case where social censure is forthcoming, even in childhood. Thus when lisping occurs in a grownup, it is much toned down, though it must have some diagnostic value as a childhood carryover.

Lisping plays an unexpected role in the process of a foreigner acquiring the English language. Invariably he has a great struggle to achieve the English "th" sound, as in "thick," "health," and so on. When a child lisps he usually pronounces a fairly acceptable version of the English growup "th." This is as true in most European languages as in English. So European children pronounce English "th" sounds when they lisp. But since apparently every grownup *can* lisp if he wants to, every foreigner has the English "th" sound down pat! Still I haven't yet seen in any book the simple instruction given to the student of English: "lisp an 's' and you have the English 'th' sound." This humble insight, I believe, has not yet been publicized.

I might add that I have become interested in the psychological background of the difficulty with the English "th" sounds. For years I thought the reason was a shying away from making the tongue too visible. Now I think this probably was a wrong explanation. To follow one more ramification here that leads to social psychology of nationality: Germans who have been told quite correctly that the English "th" sounds are related to "s" and "z" make conscious efforts to force their "s" and "z" to do the job. The result is an odd half-lisp sound that I think you all know. It has become characteristic of a heavy German accent.

On the other hand, the less conscientious procedure of Italians, Hungarians, Latins, and others is to seek a substitute "t" or "d" which gets by more easily, in part because "t" or "d" do occur in substandard or dialect English.

I have gone into some detail about lisping because it is a simple phenomenon, and because it shows the wisdom of considering the so-called specifically linguistic factors. Also, it has a rich psychological-personal background.

Unfortunately we know little about occurrence of similar features in a cross-cultural perspective extending beyond western civilization or other complex civilizations. We don't know in how many primitive societies lisping occurs. We do know that in many languages children substitute rather systematically certain sounds for others; these are very casual. We know little about whether these sounds are picked up from other children, or whether grown-ups teach them to their children. We do not know whether there is sex differentiation, how long a child is likely to retain these features, or what tolerance there is for maintaining it, even in attenuated form, in later life.

We would like to know what other elements are brought into a constellation with lisping in different cultures. To mention one example, among the Pima Indians of Arizona the mythical figure of Coyote lisps still. When the story-teller refers to him, he may do so with lisping. As among other Indian tribes, Coyote is a very ambivalent figure. In the Pima he often furnished comic relief, as imitator of the more dignified, even tragic heroes of the action. He is also highly sexed. The lisp sounds of the Coyote and of the Pima children occur also, however, as regular sounds in neighboring languages. The speakers are people with whom the Pima have been in violent warfare in the past. No doubt there are similarly complex cases elsewhere which equally tempt one to explore and interpret.

This leads us to consider briefly the more general area of so-called baby talk. Baby talk, when formalized into a system, is not only its own phonetics but also its own grammar and vocabulary. Since a child must learn speech gradually, a mass of imperfect and substandard but somewhat patterned material emerges in any language or society.

Baby talk may be defined as a systematization of the language efforts of the small child into a special dialect, so to speak; a dialect which may be imposed by a grownup as it is developed by the children themselves. As Comanche informants said when they were asked about baby talk, "Oh, you mean the first words we teach to the baby?" It turned out that the Comanche have an unusually rich and highly formalized baby talk vocabulary. Some features of it are just as difficult to pronounce as the corresponding features of the grownup Comanche vocabulary. An attempt to draw some inference from baby talk, from its presence or absence in different cultures, its content, its different degree of elaboration in different languages, is difficult because, unfortunately, our data are exceedingly scant and scattered.

However, one general tendency may be mentioned. If a language does have some grammatical devices for forming diminutives, the baby talk of the language tends to make heavy use of these forms. In grownup usage, diminutives in English may be restricted to affectionate or intimate terms. "Doggie" or "mousey" are baby talk, but "Billy" or "Katy" are not, or do not need to be. As for the child, the phenomena surrounding him are reduced by this device of diminution to the child's own stature, so to speak, and they may be enveloped by this affectionate atmosphere which surrounds the child. In this respect we may say baby talk has a protective function as reflected in the language mechanism which operates in it.

As to extension beyond babyhood, again our data are all too scarce. Some interesting observations were made by Jules Henry in a South American tribe, the Pilaga. There, persistence in using baby talk was an important symptom of personal disturbances among children. In extreme cases, of half or full orphans, baby talk persisted until the ninth year and even beyond. In the most severe cases of personality disturbances, phonetic substitutions were rigidly followed through, and at times resulted in very serious distortions of speech.

Another disturbance of interest at the cross-cultural level is stuttering and stammering, partly because its incidence in the western world is so much higher among men than among women. In less elaborate cultures than our own it seems to be rare, on the whole. While there have been no systematic surveys in the field for a couple of generations, we have had intensive observations of many North American Indian groups by anthropologists and linguists. The only cases on record are a couple of bilingual or trilingual individuals in the modern younger generation. Incidentally they also are men.

Let us now turn to the most directly meaningful phase of language, the vocabulary. The techniques through which we can attempt to explore the social experience of the individual are well known. We can locate, for example, a word that carries an especially heavy affective meaning for the individual, because these meanings are somewhat standardized expressions of group attitudes and values. I am not unaware that the importance of native terms is indicated by the extent to which some of the anthropologists' monographs are interlarded with such terms, and with commentary on them. In older days monographs had a profusion of such terms with no commentary.

Digesting or even recording the entire vocabulary of a primitive culture is a considerable task that is likely to call for the linguistic specialist. However, certain special types of words could be listed and analyzed without involving full technical study. I would like to mention some which obviously would be quite fruitful or suggestive for culture and personality. In the first place certain words serve in a culture as the vocabulary for discussing and distinguishing between different kinds of individuals, according to their various character traits or modes of behavior. We may as well assume that every word for a character trait in a given language represents potential social approval or disapproval. Every word applying to certain kinds of people as against others represents one potential category for classifying, albeit unconsciously, the variety of personalities actually found. Through this material the group becomes aware and articulate on matters we discuss under headings like "character" or "personality." It seems important that this type of vocabulary should be collected; such words are a useful point of departure.

Terminology of age seems also suggestive for our purposes. Words like "infant," "child," "youngster" and "grownup" do not by any means divide the life span of the individual in the same fashion in every language. The duration of every term may vary considerably, and the number of periods assigned to a term. Of course it is better not to assume that every term of this kind necessarily indicates a point of special social and psychological significance for the individual. Yet potentially every such word represents part of a system of differentiating people both as to age status and as to appropriate behavioral standards. Among the Comanche where I studied terminology, informants found it difficult, more difficult than we do, to define each term by the approximate number of years to which they apply. So the terms were given a meaning naturally and easily by describing the physical appearance and the behavioral differences that are taken by the Comanche to distinguish the members of one group from those of another.

As we know, behavior that the society expects of an individual at one age level often differs from what it expects in a subsequent one, so different facets of the personality must be brought into play. Thus the vocabulary of age seems a useful additional tool for locating reference points for personality norms.

Other terminologies of special value may be those relating to approval and disapproval. It should be stressed that the mere listing of such words out of any context is questionable. Naturally the more intensive the commentary and analysis of such words can be, the more it is possible to give emotional frequencies their weight, their effective connotations. The more observations we can make on actual use of words, on the setting in which they are rooted, the more reliable and constructive such materials will be. Sometimes words of this type actually cluster in some segment of special development, the so-called "pre-literate language," so they can be located more easily and given a larger and more meaningful framework.

In Negro Africa, for instance, social ideals and values are intimately reflected and phrased in much detail in proverbs. Proverbs in Africa are quoted profusely on many occasions, especially when there is social friction or when heightened tension in the individual threatens to lead to social friction. In Negro Africa, proverbs are actually the chief device for expressing or coining generalizations, including commentaries on social conduct, human nature and interpersonal relations. It is noteworthy that these proverbs rarely are in the form of actual commands. In the material from Liberia which I had an opportunity to study and collect, the standard formulas in proverbs are: we do not do so-and-so; or, we don't do this way, we do that way; or, one doesn't do this way; or, if you do so-and-so, such-and-such will happen. Rather significantly, this last formula predicting the pleasant or unpleasant effects of a given type of behavior is used very flexibly. It can have the sense that the result *must* happen, or that it *will* happen, or that it *is likely to* happen, or that it *may* happen. The grammar of the languages involved makes it possible to distinguish these relations. It is important that the proverb is used consistently in noncommital form. This can indicate a lack of pressure with which these values are conveyed to the individual. He is offered an insight, and he may take a chance in acting on it, or not.

Lack of pressure appears on two other points in these cultures. When an individual is exposed to social censure, he answers in proverbs; that is, he can rationalize his conduct, no matter how deviant it is. In such situations it is quite permissable to use a judicial proverb in a new sense, even in a sense that reverses its meaning entirely. This skillful manipulation and play is highly appreciated for its own sake. While children begin to use proverbs fairly early there is no special effort to instruct them in the art of quoting proverbs, nor is there any effort to convey to them rules of conduct by concentrated quotations of proverbs.

The role of proverbs in Africa can be contrasted with the role of formalized verbal instructions given in many American Indian tribes by the parent to the child or adolescent. These instructions or speeches are given in some tribes over several consecutive evenings and the child must listen with intent and concentration. The instructions, in contrast to the African proverbs, use an emphatic categorical style. Often the formula is this: Do not do this. It is not good. People will not respect you. Or, Do so-and-so; it is good. Commands, phrases, actual imperatives in the grammatical sense are frequent. The language is complex and can distinguish between necessary or potential results of given behavior. The forms in the instructions express rigid prediction. No machinery exists for the individual to express a verbal comeback. The values are laid down for him to accept. Incidentally, "good" and "bad" are rare words in West African proverbs.

I believe this contrast shows that the anthropologist can learn a good deal about the value systems of so-called primitive societies from language sources, from the way language is formulated and conveyed to the individual. We see that observations of what we might call "style" gain considerably if we inspect matters included under the heading of grammar. The meaning of this contrast and pressure, which appears both in the language and in actual use of the two devices I mentioned, can be extended, even if it leads into necessarily speculative directions. Think, for instance, of public confession, which, as Weston LaBarre recently pointed out, occurred among numerous North American Indian tribes. In West Africa public confession seems to be unknown or rare.

To sum up my remarks, the use of data drawn from language and behavior connected with language, is very promising for studies in culture and personality. In cross-cultural perspective, especially when we deal with non-literate cultures, we face practical difficulties because the languages are numerous and varied, because many of them are difficult to learn, and because only a small number of persons are both language technicians and students interested in personality and culture. Ideally, the field investigator should be able to communicate in their native language with members of the societies he studies. He should be able to recall all his data in that language, and to analyze his material with an understanding of the specific language factors involved. Although ideal procedures can not always be followed, the practical difficulties should not keep us from realizing that until we can cope with them better, a linguist can do much to expand and interpret this material for the social anthropologist. The field anthropologist can achieve much on his own by making gross observations on language phenomena and by making modest though systematic studies, for which he doesn't need the technical sophistication of a professional linguist. But increasing cooperation between different specialists is the keynote of future work.

I quote from a classic article by Edward Sapir, "Speech and Personality," which he wrote some 20 years ago:

"There is one thing that strikes one as interesting about speech. On the one hand we find it very difficult to analyze. On the other hand we are guided by our actual experience." My plea is that we should not let the difficulties prevent our working with language, and that we should be guided more than heretofore by the light that language phenomena can give to our problems.

102

GENERAL DISCUSSION ON METHODS

Dr. Otto Klineberg: There is one technique I should like to say just a word about which has not been discussed as yet—that of experimental psychology. There are at least a few occasions where methods of the rather narrowly experimental type may be useful in indicating differences in which we would be interested. For example, in two groups we studied we found rather striking differences in reactions to assigned tasks: one gave a very much more enumerative, summative account of things, while the other gave a much more organized and Gestalt-like report.

Another type of experimental approach that I don't think should be entirely neglected is the much despised paper-and-pencil test of personality, but not for the reason it has been used in the past. A rather detailed item analysis of some of the results obtained by these paper-and-pencil tests of personality might be very revealing. I just want to give one example. Some years ago a group of Chinese psychologists applied a number of the standard inventories like the Bernreuter, Thurstone and others to Chinese students and arrived at the sad conclusion that the Chinese students were very neurotic. One of the investigators closed with a plea for more mental hygiene in the Chinese universities to overcome this unfortunate situation.

What had happened, of course, was that the specific items in the inventory were interpreted quite differently by the Chinese. One question went like this: "Do you allow others to push ahead of you in line?" Of course all the Chinese said "yes," which apparently is marked on the neurotic side. Well, there are no such lines in China; they all gather around together. So everybody turned out to be neurotic!

That is only one item, of course, though there are many others. But it seems to me that kind of analysis could be carried through and would give additional light on the distribution of certain types of character traits, or different types of response. In any case I want to make this small plea for some of the methods of experimental psychology as not being entirely out of place.

Chairman: I think it is of interest that each person who has discussed his technique for studying culture and personality has expressed dissatisfaction with it and calls for its refinement. Perhaps the road to improvement in our techniques lies in another direction than in the field of the techniques themselves. It seems to me we will improve our tools when we have a greater cross-fertilization in our conceptual thinking. For example, psychoanalysts who are interested in this field can be trained so they are sensitized to culture and all the implications of culture; this also holds for psychologists. Anthropologists can become sensitized to psychoanalysis and thus new dimensions open up in their thinking. All this is on the conceptual level, it seems to me, and should become part of the training of students in these various fields. If this happens to a large number of people who are interested in culture and personality, we shall then have the forging of new techniques. Techniques are not static; they must be invented. Dr. Kluckhohn made a plea for experimentation in the development of the techniques of biography. But we cannot experiment purely on the tool level; the experiments will have to come within a rather broad conceptual framework. I think the most hopeful thing is the attempt to give this framework to students, so they will grow up with several levels in their thinking, not just one or two.

EVALUATION OF STUDIES

L. M. HANKS, Jr.

The Locus of Individual Differences in Certain Primitive Cultures

My interest is in the relation between the living dimensions of people and the equally living but less labile structures which are the organized institutional ways as revealed in studies of primitive societies.

Here is the dilemma, as I see it: On the one hand we receive accounts from psychologists of individuals in our culture whose reactions are clearly interpretable in terms of such psychological variables as weak ego formation, inadequate identification with the parent of like sex or inadequate development due to certain childhood traumas. The resultant picture is of an individual with lability, with skepticisms and beliefs who is in part a person of the culture and in part a person unto himself.

On the other hand we receive accounts (vide Fortune's Dobu as one example of many)[1] of primitive cultures with clearly specified institutional patterns where life processes appear to be rigid and clearly predetermined by institutional patterns. Indeed, from the nature of culture, we infer that these are institutional ways inherited from a preceding generation and that alteration of them means a disorganization of the delicate adjustment of man to man and man to environment.

My question is: How can these two pictures be reconciled? We have the psychologists' picture of personal flexibility, reaction against the established pattern, and choice governed by psychological motives. We have the ethnographer's picture of institutions mainly determined by geographical and socio-historical factors, serving the needs of individuals yet alterable only at the peril of social collapse.

Since I am not the first to be troubled by this problem, many theoretical answers already have been suggested. One style of answer suggests that the individual is not merely so flexible a crea-

---

[1] cf. Fortune, R. F. *Sorcerers of Dobu*, New York, E. P. Dutton, 1932.

ture as we might at first believe. Such sociologists as Davis and Havighurst bring this picture home to us in their book entitled *Father of the Man.*[2] Another answer is provided by anthropologists who point out that institutional ways are not so rigid as we would first expect. Linton, for instance, suggests that the culture pattern which anthropologists describe is really on the modal behavior of the group, that there is considerable elasticity of institutional ways.[3] A third answer, emphasized by Bateson, Kardiner, Mead and others, observes that individuals do not come to these fixed points without preparation; hence institutions do not give the subjective appearance of rigidity but may even be deemed necessary as a result of earlier training.[4]

It is possible, without reviewing these theories, to consider this question in the light of new evidence. During the past few years there is an increasing literature of field studies with emphasis on the individual. Instead of ethnographic studies where some relevant material on personality may be found, we have data collected where psychological questions are paramount in the mind of the field worker. From a considerable body of such material I have selected two studies which bring together more than one autobiographical study from a single society. They are the eight autobiographies from Alor gathered by Cora DuBois,[5] and the two Navaho autobiographies edited and collected by Walter Dyk.[6] The latter material is supplemented by briefer case studies on the Navaho by Kluckhohn and Dorothea Leighton,[7] as well as Alex-

---

[2]Davis, A. and Havighurst, R. J., *Father of the Man*, New York, Houghton, 1947.

[3]Linton, R., *The Cultural Background of Personality*, New York, Appleton, 1945.

[4]Mead, M. and Bateson, G., *Balinese Character*, New York, N. Y. Academy of Sciences, 1942. Kardiner, A., *The Psychological Frontiers of Society*, New York, Columbia University Press, 1945.

[5]DuBois, C., *The People of Alor*, Minneapolis, Univ. of Minnesota Press, 1944.

[6]Dyk, W., *Son of Old Man Hat*, New York, Harcourt, 1938. Dyk, W., *A Navaho Autobiography*, New York, Viking Fund Publication in *Anthropology*, number 8, 1947.

[7]Kluckhohn, C. and Leighton, D. C., *Children of the People*, Cambridge, Harvard Univ. Press, 1947.

ander Leighton.[8] It has been necessary to pass over excellent auto-biographies such as Simmons's *Sun Chief* or Ford's *Smoke from Their Fires,* since one example is useless in studying individual variations.

I should like to present my reflections on these materials as a series of propositions based on evidence from the biographies. Subsequently I shall present three additional propositions as conclusions loosely derived from these first observations.

1. These autobiographies resemble personal documents from our own society in that they show similar strains and stresses, freedom of expression and lability, and individual variation.

This proposition is evident to anyone who has plowed through these documents. Mangma, the geneologist of Alor, as Kardiner has pointed out, seems to be a person who is trying to appear in a favorable light and so omits telling considerable sections of his story so as to make himself appear more favorable to the ethnographer.[9] The fact that he is in a society that reckons success in mokos and gongs needs to be explained only briefly to a psychologist, and he will be able to observe many of the same psychological mechanisms in operation that he observes every day in our own society.

Or take almost at random a section from one of the autobiographies and it will show the same freedom and elasticity of life that we find here in our own culture. Rilpada the Seer, a man, is speaking:

> "Once mother and I went to the garden; there was a large field house, and we lived there. One day she told me to carry Senmani (the younger brother) while she worked. At noon he was hungry and wanted to nurse. I gave him food, but he only vomited it. He cried and cried and wouldn't stop. I cried too. Finally I went and told mother to nurse him, but she wouldn't come. So I took Senmani in the house and laid him down on a mat and ran off to Folafeng. From there I shouted, 'Mother, your child sleeps in the house. If you want to care for it, good; if you don't want to, also good. I am going to Atimelang to play'."[10]

[8]Leighton, A. H. and D. C., *The Navaho Door,* Cambridge, Harvard Univ. Press, 1944.

[9]DuBois, *op, cit.,* p. 226 ff.

[10]*ibid.,* p. 251.

109

Here we see no strange compulsions. This is only a child who finally rebels at caring for his little brother after a trying session. Comic strips and our own experiences quickly furnish us with comparable examples. One notes, to be sure, differing devices than would occur in our own society. Rilpada could not have escaped so easily from his task in homes of our culture, and he might have used deceit to avoid this unpleasantness. Nor would the action have progressed so far with the mother in the offing, had a middle class home been the setting. Yet the feelings of Rilpada are clear and the motivation evident. In general the autobiographies as a whole show us nothing psychologically foreign.

2. The main social effect of the individual differences seems to be a qualitative difference in the type of interpersonal relations.

Here we may compare Left Handed, i.e. the son of Old Man Hat, with Old Mexican. Though the two tales cover differing portions of the life cycle, there is enough common experience at the same age level to permit some comparisons. As Dyk has indicated, Left Handed's father was a man who, despite battles with and separations from his wife, always returned to the family, provided an adequate subsistence and had a close, warm relationship with his son.[11] Due to this and other influences, we infer as psychologists, Left Handed grew up to be a relaxed, secure person who could look objectively and humorously upon his own life. Old Mexican's early existence was without such steadfast props: His father and mother separated early, and while she never remarried to present him with the problem of adjusting to a step-father, the boy grew up in poverty with a fight for the bare necessities of food and clothing. The end product is an insecure man, angry in mood, who blows his horn of virtue throughout the relating of his story.

The effects, if they may be so described, are easy to observe. In relations with women, Left Handed as a young man showed genuine interest. While we do not know how many ephemeral moments in the bush he may have failed to mention, there is an openness in discussing many, and there was a period of considerable devotion to at least one, Woman-Who-Flips-Her-Cards. Old Mexican is more tightlipped on his youthful escapades. He does not mention returning to the same woman more than once, and he

[11]Dyk, *A Navaho Autobiography*, p. 7.

seems not to have formed any enduring liaisons. The first meeting with the woman who later became his wife was a strained and evasive encounter, where he was thoroughly suspicious and on guard.

In married life we have no strictly comparable incidents. However, both were married officially for brief periods to widows with children on grounds of charity. Left Handed was plainly in a conflict situation. His mother had validated the marriage contract with gifts, while other relatives maintained openly to the young bridegroom that this woman was still married and had a bad reputation. Nevertheless, he lived with her briefly until he chanced upon, an unknown man in her hogan. Even after this he slept with her a final night without recriminations, and awakening in the morning, he said simply in his own words, "She was still sleeping. My blanket was way underneath, so I let it go and started home."[12] He blamed neither the woman nor his mother for the incident. Old Mexican, on the other hand, stressed in his first marriage the great favor he was doing to help a poor widow with children, who never appreciated him, who later was faithless, and whom he forgave, but all for naught. Indeed, his marital relations were a constant source of vexation, and he complains of having his honorable intentions misunderstood and misconstrued.

We find quite comparable incidents in growing corn. Left Handed found his field choked with weeds, and like most Navahos, sent word to his relatives to come lend a hand in clearing them away. They came, and in one day most of the work was done. That evening they parted with words of gratitude, "Thank you very much for hoeing up the weeds. You've done a great deal for us. If you folks hadn't come, the weeds would still be in the corn . . . I'm very thankful to you all."[13] Old Mexican presents the dogged, painful picture of a man who hoed alone with his wife day and night, complained about his wife who finally went home to sleep, and drove away a clanswoman coming around to claim parts of the land that he had cleared. When finally some clansmen themselves took pity and offered help, he could only remember the jest of one man, "Eat a lot. Eat of these fat, San Juan sheep, and

---

[12]Dyk, *Son of Old Man Hat*, p. 312.
[13]*ibid.*, p. 246.

drink some of their coffee, that they drink only themselves, and eat bread. Get filled up."[14] They just helped him in order to fill their bellies.

Many other similar comparisons could be made in the gaiety or coolness of relations with others, attitudes toward ceremonials and reactions to people in distress. But all seems to have a social effect mainly in the amount and kind of interpersonal relations. Left Handed seeks out people, enjoys them, participates in their activities and they in his, while Old Mexican is the individualist going his own way, at a loss for help when he needs it, shunning people and considering life a struggle, with mankind as the chief antagonist. Both made their livings as Navahos do, both married and, we may believe, raised families. Both participated to some extent in ceremonials and moved seasonally in accordance with their occupations. But Old Mexican was alone, while Left Handed moved among gay, good-humored friends.

Yet this is precisely a main claim of many psychologists: That individual differences arise from the varying kinds of primary-group influences which determine attitudes toward life and people. Our evidence agrees that Navahos, too, may be gregarious or withdrawn and that this important difference seems to have originated in the early conditioning. Despite comfortable wealth at a later age, Old Mexican did not appreciably alter his attitude toward life and people. Though it is advantageous for Navahos to be friendlier than Old Mexican, there is no imperative, but Old Mexican must accept the rankling consequences. The psychologists' observations seem substantiated.

We may now inquire: If these Navaho and Alorese are individuals like those in our own society, what effect does this have on society? We hold the following proposition to be true:

3. These individuals have not noticeably altered the institutional ways of their societies.

We have the story of the Alorese Malafela the Prophet who seems to have come as near as anyone. He was notified in a sequence of dreams that Good Beings were coming to free the people. Though the exact state of affairs after their arrival was

[14]Dyk, *A Navaho Autobiography*, p. 52.

not disclosed in detail, the implication was that life would no longer be difficult. People would not have to pay taxes or do corvee labor. Through his influence people built a house for these Beings; the exact amount of labor that this involved was not clear, but I guess that two or three days would finish the job. Events might have worked out so that Malafela would have shared the fate of equivalent persons in our society who predict and prepare a few for the end of the world. They merely become discredited prophets in the mind of the community. As it was, the nervous Dutch administrator clapped him into jail for a year. Thereafter he continued to dream messages from the Good Beings, but no further changes in community life were apparent from his influence. We may suspect that he capitalized upon the sudden disappearance of Dutch officials a few years later and of course would like to know if there were a sequel.

Old Man Hat too had an opportunity to influence history when a company of U. S. soldiers appeared on the Navaho reserve to bring to justice the murderer of a white man. People listened to his words, and he might have induced the Navaho to defy the troops. As a result punitive measures might have been undertaken with consequent loss of life and, indeed, even more far-reaching results. In fact he counseled polite non-cooperation. A group of horsemen appeared at the camp of the soldiers one noon; Old Man Hat acted as spokesman, made a reassuring speech to the captain after a warm shaking of hands, and departed, having aided neither the murderer nor the troops. The effect of this incident on Navaho society was probably no more, probably considerably less, disastrous than a flood which was described by Old Mexican.

Fantan the interpreter, who knew Malay, who had gone to missionary school, and who had even visited a neighboring island, made no impression on the institutional ways of his society. He may have thumbed ostentatiously through his notebook, given him by Dr. DuBois, while the headman was hearing evidence on whether Fantan should reunite with his wife. This was in keeping with Fantan's striving for attention, but like any humble Alorese who had never even visited the sea coast, Fantan rejoined his wife in accordance with the decision of the headman.

Lest I confuse you, let me reiterate my thesis: It seems to be a

113

descriptive fact that none of these individuals altered the institutional ways of his society. There is an additional question which I shall not go into, namely, how much can an individual influence the institutional ways of his society?

We have shown that these people are individuals in our sense of the term. We also have tried to show that the institutional ways of their societies have not been affected by this lability. The question then arises, where in an organized society is the place for these individuals to express themselves. Our answer is in the following proposition:

4. Many portions of these materials are concerned with affairs that have no direct effect on the institutional ways of the society and may be termed socially inconsequential.

At least it is necessary to define *institutional* ways, and unfortunately the term's referent can only be indicated rather than circumscribed. *Institutional ways* refer to those societal organizations and correlated devices which are primarily concerned with organizing the relations between people and of people to their environment. They include property concepts, devices for settling disputes, economic mechanisms of exchange and distribution, systems of reciprocal obligations and duties such as kinship organizations. They also include systems of production, practices of medical therapy, cosmological systems and religion which relate people to their environment. When we describe a culture, this is the main substance of what many ethnographers bring home, if they can stay that long.

Some, like DuBois, however, also bring home such incidents as this:

> "Many of us played together . . . We broke off young corn, tore off the husks, and said they were rice baskets and rice rolls (used for feasts). They boys took a cassava stalk and made a moko out of it. They said it was a Fatafa (moko) . . .
>
> "Then we women said, 'When we women play with boys, they always hit us. We had better play alone.' We did, and some of the women made believe they were men."[15]

This incident is socially inconsequential in at least one dimension. It is inconsequential because the Alorese do not define the

[15]DuBois, *op. cit.*, p. 521.

sex of the children's play group. Girls may play alone or with boys. I further assume that if it were socially consequential, the sex grouping would be defined and regulated. Other societies do segregate the sexes and attempt to enforce a social code; this constitutes a particular sociological twist, which has a functional value for the society.

Behavior may also be socially inconsequential, not because the acts are socially undefined, but because they are socially isolated either in time or space. For instance, Left Handed recites a Rabelaisian incident when he had a contest with two girls to see who could piss the farthest. Assuming that this is offensive behaviour in Navaho society, it is socially inconsequential as long as it is uncommunicated. A good deal of intimate behaviour is nonconformist in this sense but, being socially isolated, becomes socially inconsequential.

Thus those acts whose dimensions are undefined and/or which are performed in isolation we call socially inconsequential. Since this is far from being a water-tight definition, it is important to distinguish this kind of behaviour from two other kinds with which it has sometimes been confused. The following, from Alor, represents such an incident:

> "My elder sister Lonpada and I fought over a carrying basket. She took my basket and went to Alurkowati and didn't bring it back. I had stayed home to take care of her child. We fought with words and fists. After that I didn't take care of her child any more. I said, 'You have thrown away my basket and now I won't care for your child any more.' Then Lonpada made me a new basket, and about a week later she brought it to me and spoke nicely saying, 'Now I have made a new basket, so you can come and care for my child'."[16]

This behavior is socially consequential. Here we see discord arising because of a breach in approved behavior, but since this is socially recognized as a possibility, a mechanism has been provided to patch up the differences. The act is consequential since it involves a social definition and is not isolated. Our definition is not to be confused with two other possibilities: 1) The breach has been healed and is hence a settled dispute. Even assuming that the difference is psychologically as well as sociologically settled,

[16]*ibid.*, p. 444.

115

a settlement mechanism was involved, and the incident becomes consequential. 2) This event may seem socially inconsequential because only two persons are involved. Divorce, on the other hand, is a public concern and must be sanctioned by a village headman. This distinction is not involved in the present definition of inconsequential. Some societies define an act as individual, others as group concerns, yet they are both socially defined.[17]

Hence, in so far as the society in question leaves areas of behavior socially undefined or through lack of communication reduces the social consequences of certain acts, there is room for individual variation.

If variation characterizes certain aspects of individual behavior, we may inquire further whether variation may not also characterize certain aspects of institutional ways. With relation to this question, we maintain the following: Are the institutions then flexible too?

5. Parts of these autobiographies reveal behavior which seems to be socially important and which admits no exceptions. These seem to concern the institutional ways of the societies.

Inflexibility of institutional ways does not mean here that there is no breach of the ways nor that all behavior concerned with them is stereotyped. This may be true, but it is not necessary, even though socially simpler when it does happen. Inflexibility occurs in terms of achieving social ends in a functional sense that there is a necessary job to be done. It is furthermore inflexible in that it usually is phrased as "conform to this way or accept the consequences." A good example is furnished by Llewellyn and Hoebel in *Cheyenne Way*.[18] Buffalo hunting by individuals at certain times jeopardized the meat supply by driving the herd away. It being necessary to maintain the food supply for the camp, individual hunting for buffalo was prohibited. The end was fixed that no one

---

[17]The word *individual* needs to be refined. While I have tried to restrict its use to the one sense of variation from a norm, I may unwittingly have brought in some of the other senses, *viz*, an individual act is: an act of no public concern, an act of infrequent occurrence or an act socially defined as concerning only one person.

[18]Llewellyn, K. and Hoebel, E. A., *Cheyenne Way*, Norman, Univ. of Oklahoma Press. 1941.

116

should hunt for buffaloes without permission, but the inflexibility was not phrased that way. Rather, the Cheyenne said, hunt when it is approved by the chiefs, or accept the consequences of having your property destroyed. Thus institutions, to be effective, must and do allow for all types of behavior that the society produces.

Let me quote two examples. The first case is about Fantan's obligation to keep up a flow of gongs and mokos with his mother-in-law. He said:

"(my wife's) mother gave a lot of little feasts and expected me to give her things all the time. If a man is old or rich, he can bring gongs and mokos, but we children can go free if we don't have anything. She wanted to be given a great deal. But her husband said, 'We are rich people. If we get gongs and mokos that is all right; but the rest of the things don't matter.' (Informant very disturbed) I wanted to separate but my wife didn't want to. She wanted to use me right through."[19]

The force of this social compulsive is clear. Fantan recognizes the obligation to contribute to his mother-in-law's feasts but is trying to avoid it by having himself included in the category of children where this obligation does not apply.

Another example is from Old Mexican's story:

"After we put in all the crop, my daughter got sick. We had some singing done over her, and after she got a little better I went across to see my folks . . . One of my stepsons came over from the other side of the river and told me my daughter had got worse. He said, 'We are figuring on giving a Squaw Dance for her.' I started back alone, while he went on to Carrizo. I got back there the next day, and then started this way toward the river, to ask a man there to take the dance for one night. He told me to bring the dance over in three days. My daughter wasn't any better. When three days were up, we went to this man. We sang there that night and danced. That was all we did. There wasn't a very big crowd. The next morning we got back to our camp. We kept it up as usual the other two nights. Eight days after we quit dancing the Squaw Dance she got worse again. My wives decided they would give a sing there on my stepson's farm, where there was a big hogan . . ."[20]

As we have already observed, Old Mexican regards Squaw Dances as unpleasant and probably too expensive. Yet here there was no hesitation about the proper action to take. He recognized the obli-

[19]DuBois, *op. cit.*, p. 336.
[20]Dyk, *A Navaho Autobiography*, p. 150.

gation to help his kinsman to recover. Though he played his role without interest or enthusiasm, much as we may submit to an operation, there was no question that the sing was the proper means to this end.

This is not to say that all institutional ways act as effectively as did the rigorous prohibition of individual buffalo hunting for the Cheyenne. Most institutional ways, if attacked, are not attacked at the point of their main intent; this is rarely questioned. Within a given society that frowns on intra-group murder it is always punished. Evasion occurs by trying perhaps to show that the principle of punishment does not apply: "True the man died at my hand, but he attacked me first with an axe." Even under the unpopular and memorable Volstead Act prohibiting alcoholic liquor in this country, no sane person questioned the right of the government to seize and prosecute violators. Rather it was the ease of violation, the unlikelihood of being prosecuted and the attendant implications for the authority of the state that became the chief social reasons for condemning it. Thus, I see institutional ways as inescapable once established in society. The effectiveness of a device for achieving its purpose is another question.

We have confirmed through these autobiographies the picture of individual flexibility in two primitive societies. It is seen to occur in cases where the society leaves the behavior socially undefined and where communication of a breach is unlikely. Institutions are inflexible to the extent that a device is prescribed for achieving a given social end. However, since few institutions apply without exception to every member of a society, evasion may occur, and to the extent this is possible, further degrees of freedom for individual flexibility are permitted.

Can we now make any suitable generalization on the place of individual variations in society? First I assume that:

1. The raw data of anthropology and psychology are the same.[21]

[21] What these raw data should be called is perhaps a matter of taste. Bidney ("Human Nature and the Cultural Process," *American Anthropology*, 1947, 49, 375-399) appears to call them all "culture," while Kluckhohn and Leighton (*op. cit.*) dub them "life ways." My objection to the term culture in this connection is that it implies under the usual conno-

2. The elaboration of these raw data may be toward institutional ways or toward the psychological person. Both possibilities are included within the data.

With this as the basis I make the following generalization:

3. We may think of behavior in a society as falling along a continuum in terms of variation. At one end all major dimensions of behavior show little variation; at the other end all major dimensions show considerable variation. If so, the items of behavior with less variation will be more institutionalized, more nearly continuous or permanent historically, and more socially functional.

Into this proposition I have smuggled several assumptions. The ones of which I am aware are: 1) institutionalized behavior is less variable than non-institutionalized, 2) institutionalized behavior is more perfectly transmitted from generation to generation; 3) behavior is institutionalized to serve social needs.

I picture this proposition in terms of the accompanying chart. Here is a single line on which we arrange all behavior of a given society. At one end all dimensions of behavior are invariable. At the other end all dimensions are variable. If the behavior of any society were itemized in such a manner and distributed along this line as a scale, it would probably fall in some kind of heap toward the middle. Some societies would have more, others less variable behavior. The resulting behavior would then be found to have these characteristics: The behavior toward the less variable end would be more institutionalized, vary less from generation to gen-

---

tation of the word an inheritance from the preceding generation. I believe that only part of the behavior which I have described as socially inconsequential is inherited from the preceding generation. My objection to "life ways" is not so much the term as the diagram (cf. p. 233) which, despite the intermingling of arrows, clearly distinguishes personality determinants from environmental and historical determinants. While this conception is systematically justifiable, it promotes confusion by dividing individuals from institutions. Genetically the diagram is correct but in terms of any concrete situation, analysis into these parts seems to me unfruitful.

The concept of social behavior here would probably have to include both overt and covert behavior in order to be inclusive. Also it may be questioned whether the term "social" makes any contribution, since it so obviously refers to all behavior.

eration and more clearly serve social ends. Contrariwise, the be-, havior toward the more variable end of the scale would be relatively less institutionalized, more variable from generation to generation and socially less consequential.

GRAPHIC REPRESENTATION OF GENERALIZATION 3 OF CONCLUSIONS

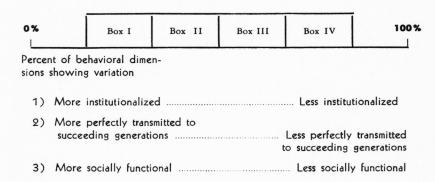

What specific kinds of behavior would lie on the various portions of the scale? Starting from the least variable end, we would be inclined to think that in Box I falls behavior which is assumed, on the level of the unconscious. The Navaho assumption of a nomadic life in pursuit of any means of subsistence. The Alorese assumption of life in a village with financial transactions as the chief male aim. Perhaps forms of behavior in the kinship system would also fall in here, that an older sister looks after her brother's livestock among the Navaho or in Alor that women know nothing about finance.[22] Moving from Box I to Box II we would

[22]Prof. A. L. Kroeber raised in discussion the question whether I have not run afoul of the form-function dilemma. Certain behavior may be inherited, as grammatical form, yet its social function is ambiguous, if not non-existent. It is the question of the extent to which a functional view of society is applicable to the data. Certainly, if functionalism be considered a methodological conceptualization, rather than a statement about the nature of society, the danger of forcing data into an unreceptive mold is somewhat reduced.

find a group of institutions that are mainly consciously organized. In Alor we note the legal institutions under the headman and the death feast. Among the Navaho the various methods of earning a living by herding or agriculture, the use of the Yebichai to discipline children would probably fall here. There may sometimes be a compulsive element in this group, since the behavior is not necessarily in keeping with the mode of training the young. These types of behavior are again mainly inherited from the preceding generation.

Approaching the more variable end in Box III, I would expect to find behavior where succeeding generations do not agree. Within our society this type of behavior is so frequent as to attract little attention today, being found in educational practices, in styles of art and music and in political and economic creeds. There is little evidence of such behavior among the people concerned in the autobiographies, though we note that Old Mexican became involved in white ways. Unlike his father, Old Mexican owned a team and wagon, raised horses and followed in many ways the latest word from the agency. Yet we do not know the attitude and behavior of the older generation toward this. Distinctly in this category are fashion changes such as the differing style of hairdress among the plains Indians. The Northern Blackfoot began wearing their hair in braids about 1890, though formerly it was worn loose. At the extreme end of the scale in Box IV lies the category which we have called socially inconsequential. Here is a good deal of child behavior, most of the dreams, various idiosyncracies such as Fantan's behavior with his notebook while in session with the hearings of the headman. Here there is a complex reaction to the preceding generation which makes prediction of concrete behavior difficult. Where there is positive identification, we would expect similarities between generations; where there is more or less repressed antagonism, we would expect less similarity.

Viewing the total gamut, you will have observed what an hypothetical affair this is.[23] We have no way of getting at the total

[23]Prof. R. Linton observed in comment that empirical investigation is necessary before this generalization can be validated or invalidated. I would agree and add that for many parts of the investigation data from our own society could be used.

dimensions of most acts nor any way of defining a unit of behavior. Also these categories should be considered as analogous to spectral colors rather than distinct categories. Yet certain advantages seem to come from this type of consideration. For instance, all behavior may be considered as functional in terms of need satisfaction, even though some needs may arise from a particular social consideration of other persons and be compulsive or indifferent to the individual concerned. Other items of behavior may be regarded as serving unique needs for expression or repression of particular constellations of hostility or anxiety. At the invariable end behavior may be viewed as organized into a strong gestalt, though certainly at the variable end the organization can only be described as socially diffuse and weak.

In answer to the question of the locus of individual differences, I feel able to reply that they are mainly concentrated in those parts of society which are least institutionalized, least continuous historically and least socially functional. However, some dimensions of social behavior will be found to vary throughout most of society.

The question of the relation between individual flexibility and the rigidity of the social structure is partly solved by observing that individuals are neither so flexible nor institutions so rigid as we first supposed. Institutions do cover as much of the total range of society as is necessary to achieve their purposes.

Finally, I would thank the authors of these autobiographies. They are far richer documents than my superficial usage of them indicates. I would add that the well-annotated work of Dyk with its chronological order is far easier to read and understand than DuBois' unorganized field notes.[24] But above all I would like to have more from the same society but taken from the same social group. Occasionally I have the feeling that many of the differ-

[24]Prof. C. Kluckhohn in his methodological statement at the meeting indicated that for interpretations of personality a continuous document from birth to death is not necessary. Biographical data may also reveal the cultural attitudes toward the life cycle, indicate the way that a human existence is conceived and show the experience of a person who is participating in the culture. To the extent that these demands are made on personal documents, the associative form with its gaps and incoherences is not completely satisfactory.

ences between Left Handed and Old Mexican are due to growing up in differing parts of Navaho society. To study individual differences in a true sense of the term, status factors must be reduced.

The materials are also influenced by the focus of the collectors. Dyk seems to have focussed more on the total life cycle, while DuBois was more interested in the idiosyncratic. With my interest I would seek autobiographies from successive generations within the same family. This might reveal modes of transmission of institutional ways to be more complex than has been allowed for. The psychological importance of varying relations between parent and child might be more influential in cultural transmission than we have yet credited it. Hence I would hope to see perhaps under the editorship of Mr. Dyk at least two more autobiographical studies, one entitled "Grandsons of Old Man Hat" and the other, "Sons and Stepsons of Old Mexican".

DISCUSSION

Dr. Ralph Linton: It seems to me that in this thesis of the concentration of individual differences in various parts of the range of culture patterns, it is necessary to start from actual observations rather than from an *a priori* theory. Different cultures show a tremendous amount of difference in the degree to which their patterns are consciously formalized. My experiences with Polynesians and Comanches illustrate this: Polynesians can give you practically an Emily Post statement of what proper behavior should be on all occasions, whereas Comanches, when asked how they do anything immediately answer, "Well, that depends." They genuinely think of behavior as a range of unlimited, individual, freedom of choice, although when you take a series of examples of behavior, as Hoebel did, you find actually quite a high degree of uniformity. But you have to check Comanche behavior to arrive at this.

In addition, when it comes to the matter of institutional rigidity, I think you will find that where an institution has ceased to be effective, in terms of either the external environment or in terms of the changing value system of the society itself, that it will remain fixed at a certain point, and then will break abruptly, some individual finally taking the first step in direct opposition to the pattern, but finding an already prepared support. I hate to cite such a little known example, but one case of this occurred when a single Comanche finally broke up the Morning Star ceremony (a human sacrifice). Previously, there had obviously been increasing opposition in the tribe. The captive girl was kept for many months before the time of her sacrifice arrived, so that she came to be known as an individual, made friends, etc. Finally, a man of high status—he was the next in line to the chieftainship and son of the head chief's sister—broke in, carried the girl off, and said, "We will not have this ceremony any longer." Apparently, he had majority backing in the tribe, for the ceremony was discontinued.

Another interesting example came under my own observation among the Tanala. For a long time they had permitted sororal polygyny in connection with a strong pattern of responsibility for cross cousins. A man could marry two sisters if they were cross cousins and if no adequate partner was to be found for the second one within the system of cross cousin marriage. Interestingly enough, this had persisted in certain gentes, but with a general recognition that sisters are more jealous of each other than strangers. It was, therefore, *not* a good idea to have them as plural wives! While I was there, the tensions in one gens finally culminated in a case in which one sister poisoned another who was a plural wife. This brought the dissatisfactions to a head and the old men of the gens met together and officially tabooed marriages of this sort. And they got the backing of the bulk of the population!

I think you frequently have in connection with rigid institutions, something that would almost correspond to traumatic experience in the individual life history—discomforts build up, and then suddenly are touched off by some episode resulting in an actual change.

After all, a culture pattern is never a point, but always a range. Percentages will tend to move over from the center toward one end or the other of the permissible range, and in fact, the whole range itself may be displaced in certain directions. I think this actually is the agency by which most culture change at the institutional level takes place.

DR. HANKS: I would agree that there is certainly necessary flexibility in the institutional ways and that you might say the amount of any particular one of these categories in a culture would vary considerably, as in your example, the Tanala.

DR. LINTON: The point that I want to explain is that of the degree of verbalization of the patterns. Many patterns are regularly honored in the breach rather than in the observance. The fact that a society has developed an ideal pattern, a verbalization as to what should be done under certain circumstances, does not mean that the people adhere any more closely to a norm than those of some other society which has never bothered to verbalize a pattern.

DR. HANKS: Then you say it would be necessary just to get out and make descriptive studies?

DR. LINTON: Yes, take case histories. Find out how certain people behave under particular situations.

Dr. Lawrence K. Frank: The last few remarks Dr. Linton made seemed to me to point in the direction of a methodological matter that your paper brought up. Do you think there would be some advantage in ordering our observations to think in terms of the usual frequency distribution rather than this linear continuum? The best you can say is that there are certain local conducts which we have observed which may be institutionally sanctioned or may not be. At both extremes, as we see today in our own culture, we may have either the criminal, anti-social, or the idiosyncratic neurotic and psychotic. And I think to give that kind of a picture is important because then we begin to ask ourselves, "What happens when we have bi-modal societies and cultures?" It is that part of the dynamics of change that Dr. Linton has pointed out; it gives us something we can get at. It also gives us a clue to the situation that we find in the social science field today: because the classic social sciences, economics, political science and sociology, have until recently been concerned with modal behavior, and have ignored the two extremes. We find we cannot get the two together; they are concentrated on central tendencies.

If we are going to use the benefits of all the social sciences, I think we are going to have to ask ourselves: How can we use both the modal observations and these idiosyncratics and deviants? Now part of the picture is to recognize that each individual may occupy a different rank order position in each frequency distribution on which you could make observations. That's the thing it seems to me we have often forgotten. It's very important because if we recognize that an individual occupies such an extraordinary range of positions in these frequency distributions, from one end to the other, *how* does he reconcile and maintain his private world, so that he can continue to function in society, despite the fact that he may be way low on one end, occupy a lot of median or modal positions, and be quite high in the idiosyncratic neurotic? That gives us, it seems to me, a dynamic way of ordering observations. It may be very useful in using data that come from all the social sciences. And I suggest it as another alternative to the linear way of looking at things which you have suggested.

Dr. Joseph Stone: I think the methodological problems are the crucial ones here and it seems to me that all of our methodologies involve difficulties. We're not entirely satisfied with autobiography. We're not entirely satisfied with the longitudinal case study: it stands by itself and is retrospective. A number of papers, some of which I didn't hear, are concerned with that. I thought it might be worth mentioning now a study which is just getting under way. I feel free to mention it because I am not helping do it. Some of you may know a study which Dr. Roger Barker of Kansas is undertaking—a field study of the behavior and the impact of society on children in a small community which he has named Micropolis—a community of about one thousand people. He's trying to insinuate carefully selected observers who will be accepted in the community. He is con-

cerned with the kind of study which I think reflects the enriching awareness of what's going on in these parallel fields we are considering. I think
we have reached the point where psychologists, anthropologists, sociologists and psychiatrists are beginning to have not merely verbal respect
for each other, but working relations with each other, and I think this
kind of field study is one evidence of the methodological virtues of com-
bining techniques of different fields.

DR. A. L. KROEBER: I am much interested in the scale Dr. Hanks has discussed and in Linton's comments on it. A comment on the latter first: if
we visualize, as he said, on one end of the scale, for instance, the sharply
institutionalized form of life of the Hopi, pretty rigidly adhered to, next
the Navajo, and beyond that, the Walapai, with whom I also have had
some personal contact, it strikes me that one reason for the differentiation
which makes this possible is that these tribes are all on the same level of
development. Perhaps the reason for that is economic. The Pueblos are
the aristocrats. They have prospered economically; therefore, they have
preserved the luxury of institutions in their life. The Walapai are living
on Tobacco Road, so to speak, and they never have margin enough to
adopt a rigid pattern. They try to begin, but they have to make exceptions
right away because everyone is so hardup. Of course that is not necessarily the only factor, but I think the economic factor *does* enter in. It is
obvious that they have to have a certain basic security to pull them together, and, as I said, indulge themselves.

One reason there has been so much discussion as to the merits of the
functional and historical approaches is that we do have enormous range
in any culture. For instance it's hard to make out very much of a case
for the particular forms of language having particular functions. The
people who know most about it don't believe that. If you want to go
seriously into language patterns, forms, and grammar to see whether you
can explain it well or not—you get away at the opposite end of the scale
from that where you work with the conscious motions in which institutions
are involved. In that area, the functional explanation is going to work by
far the best. People who began for some reason or another to be concerned
with the forms of culture, saw relatively little in functionalism, or, admit-
ting it was there, did not occupy themselves with it. At the other end were
people who did not begin with strongly patterned forms but with how the
individual lives—behavior, let us say—and who tended to be functionalists
and to overlook the forms, or just consider them a background against
which behavior operates. In other words, we do have a scale. Dr. Hanks'
remarks have illustrated it very beautifully—which shows why we have
so many differences of procedure and of methodology.

126

OTTO KLINEBERG

Recent Studies of National Character*

Most of the methodological and controversial points I wanted to raise for discussion have been raised by Dr. Hanks and those who followed him. In spite of that, perhaps the situation is a little different for the larger, more complicated groups we deal with under the general head of national character. So I would like to present some recent studies in this area, and make some critical suggestions and comments.

Of course the problem is almost as old as history, but until recently social scientists gave little direct attention to methods of studying the relatively large and complicated modern societies or nations. The whole approach might be regarded as having a relatively brief history. However, a few years ago when I tried to review the materials available in this area there already were a number of striking and interesting suggestions. Attempts are made by psychiatrists, such as Brickner in his well known book, "Is Germany Incurable?", and by ethnologists, as in Margaret Mead's account of our contemporary American society in "And Keep Your Powder Dry". There is Geoffrey Gorer's suggestion about the relation between child training of the Japanese and adult personality structure in "The Japanese Culture". Or there is Erikson's article on the attempt to relate certain images used by Hitler to the nature of German youth, particularly adolescent strivings and impulses, and German revolts against authority, which helped him understand, he thought, why German youth accepted so readily Hitler's point of view and imagery.

It was interesting to me that the journal, *Psychiatry*, should have been the home of so many recent attempts. I don't know

*Owing to Dr. Klineberg's absence from the country when this paper went to press, he was unable to rewrite or revise his remarks. The present paper was made from the wire recording, with slight changes by the editors.

whether this represents a special interest of the editor. But looking through *Psychiatry* for the last few years, one is impressed with the number of studies dealing directly or indirectly with the problem of national character.

I mention one as a sort of footnote to Dr. Herzog's paper, an article by Thorner on "German words, German personality and Protestantism" in *Psychiatry*, in 1945. He attempts to get hints about German national character from words that appear rather frequently in German conversation and writing. He contrasts German and English, for example, in the words "Herr" and "Mr." "Herr" represents a kind of position of authority; "Mr." does not have that authority. He believes this indicates the hierarchical arrangement in German society. Another example is "Schadenfreude", the joy in somebody else's hard luck. He points out there is one word for this in German, but no one word for it in English. Unfortunately for his thesis, he shows that the Scandinavian languages have almost exactly the same word for this, but he thinks it is borrowed directly from the German and therefore hasn't any great value. I think most of us agree, in view of what happens in acculturation, that if people borrow, there probably are reasons for their borrowing. If the Scandinavian equivalent of "Schadenfreude" comes from the German, probably the Scandinavian people aren't entirely absolved from responsibility for having it in their vocabulary.

So this kind of analysis leads to complications that I don't have time, and probably not the capacity, to deal with fully. However, I give one more example from Thorner's article. He mentions that Luther's translation of the Bible has a German phrase "ohne meine Schuld"—"without my responsibility" or "without my being to blame for it"—that isn't in the original, or in the original has a somewhat different flavor, without the notion of absolving oneself of responsibility. Thorner thinks that, too, might tie up with German attitudes—the assumption that whatever happened is somebody else's fault and not theirs. My feeling about this kind of material is not that it is useless, but that penetration of a people's mentalities in terms of its language, as Dr. Herzog suggested yesterday, might be fruitful; but what we have here are only very tiny samples which leave me unconvinced. One would need a much more thorough study of the language and of the integration of the language with the whole character of the people before knowing just how much weight to put on it.

Another recent study, presenting a different attempt to get at national character by analyzing a cultural product, is the book by Kracauer, "From Caligari to Hitler", which analyzes the history of the German movie. Kracauer tries to get some indication of German characteristics by analyzing nearly every film ever produced in Germany. (We know a lot can be said for analyzing German films carefully. Gregory Bateson's analysis of "Hitler Junge Quex" and other pictures show how the Nazi philosophy reflected itself in German-produced pictures.) Kracauer's aim is ambitious. He believes one can really learn about German national character, and that movies are a particularly happy medium for this study because a number of people collaborate to produce them, and, being meant for a multitude of people, they are not the private property or private productions of individuals in the community.

I give an example of his technique. The famous movie "Caligari" many of us are old enough to have seen and to remember. Kracauer points out that the original theme of "Caligari"—the script of the first movie—was quite different from the "Caligari" as it finally appeared. In the original, apparently it was a kind of revolt of the individual against certain types of brutal and unfair authority. In this, Caligari was really the head of a psychiatric institution and at the same time was a criminal who sent the man whom he hypnotized to perform his murders for him. When it reached the screen all of this became a story within a story. It was the dream of the diseased individual who saw all of these things happen. In other words, as the story emerged there still was respect for authority! In the original script, written by two rebels, you might say, against the system, there was an attack on established authority which seemed so criminal and insane in many cases. But in the picture released to the German public, authority no longer became insane. It was a real, genuine, reasonable authority and the insanity was in the mind of the individual who imagined this authority was insane.

I picked this as one of the most favorable examples for Kracauer. It reveals his method in its most favorable light. The book is too complex in its general treatment for easy summary. The

129

only general criticism I would make is that this kind of "post hoc" reasoning is relatively easy in the sense that when you know what happened to Germany you can look back and find all kinds of justifications for the situation you now find. I should guess that if tomorrow or next year or ten years from now a similar revolution took place in the United States (God forbid!), we could find in our movies bases which would help explain it. In other words, the picture isn't clear or uni-dimensional, but complex. And it seems to me we must be wary of the kind of reasoning that follows or depends on earlier knowledge of what had happened to Germany.

Recently attempts have been made by anthropologists to direct their techniques to analyzing more complex societies of the types we may legitimately call nations. Many have not been published; that is, they were published in mimeographed form for various war agencies and although they are now declassified and can be referred to freely, they are not readily available to everyone. I want to refer briefly to one or two. Ruth Benedict's studies of Roumania and Thailand, and Geoffrey Gorer's study of Burma stand out among these unpublished studies.

The general problem that emerges from them occurs again and again in studies that must be carried out under relative difficulties, far from the original country, sometimes with a group of informants relatively limited in number and variety. This is not criticism of what was done, because I believe it was the best that could be done. It is criticism, perhaps, in terms of an ideal situation, which of course would require a more direct participation in and knowledge of individuals in the culture.

For example, Gorer's study of Burma he quite frankly admits was carried on with three informants, none Burmese. All had lived in Burma and come back with presumably a good knowledge of certain aspects of Burmese culture. Gorer, I am sure, did the best he could with those informants. But that is a far cry from the ideal situation in which an ethnologist could be placed where he could study this community at first hand and check, himself, the individuals' behavior against the verbalized reports of his informants. That point has come up before and will come up again.

Dr. Benedict's study of the Roumanians was carried on under

130

much better conditions than Gorer's. There were, she tells us, 25 informants, all having some direct participation in Roumanian culture. Therefore, methodologically speaking, the material is much more helpful. I shall not go into the details of these because I think a summary of the actual findings is less important than the methodological problems which I hope will come up in a few moments.

Coming back to psychiatry, Dr. Weston LaBarre recently published three papers, one dealing with the Japanese and two with the Chinese. In his Chinese studies he describes first the Chinese as *not* being a number of things. They are not militaristic or imperialistic. They are non-mercantile, non-industrial and non-urban. When I read this list it sounds worse than it really is because he does try to take care of certain objections one might raise. Having a little knowledge of Chinese history, I find it rather difficult to say "non-imperialistic" for China, when one considers its size and population and the number of different communities that united to form the Chinese. It is difficult to say "non-mercantile" when we know that in the Straits Settlements the Chinese have taken the lead in mercantile activities. Certainly in Singapore, Penang and other communities one gets the impression that the Chinese represent one of the most highly developed mercantile classes one can find almost anywhere.

LaBarre mentions the easy toilet training of the Chinese; boys, for example, are just given a pair of seatless trousers that allow satisfaction of certain impulses with a minimum of difficulty. He points out that human feces are not regarded with the same repulsion as in other communities. We know that human feces are collected and used as "night soil"—as fertilizer. He believes that this general attitude toward evacuation results in the Chinese being free from compulsiveness, unobsessive, with none of the characteristics you get in a compulsive society. They lack any strong visceral discipline. The "id" demands get all the gratification they need. I wonder whether, in terms of the tremendous amount of famine in Chinese history for so many generations, one really can speak of "id" gratification in any perfect manner. I should guess that the need for food still is part of the "id" demand. In that respect, certainly, one can hardly describe the Chinese as having a complete "id" satisfaction.

131

LaBarre points out that no true national patriotism exists in China because loyalties are to the family, the extended family or to the clan. Here again I ask, perhaps naively, if there is no national patriotism, isn't it a little difficult to explain why the Chinese have retained the largest population the world has ever known in any one nation under one political organization? Certainly a more detailed analysis of what is meant by patriotism or cohesiveness is needed to reconcile the fact that more than 450,-000,000 Chinese live in one community, that there has been only partial breaking away from central authority.

To quote one brief statement:

"The Chinese ethos is that of the artist, scholar and gentleman; not of the soldier, scientist, the entrepreneur, the metaphysicist, priest, lawgiver, or even of the statesman. He has an uncompetitive attitude toward the real world. He has accommodated himself to nature and does not compel nature to accommodate herself to him. Inhibition, tensions and aggressions of the west are not part of his genius. His temperament is kindly, gracious and responsive; unpolitical, unaggressive, unfanatic, unobsessive, cheerful, poised, enduring, rational, secure, calm and deeply considerate of others. He has a healthy ego and a satisfied id, and none of the overgrown mastery of the super-ego."

One gathers that LaBarre likes the Chinese! I like them too, very much, but this description seems to me a little extreme. There have been quarrels in China. There has been trouble. There still are problems to be solved that would seem easy to solve if this kind of Chinese ethos were as widely distributed as LaBarre suggests.

For the Japanese we have both LaBarre's brief account in *Psychiatry* and Ruth Benedict's book, "The Chrysanthemum and the Sword", which for me, and I am sure for many others, it is a pleasure to acknowledge as an extremely able, interesting, informative book that leaves us with considerably more knowledge about the Japanese than when we started. I believe it a real contribution in this field and an example of what a careful anthropologist can do when she turns to the problem of national character.

We have here an account of some important problems the

132

Japanese have to solve: the importance of having a safe position in the world, and of adapting to the external world and to people; the importance of duties and obligations one assumes because one is a member of the society; the indebtedness one incurs to others, and life viewed in a large measure as paying off that indebtedness. We get a good picture also of child training, and some of the relationship of child training and adult personality.

I repeat: the study seems to me extremely valuable and important. If I raise certain questions, they concern things that might have been added to give a complete picture of national character, rather than a criticism of what has been done.

We are told in the book that filial piety and, in general, family relationships are limited to the face-to-face family contacts, in contrast to China where one's loyalty and one's contacts are with the whole clan, with everybody who has the same surname. Yet we learn that when a betrothal is arranged, a conference on the betrothal is held with members of the family coming from distant parts of Japan to participate in the decision. This seems to me a certain extension of the family relationships from the immediate face-to-face family to others less directly face-to-face.

A few other points have to do with certain contradictions between Dr. Benedict's and Dr. LaBarre's statements. I do not compare the two studies, but I think we need a methodology to distinguish between the results of two such studies done by persons trained in anthropology, who arrive at rather different and sometimes contradictory conclusions.

One gets the impression from Dr. Benedict's book that there is very little super-ego with the Japanese, in our sense of inner conscience. There is, instead, a feeling about shame in relation to others, to what others will think about what we say, rather than any feeling about having to do or not having to do certain things because of inner conviction.

From LaBarre, on the other hand, one gets the impression that the super-ego in Japan seems tremendously important. Is this perhaps a question of the meaning attached to the term super-ego? When we use it we think of it in our sense, but does it perhaps mean super-ego in the sense of shame, not in the sense of inner compulsion? LaBarre gives the impression of a super-ego in our

133

sense. Dr. Benedict describes it as a sense of shame in relationship to others, instead of an inner feeling of wrong.

LaBarre's account of Japanese toilet training seems much more rigid and painful than the one Dr. Benedict describes. He speaks of actual severe punishment for breaches. Dr. Benedict, on the other hand, describes a rather rigid discipline in which the child is held firmly outside the house at certain intervals. LaBarre shows that certain things are clearly expected of children, but Dr. Benedict seems to find little actual physical punishment for breaches. (LaBarre's informants, incidentally, were Japanese in a United States relocation center; he used only people born in Japan.)

LaBarre speaks again and again of a Japanese inferiority complex. From Dr. Benedict we get the notion that the Japanese are relatively free from what we call an inferiority complex. She doesn't use the term, and tends to suggest that the Japanese have a certain self-assurance and certainty that is hard to reconcile with the idea of true inferiority feeling.

Two little points about Dr. Benedict's account of Japanese reaction. She tells us (and here again is a footnote to Dr. Herzog's comment) that in Japan to speak of conscienceless individual does not mean the same as a conscienceless individual in our society. With us it's a person who can do wrong without seeming concerned about it. In Japan apparently it is a person who does things free from the trammels of outside consideration. His conscience acts in a manner true to himself without outside interference or too great concern for others.

I wonder whether we aren't getting into the realm of language or semantics. I recall that in Brazil the word for conscience is the same as the word for consciousness—"consciencia". When we speak here of "conscienceless" do we really mean "consciousnessless" rather than "conscienceless"? In this case isn't it perhaps misleading to use a term like "conscienceless" for the Japanese?

One other point. Dr. Benedict believes that teasing in early childhood probably explains the great fear of ridicule in later life. Could one not argue that exposure to considerable teasing in childhood might, on a purely logical basis, make one relatively immune to that sort of behavior in later life?

I am reminded of Dr. Bateson's suggestion in his article on

134

"Culture in Relation to the Frustration and Aggression Hypothesis" that in Bali there seems to be little aggression as a result of frustration. The reason, he suggests, may be that the Balinese become used to frustration in childhood, so in later life frustration doesn't lead to aggression, as Dollard and his Yale collaborators would suggest.

Here again we have a methodological problem. When can we assume that exposure to certain behavior in childhood will make us more sensitive to that behavior in adult life, and when can we assume that it will make us negatively adapted, so that in adult life it won't mean much to us?

The kind of material presented us by Dr. Benedict and other careful anthropologists seems to me of the greatest value, showing us the general patterns of behavior and culture and their influence on what Fromm would call "social character". But the question we must ask is, and I echo in different words the point already made by Hanks: how basic, how similar, how universal are these traits? It seems to me that it is something we must know.

I repeat: How basic? How universal? In what direction do we find deviations, and how commonly? As Dr. Kroeber and Dr. Linton pointed out, degrees of consistency apply to nations as well as to the communities anthropologists study. I am reminded that long ago when Halbwachs studied suicide in different regions of England, he found the frequency of suicide relatively consistent. When he did the same thing for regions in France, he found a marked variation in the number of suicides in the various communities. In other words, we get the notion, from the statistical data in this case, that possibly nations differ in their degree of homogeneity.

We must also be able to separate national character from national mythology. This is often difficult because people will tell you things about their behavior and characteristics which may not reflect their actual behavior. The point has already been suggested in the study of primitive cultures.

Now many of these questions, I think, can be answered up to a certain point by the anthropologist himself, within anthropological field work. When an anthropologist tells us about a culture pattern and its relation to individual behavior, we also would like

135

to know, and this is what we miss in these studies: does *everybody* do this? Is this the sort of thing people *should* do, or what they *actually* do? Do *you* do this? Do you *always* do this? Do you *usually* do it? What would happen if you didn't do it? In other words, if the anthropologist asked the informant a whole series of questions, perhaps the answers would enable more psychologically oriented persons to find value in the material and gain insight into how it touches the individual.

In national character studies we need also more detailed information about the informants, I believe. The studies with which I am familiar have, without exception, too little description of the kinds of individuals who gave the information. What is their age distribution? Their sex? Their class? And here again, on what do all the informants agree? (This is different from asking, "Does everybody do this?") On what points do they differ? How do they differ, and how much do they differ? Was the same information requested of all the informants, so that when an item is told us about the national character of the Roumanians or Americans or Japanese or Chinese or any other group we know whether the informants answered more or less the same kind of questions and gave information on the same topics.

These questions are just suggestions. The anthropologists themselves, if they feel it worthwhile, can add or subtract from them. But I think they would make it possible to evaluate the studies much more successfully than we can at present.

This kind of information would enable the unbiased external observer, for example, to choose between statements by Benedict and LaBarre, or even by the general consistency of Benedict or LaBarre, or even by the general consistency of the report (which I admit is an important source of internal evidence), but by the methodological information enabling us to say "this is an important study" and "that is an unimportant study". It is like our saying in psychology that, other things being equal, a study based on 2000 cases is worth more than a study based on 20. I repeat, *other things being equal!*

Another suggestion I make is that wherever possible these ethnological studies should be supplemented by psychological techniques. I referred briefly to one in my previous discussion. There are other techniques, many of which, of course, the anthropologists know well and are beginning to use, especially the projective techniques. Dr. Benedict's book encourages the psychologists by reporting studies of competitiveness between Japanese, using methods of experimental psychology, Rorschach results and other projective techniques. Here is a beginning of integrating psychological and anthropological material which many of us regard as so valuable.

Let me give two examples of other types of study that I think occasionally can be useful. In Bruner's book, "Mandate from the People" there are incidental but interesting indications of certain aspects of American national character. For example, Bruner reports:

"In March, 1943, the president sent to Congress an omnibus plan for social security after the war. A week later, in a public opinion study, 76 per cent approved, 15 per cent disapproved, and 9 per cent expressed no opinion."

Nothing happened. Nothing was done. Why, asks Bruner? Because Americans have almost incomparable faith in their own personal future. No one believed that social security was *his* meat. Bruner goes on to give the percentage of people who believed that even though it might be a good thing, they did not care whether it was implemented now or later because it didn't touch them personally. He reports that only about 39 per cent favored immediate action on the plan, while only about a third of the population (32 per cent) believed the social security program would make any difference in their lives.

Now you can say this is what we have always known. Any ethnologist and sociologist knows that Americans are optimistic and expect to rise on the ladder of opportunity. That is the American dream. You don't need public opinion studies to find that out. But we have here a minority of 40 per cent of the people who *did* want this done. We have a group of 32 per cent who *did* believe it would affect them. Well, that's part of the picture of America. It is the substantial minority that doesn't fit into the American dream. And in the future any change that may take place in the social structure may come out of minorities like these who would be completely neglected if we didn't have some kind of quantitative study to help us know not only the American culture pattern but also the character of the deviants. By deviants I mean not just

137

those people at the extremes, but those who would not quite fit into the major pattern.

We can say, of course, that the Germans have shown more desire or tendency than Americans to obey their fathers,—"authority in the family", and so on. That is true. But McGranahan, in a recent study, points out answers to a question: "Do you think a boy is justified in running away from home if his father is cruel or brutal?" The American sample said "yes" much more frequently than the German sample—that a boy *is* justified in running away from home. In the American sample, 68 per cent said yes, but *30 per cent said no*. A substantial minority accepted the father's authority, therefore, even when he is brutal. Although in the German sample 50 per cent said "no", which is a larger proportion than in the American sample, there still was 45 per cent (almost half) of the Germans who said that a boy *is* justified in running away from home if his father is too harsh on him.

One other question: "Which in your opinion is worse, the boy who tyrannizes and beats up smaller children, or the boy who disobeys his superior?" The idea here was that presumably American boys would say the first is worse, and German boys would say the second is worse. Of those who made a choice, 68 per cent of the Americans said the bully is worse, and 29 per cent said the disobedient boy is worse. In the German sample, 41 per cent said that the bully is worse, and 30 per cent said the disobedient boy is worse. In other words, it didn't come out quite in the manner expected. The tendency was in the expected direction, but the difference was not very marked. Here the psychologist had a hunch based on a general knowledge of Germany. It turned out not to be nearly as certain as he had believed.

Now I am not suggesting that these methods are superior to ethnological methods in studying national character. I will be faithless to my occupational identity to the extent of saying that if I had to choose one or the other method, Dr. Benedict's would seem to me definitely superior to Dr. McGranahan's.

But I think there is no need to choose. The method McGranahan used, and that Bruner used indirectly, can be a very valuable supplement to the general description of a community's culture. In studying the culture pattern, we need to know both the degree of agreement and the individual variations within it.

DISCUSSION

DR. RUTH BENEDICT: I want to say that I agree entirely with Dr. Klineberg, that there are difficulties in doing a national study of the Japanese without having been in Japan. Let me say that after V.J. Day I made every effort to go to Japan. All my male friends went, but the American army and the American government insisted that the Japanese would all rape me. I assured them that the Japanese would not, that the Japanese were going to accept Americans and they would accept an American woman. By the time they were convinced of that, after four months, I was no longer free to go. But it was not my fault that the American army and American government thought a woman would be in danger in Japan after V.J. Day! So all the studies I did during the war were admittedly done under great disadvantages. Everything that *was* done is that much ahead in hypotheses, I hope. Now there should be field work; the anthropologists' whole method is based on field work.

I should like to discuss what Dr. Klineberg says are the differences between Dr. La Barre's and my work on super-ego and inferiority complex. I feel that the great advantage one gets out of studying different cultures is the realization that super-ego has so many particular different kinds of components in two cultures. Hence I omit the word "super-ego". I try to explain how the Japanese are not concerned with the problem of sin but are terribly concerned with the problem of being ridiculed—of shame. So I have not used the word "super-ego" and I have not used the words "inferiority complex," because a Japanese inferiority complex is so different from ours that I think I can describe it better by *not* using the word. So I have omitted a great many words used in our language because they have all the connotations of western culture. Therefore I find it better to describe the high level of aspiration in Japan, which is true, and not discuss inferiority complex as we use it. That brings up the problem of why I have used "conscienceless." The same problem was raised by using "responsibility" as the translation for the Japanese word "makoto." The Japanese universally accept those translations; they have appeared in every record, every newspaper. Therefore it is terribly important for an Anglo-American audience, as I have said in the "Chrysanthemum and the Sword," to understand the differences in usage when you read the word "conscience" and when you read the word "responsibility."

Just one other point: when can you assume that teasing will make a child more teasable or less teasable when he gets older? You don't assume anything about that, to my mind, from the fact of being teased. Being teasable in adulthood does not arise wholly from whether or not you are teased as a child. If you establish from your total familiarity with the culture that there is great shame in the face of others, great tension due to ridicule, it does not necessarily arise from childhood teasing, since there are so many other developments in the culture.

139

DR. KLINEBERG: I hope no one thought I was criticizing these studies because field work wasn't done. I realize of course that what was done was the best that could be done. On this last point, about teasing, I was raising a methodological question. Sometimes we seem to find the casual relation between childhood and adult life going in one direction, towards congruence. Sometimes (and I hope Gregory Bateson will say a word about this) we seem to find that the adult life goes in the other direction, toward compensation for what happened in childhood. I was wondering how useful this kind of thing is, when sometimes it seems logical to come out with one kind of relationship between childhood training and adult life, namely that adult life extends and continues the same kind of behavior, and at other times to come out with the view that in adult life one gets a reaction to and compensation for what one had in childhood. That seems to me an important methodological problem.

DR. BENEDICT: Yes. Some ten years ago in "Psychiatry" I discussed that same problem—on the differences in cultures which have continuity and discontinuity between childhood and adulthood. It's a constant problem in any culture. You never start by assuming that there will be one kind of relation between adulthood and childhood. That is methodologically impossible, I think, for a trained person.

DR. BATESON: It seems to me we come up against, first, the problem of communication. Apparently we have on the whole failed to get across to Dr. Klineberg what we are trying to do. It may be that we anthropologists are not very clear about what we are trying to do! His demand that we quantify is salutary. Not in the sense that in the next ten years he is going to get important quantitative data; I don't think he is. But what in God's name would he quantify? Twenty years hence that challenge may be a very important one. I think it is underlined by our difficulties in communication. I have not the slightest idea personally (and I agree with Klineberg in this), what La Barre meant by "patriotism," "mercantile attitude," and so on. He may have meant they are very important; I'm not sure.

Dr. Klineberg quoted me in saying that the Balinese in childhood became used to frustration. I really don't think I said that. The point is that the Balinese child suffers very sharp and very specific types of frustration in childhood and reacts very violently to those frustrations; not that when he meets those frustrations in later life he accepts them, which would be the natural interpretation. But later life behavior in Balinese culture follows such courses that in fact these frustrations do not appear. It is not that the Balinese, when they get into a conflict situation and can't meet certain demands, accept that failure, but that they avoid conflict situations. And that is a very different picture.

We are out to quantify and the question is, what do we quantify? We are dealing with very complex Gestalten, with propositions which go to make up a basic personality description. They are in practice a mixture

140

of illustrative material and adjectives of various kinds derived from psychiatry, descriptions of human relations of various forms, and soon it's a mixed bag. That whole set of propositions about basic character structure is an attempt to say things that are very highly abstract. They are not of the order "mercantile," "patriotic," etc. I have been trying in the course of these meetings to get some idea of what the relationships are between the whole systems of propositions that go to make a basic character structure description of a human being. I was horribly shocked to find that both Fromm and Kardiner were willing to accept the notion that basic character structure is created by a subtractive process—that it is the characteristics of human beings *minus* those characteristics which they don't hold in common. And that leaves a thing with holes in it and no integration, unless it be a core or nucleus as Fromm suggested.

One can attempt to define the measurable by dealing with highly simplified hypothetical situations, with grossly simplified value systems reduced to a single scale, but one is then dodging most of the things we will be interested in. Qualitative or quantitative descriptions of types of strategy, for example, get chopped out of the picture because they are too difficult. The propositions which go to make up a basic personality structure description are going to be much more difficult to quantify. And preliminary to that quantification, comes an enormous task of trying to find out what orders of abstractions we are dealing with. Are we dealing with the degree represented by asking, "Is the melting point of water 0 degrees centigrade?" A uniformity? Are we dealing with a degree, "the melting point of water varies in such and such a way with the pressure" —a statement of the regularity of variation? Or higher orders of complexity, or regularities and variations under different circumstances, as we must assume from what Gardner Murphy said and what Dr. Bidney said? To ask us to quantify tomorrow is healthy in that it may make us try to think a little more sharply about where conceivably quantification might lie. It certainly does not lie in looking for simple uniformities or in answers to questions whose meaning is not clear.

DR. HORTENSE POWDERMAKER: I want to raise a question related both to the Kracauer book and to anthropological field work. It would seem logical that a movie made collaboratively by several hundred people, as it is technically, would perhaps represent better collective imagery than a novel or play made by any one person. But if you do field work on how movies are made you see that this doesn't hold true. In Hollywood, at least, movies are collaborative in the sense that several hundred people are concerned in the making of each production. However, the imagery of the movie—the thing that goes on the final screen—is not the work of several hundred people but is the concern of one or two persons, or at the most, three. It reveals the imagery of the person who is earning the biggest salary—the producer, the director, or sometimes the star. Whether it indicates the American internal character structure is a matter for study.

141

MIRRA KOMAROVSKY

S. STANSFELD SARGENT

Research into Subcultural Influences
upon Personality

The term "subculture" refers in this paper to "cultural variants displayed by certain segments of the population".* Subcultures are distinguished not by one or two isolated traits—they constitute relatively cohesive cultural systems. They are worlds within the larger world of our national culture.

While we know in general that social classes, racial and cultural minorities, urban and rural communities, and regions all form "subcultures"—much remains to be done in describing and distinguishing them. The more analytical work, tracing the influence of subcultures on personality, has only begun. Recent studies such as West's *Plainville, U.S.A.*, Warner and Lunt's *Yankee City* series, Drake and Cayton's *Black Metropolis* all have to do directly or indirectly with *human behavior,* but by no means all can be said to deal with *personality.* They describe the mode of life, the cultural patterns or the social structure of the respective communities, staying on the level of the more explicit sanctioned patterns. These community studies come closest to personality when they discuss social attitudes and values. The Lynds in "Middletown in Transition", for example, devote a long chapter to the enumeration of the dominant Middletown values.

Other studies have concerned themselves directly with one or another aspect of personality but usually with some specific attitude. Newcomb's *Personality and Social Change* is an intensive study, covering *several years, of the effects of a particular subculture*—Bennington College—upon the students' attitudes toward public affairs. Again, many of the studies of depression, unemployment, and low economic status have been concerned with effects upon such aspects of personality as attitudes, interests, and

*The authors are indebted to Dr. Conrad A. Arensberg for this phrasing.

morale. Dalton's recent study of worker response to a wage incentive system in relation to his social background* is another example of this category.

Finally, other studies of subcultures deal explicitly with personality in a fairly inclusive sense. In the American Council on Education series on the Negro the authors address themselves directly to personality after explaining what the term means to them. Waller's *Sociology of Teaching* and Lewis's *Children of the Cumberland* are other examples.

We shall limit ourselves to an evaluation of the last-named group of studies, "those dealing explicitly with personality in a fairly inclusive sense".

Of the subcultural factors we have chosen occupation, social class, and certain ethnic variables.

In discussing separately the influence of occupation, social class, and racial or ethnic status this paper merely reflects the nature of the original studies. It is well to remind ourselves (as was pointed out by Milton M. Gordon in the October 1947 issue of *Social Forces*) that "a child feels the impact of a subculture as a unit". Thus a Negro is not a member of three separate subcultures: lower class, Southern, and rural, but is a Southern-rural-lower-class Negro. This integrative view has guided the work of Frazier, Dollard, Powdermaker, and Davis on the Negro and Warner in the *Yankee City* series. It is often lacking in other studies.

The evaluation of studies will be made in terms of such questions as the following:

I. Which aspects of personality are being considered and how are they defined and ascertained? (Values, social attitudes, roles, personality traits, etc.)

II. Which particular features of the subcultural variables are taken as the decisive ones for the determination of personality? Thus, for example, studies of occupational personality have located the determinants in the social structure of the work situation, in technological factors, in the family practices characteristic of the occupation and so on.

III. What methods are used to relate the personality charac-

*Journal of Political Economy, Aug. '47, pp. 323-332.

teristics to the imputed determinants? Speculative inference without attempts at rigorous verification? Case studies and interviews, correlation or other statistical methods, or other approaches?

Occupation and Personality

The class of writings richest in reference to what might be called "occupational personality" is one which this survey will omit entirely. We refer to the perceptive discussions of the problem in social science classics such as Adam Smith and Durkheim on the division of labor, Herbert Spencer on the military mind, Max Weber on bureaucracy, Veblen and others. Veblen, indeed, can be said to have devoted much of his writings to the elaboration of his guiding principle that "the kind of work by which men live and particularly the kind of technique which that work involves . . . is the influence which shapes men's thoughts, their relations with one another, their culture and institutions of control"*

This paper dealing as it does with the more empirical studies must leave the masters with this brief acknowledgment.

A comparison of a pioneer study of occupational types like F. R. Donovan's *The Woman Who Waits* (1920)[9] with such a book as Waller's *Sociology of Teaching*[19] or Whyte's chapter on the waitress in *Industry and Society*[21] shows the distance we have traveled.† Credit must be given to the early studies for opening up the field but they were impressionistic descriptions with a minimum of conceptualization. Donovan's study for example is an autobiographical account of the author's experience in that occupation. Progress has been made not merely in more rigorous methodology but in the rise of more incisive and scientifically sophisticated systems of concepts.

One such system derives the occupational personality from a sociological analysis of the occupational social systems. This book is Waller's *The Sociology of Teaching*[19], especially part V entitled "What Teaching Does to Teachers". Waller describes the social structure of the school in terms of the acknowledged, socially sanctioned patterns (roles, values, practices) involved in the rela-

---

*MacIver, R. M. Society, *A Textbook of Sociology*, p. 453.

†Numbers refer to bibliography at end of paper.

tion of the teacher to student, to colleague, to the administrator, to the community. But he does not stop there. He also discerns the unverbalized codes and the unintended emergents of these social situations. The dynamic social situation of the class room refuses to be bound by the sanctioned patterns. A teacher must be a taskmaster, an agent of social control. That means that the wishes of teacher and students are often divergent and the classroom situation is one of conflict and hostility setting up in turn a chain of further reactions.

Again the teacher is not an automaton playing out mechanically the teacher's role. He is a total personality and Waller is at his best when he describes the interaction of this personality with the occupational role; how teachers learn it; the techniques of maintaining it; the tensions and distortions in the total personality produced by it and then, in turn, the ways of escaping and resolving these tensions.

In the total social process of the school Waller isolates certain features as most significant in determining the peculiar personality of the teacher. One is the incomplete personal participation in a dynamic social situation—"the ever present need in the classroom and even in the community at large to inhibit the total responses in favor of a restricted segment of them", to inhibit tendencies inconsistent with the "teacher's role".

Another element in the teacher's life situation is the need of maintaining authority. The classroom is an "unstable dominance-subordination" situation and much of the teacher's personality is devoted to securing and maintaining his authority.

The end result of these experiences includes, among other things, a certain inflexibility, a stiff and formal manner, a flat didactic tone of voice, dignity, lack of spontaneity and on the whole a lack of creativeness, and a strong desire for security.

That different psychogenetic personality types react differently to the teaching profession is recognized by the author in a chapter on "Teacher Types".

Methodically the book is a work of interpretation based on experiences of a highly sensitive observer, a disciple of Cooley, Park and W. I. Thomas. It is an empirical study in the sense of utilizing many personal documents, case studies, and concrete illustrations.

146

The topic, however, calls for more rigorous research methods. We must face the problem of the relative frequency of the discerned processes which, in turn, always calls for greater precision of definition. To be forced to count the incidence of certain occurrences brings us face to face with the phenomenon of variation and brings about further refinement of generalizations. For we must now explain why or under what conditions this or that result follows.

But whether or not future studies will confirm the teacher's profile as developed in this book, it seems highly probable that Waller's subtle descriptions of the teacher's occupational experiences will stand the test of time. He has succeeded in bringing to light and conceptualizing many unformulated processes (such as, for example, the alteration of roles in the classroom to maintain authority), and on the other hand in interpreting some very familiar but hitherto puzzling phenomena. In a word, if the methodology of the book was not rigorous enough for the findings to be more than hypotheses, they are nevertheless brilliant hypotheses in an unexplored field and they will surely serve as a point of departure for future work.

An approach in some respects similar to Waller's is being developed in the growing literature of industrial sociology. The social structure and interaction of the job is the primary concern of this literature and we may expect from this source new light on occupational types. Whyte's study of the waitress in *Industry and Society*[21], a part of his forthcoming book on *Human Problems of the Restaurant Industry*, may serve as an illustration. Whyte studies the social interaction of the waitress on the job and traces its effects upon her in psychological terms, though without attempting to formulate long range effects on personality. As in the other writings of this school the delineation of the lines of communication and authority stands at the core of the analysis. The waitress must adjust herself not only to the other waitresses, to the pantry workers, cooks and bartenders but, in a subordinate position, to the supervisors and to some 50 to 100 customers a day. In the last named relations tensions develop frequently without adequate institutional outlets—hence the "crying waitress". Whyte faces the problem of personality differences in adjustment to the job and cites interviews to illustrate these different reactions.

147

Not the social interaction on the job but certain technological and economic features of the occupation are the decisive determinants of personality in *The Railroader* by Fred Cottrell[2]. Mobility is one such factor. "The influence of institutions which mold and form character, that serve to give stability to personality, that provide the nexus between person and locality are continually broken by this mobility. The creation of the family is delayed, and its formation altered by reason of a long period of rapid shifts in location. Contacts with church and school are transitory. Participation in government and the community is made purely secular and pecuniary. Status is more and more dependent upon a financial rating. In short, though the vast majority of railroaders are rural dwellers, the pattern of their social relationship is increasingly urban." (2, p. 59)

Another feature of the occupation is its extreme dependence on the clock and, on the other hand, the impossibility to 'time plan' other relationships. "Time dependence cuts the family off from other groups in the community, as well as its members from each other . . . The organic pattern of physiological rhythm is broken into unequal intervals with resulting psychological strain, intensifying antisocial, or unsocial relationships that might otherwise be disregarded." (2, p. 77) An interesting note is that *The Railroader* contains a whole chapter and a 20-page glossary on railroad language.

Class and Personality

The next two books differ from the above first of all in the fact that it is the broad class rather than the occupational subcultures that they analyze. Furthermore, both focus on the character of early disciplines to which the child is subjected as the critical differential in class personalities.

The Father of the Man: How Your Child Gets His Personality by Davis and Havighurst[5] has as its main purpose "helping the middle class mother and father see more clearly and dispassionately the powerful middleclass system in which they are training their child". This purpose is best served by contrasting the upbringing of the middle class and the slum child; this contrast becomes an important theme of the book. Middleclass child training is characterized by the tense insistence of parents on fast and early attainment of middleclass values of cleanliness, respect for property, sexual control, control of physical aggression, a sense of responsibility and a drive for achievement. The methods used to train the child instill in him "a deep anxiety that (he) will be a failure, or will not be loved if he does not learn early and well the cultural goals of middleclass life". He is made to feel constant attacks of prolonged guilt.

In contrast the psychological drives of the lowerclass child are less frustrated. He is allowed a deeper physical enjoyment of his body and is spared the anxiety and guilt produced by rigid disciplines.

Perhaps because the book is primarily a much needed popularization of recent theories of socialization and is intended for a wide public the account of methodology is not complete. A few case studies are vividly presented as illustrative material. The appendix includes the results of 202 interviews with white and Negro middle and working class mothers. There is no adequate statement of how class was defined and none at all on the sampling procedure. The results give the general direction ("more", "less", "earlier", "later") of class differences in feeding, weaning, toilet training, age of assuming responsibility, strictness of regime, etc.

These differences in child training have direct and indirect effects on personality. Each class inculcates its own class values in its members through indoctrination, identification, punishment and reward. Respect for property, responsibility, control of overt aggression, desire to get ahead are some of the middle class attitudes lacking in the slum class. In so far as rigid disciplines of the middle class engender guilt and anxiety, sap self assurance and independence, they have many indirect and unintended effects on personality of the middle class adults. These results are merely inferred and no new evidence is cited.

In *Children of the Cumberland* Claudia Lewis starts with observations of personality differences in two groups of children of widely differing social classes and then attempts to account for these in terms of respective patterns of child training. The children of the Harriet Johnson Nursery School in New York City, sons and daughters of middle class and largely professional New Yorkers, constituted one group. The other consisted of children

149

of Scotch and English ex-miners and ex-lumbermen in a small county fifty miles from Chattanooga, Tennessee.

It is clear that this contrast is not merely one of class. It probably also reflects regional and urban-rural differences. That the author finds class per se to be one of the factors is indicated in the opening sentence of a chapter on the *lower class* children in *New York:* "It is not necessary to go all the way down to the Cumberland, however, to find children who are in many ways like (the Tennessee children)".

The author found the Cumberland children to be more compliant, placid, unresisting, easy to handle, untroubled than the middle class New York youngsters. Rebellion was rare. Their play was less active, energetic. It lacked the drama, the creative ability and brilliance shown by the New York children. The evidence in support of these generalizations lies in such abundant, vivid and artistic descriptions of scenes and children that they almost create for the reader the illusion of first hand experiences.

The author explores widely the possible causes of the observed differences. She considers physical and economic factors and various features of community life. The explanation she finally arrives at lies in the permissive upbringing of the Tennessee children. In her own words "In this absence of restriction we may find one of the important keys to apparently compliant, happy life of the Tennessee child. His long natural babyhood of close physical proximity; his privilege of suckling at the breast at any time, even long after he is eating the solid foods others eat; the late begun and simply managed matter of toilet training; the few prohibitions relative to 'Do not touch this' 'Do not play there' 'Do not go in here' the relatively little insistence on washing, keeping clean; the space in the yard that is his to play about in, and especially the presence of both his parents, and the fact that he is not shut out from this life or this emotion, not told that he must stay home, go to bed, keep away from, all these things make his young childhood a time of ease. He does not often have to picture his parents as 'those grown up people who can do everything they want to but won't let me do anything'." (13, p. 156)

This is a persuasive passage and yet the imputation of causes is particularly risky in this area because we do not have enough prior knowledge concerning the influence of each one of the conditions upon personality. The permissive upbringing in Cumberland did not extend to sex. Why have not the strong sex taboos caused repressions with all their corollaries? Kardiner in his interpretation of *Plainville, U.S.A.* attributes serious effects to what appear to be very similar sex taboos.*

Ethnic Status and Personality

We turn now to studies of ethnic minority groups, specifically the Negro.

Despite much interest in the problem of anti-Negro prejudice and discrimination, it was only about ten years ago that serious attempts were made to find out what effects the Negro's status in our country has upon his personality. In *After Freedom*, Powdermaker reported on Negro-white relations and attitudes found in a Mississippi delta town of the deep south.[15] Dollard, who had studied the same community, stressed in his book the reality of both caste and class differentials as determinants of Negro personality.[6] These caste and class factors were further buttressed by the extensive statistical and case study researches done by Davis and the Gardners and reported in *Deep South*.[4]

While the above studies were in process, the American Council on Education launched its ambitious project to study Negro personality development in different sections of the country. The question they asked was simply this: "How does the fact of being born a Negro affect the developing personality of a boy or girl?"

There was general agreement upon conclusions reached by the four sets of authors of the major volumes published: being born a Negro in the United States places one in a castelike status which has, in general, a variety of unfortunate effects upon personality. However, we are more interested, for the moment, in differences among these investigators—differences in respect to their conceptions of personality, as to methods used, as to aspects of the subculture studied, and as to conclusions. Let us examine a few of these points more closely.

Frazier, in *Negro Youth at the Crossways*,[10] conceives of personality broadly, as involving motives, attitudes and traits, organ-

*See Kardiner, A., *The Psychological Frontiers of Society*, 1945.

ized and directed toward goals in the course of social interaction. He notes that physical heredity, temperament and intelligence are also involved. However, he is primarily concerned with the feelings and attitudes of youth toward themselves as Negroes. His aim is to show how these are influenced by personal contacts, groups, institutions and ideologies. Studying Negro youth in Washington and Louisville, he analyzes the effects on personality of the community and its stratification, of the family, the neighborhood, school, church, employment and social movements. He uses field work reports, interspersed with excerpts from interviews, to illustrate the effects of these aspects of the ethnic subculture. He then appends two fairly extensive case studies, one of them interpreted by Dr. Harry Stack Sullivan. In his conclusions, Frazier emphasizes the role of the family, though closely related to other social influences. In his words: "the personality of the Negro child develops in response to the family situation into which it is born. The culture, traditions, and economic position of the family determine not only the type of discipline to which the child is subjected, but the manner in which he develops his conceptions of himself as a Negro. As he grows up his contacts with the larger outside social world influence still further his attitudes toward himself as a Negro, as well as his attitudes toward white people. Because of the limitations which make impossible free and easy participation in the larger community, his attitudes and overt behavior will show more or less the influence of the isolated social world to which he is confined." (10, p. 201)

Warner, Junker and Adams, in their *Color and Human Nature*, proceed somewhat differently as they study Chicago Negroes.[26] Their major concern is "social personality," by which they mean that part of an individual's make-up which is contributed by his society and shared in large measure with all others occupying the same social position. Drawing upon prior studies of Negroes, they concentrate upon the three variables of color, class and sex as the most promising determinants of social personality. From four grades of pigmentation, four of class, and the two sexes, they obtain 32 types into which their 800 cases are sorted and studied.

In general, lightskin persons are at the top of the scale and darkskin ones at the bottom. The authors point out that "what a Negro has to say about his color and that of other people . . . may often furnish a direct key to all or most of his thoughts about himself and his very existence. Such evaluations somehow get involved in almost every incident in his life, sometimes more and sometimes less explicitly." (20, p. 293) They realize that in the case of some individuals or even whole groups skin color is not always or necessarily the most potent factor operating. In the case of the lowest level of Negroes the basic needs of survival outweigh other factors. In pathological cases temperament or traumatic family situations may be of paramount causal significance. But by and large they conclude that "inasmuch as color is the badge of racial separateness as well as, in very large measure, the basis of high or low position in the Negro social hierarchy, this factor is the most important single element that determines for better or for worse the development of Negro character." (20, pp. 292-293)

In *Growing Up in the Black Belt,* a study of Negro youth in the rural south, Johnson defines personality as the "organization of an individual's habits and behavior patterns in adjustment to environment."[12] He was particularly interested in discovering the sources of tension and conflict in Negro youth. He studied 2,000 individuals, a fairly representative sample according to section of the rural south, to sex, and to social class. All these individuals were given six tests—of intelligence, personal attitudes, color ratings, occupation ratings, personal values and race attitudes. Several hundred of the group were interviewed, and a few extensive case studies were made. Conflicts were found to center particularly in the areas of social status and occupation. In contrast to Warner's study, little correlation was found between class and color; nor was pigmentation a source of much personality conflict.

Davis and Dollard, in *Children of Bondage,*[3] have a somewhat different view of personality. For them personality is "perceived in that behavior of an individual which distinguishes him from other individuals trained by similar social controls." (3, p. 11) Thus they are interested not in those aspects of personality which a social group shares in common, but rather in an individual's uniqueness. This definition differs greatly from that of the other investigators, particularly Warner and Frazier. Davis and Dollard insist that the origin of personality is to be sought not in the culture or some few aspects of it, but rather in the history of the individual's training. Their chief data consist of eight extensive case studies chosen from different class levels within the urban south. These cases they maintain "reveal the interplay in personality formation between those factors which arise from the general family, age, and sex controls, and those which are systematically reinforced by the class or caste environment." (3, p. 16)

The authors rely on both psychological learning theory and dynamic interpretations. They define caste as "systematic interference in the efforts of a special group of individuals to follow certain biological and social drives." (3, p. 250) Resulting frustration leads to aggressive behavior, usually in a disguised form. Contrasts in the training of middle and lower class Negro children are brought out. Middle class parents put pressure on their children to study, to inhibit aggression and sexual impulses, and the like, setting before them relatively high educational, occupational and marital goals. The pattern of learning for the lower class children is very different, both as to goals and the giving of rewards and punishments. He is not rewarded for repressing aggression or other kinds of impulse gratification. He is punished severely and frequently, but the timing and consistency are such that the learning is ineffective. Often, as with sexual behavior, the example set by the parents is the opposite of their precepts.

Though aware of school, neighborhood and other social influences, Davis and Dollard emphasize the far-reaching implications of class and caste. Of the two, they find class more important in shaping the habits and goals of Negro children, because it governs a wider area of their training.

When we look at the four American Council of Education studies of the Negro we note fair agreement in their conclusions as to the very significant effects of caste status, of class, of color and of family training upon the personality of Negro youth. However, when differences occur in the interpretations made, one cannot be sure whether these reflect actual differences between the four sections of the country studied or whether they result from the varying conceptions of personality and different procedures employed by the investigators. For example, the conclusions of Warner and his associates stress color, while Davis and Dollard emphasize class. Does this mean that color is a more salient in-

154

fluence in Chicago and class in New Orleans and Natchez? Or do the respective emphases by the authors reflect, rather their differing conceptions and procedures employed in the two studies? It is to be hoped that from these four investigations and from other studies of the Negro we can arrive at better agreement as to the meaning of personality and as to research methods so that the findings in different areas will be more nearly comparable.

What impressions, in conclusion, do we have about studies of the effects of subcultural influences upon personality?

The evidence presented here, though incomplete, shows that occupation, socio-economic status and ethnic minority status function as significant determinants of personality within the broader American culture pattern. By and large we can say that the studies have been moving from purely descriptive accounts, couched in laymen's terms, toward more sophisticated conceptualizations and techniques. We note increasing use of a social interactional approach, and of a developmental viewpoint. We find emphasis upon more intensive interview and case study methods, often supplemented by individual testing or by statistical data on social influences. We discover also greater use of dynamic psychological and psychiatric interpretations of personality. On the other hand, there is still need for better agreement as to the meaning of personality and as to the most productive research methods to be used in further investigations. (For example, much needs to be done by way of validating insights obtained through case studies and personal documents.) The notable progress of the past ten or fifteen years gives hope for continued advance in these directions.

SELECTED BIBLIOGRAPHY

[1]Anderson, N., *The Hobo,* University of Chicago Press, 1923.

[2]Cottrell, W. F., *The Railroader,* Stanford University Press, 1940.

[3]Davis, A. and Dollard, J., *Children of Bondage,* American Council on Education, 1940.

[4]Davis, A., Gardner, B. B. and M. R. *Deep South,* 1941.

[5]Davis, A. and Havighurst, R. J. *Father of the Man,* Houghton Mifflin, 1947.

[6]Dollard, J. *Caste and Class in a Southern Town,* Yale, 1937.

155

[7]Donovan, F. R. *The Saleslady*, University of Chicago Press, 1924.

[8]........................ *The School Ma'am*, Stares and Co., 1938.

[9]........................ *The Woman Who Waits*, Badger, 1920.

[10]Frazier, E. F. *Negro Youth at the Crossways*, American Council on Education, 1941.

[11]Green, A. W. "The Middle Class Male Child and Neurosis", *American Sociological Review*, 1946, 11, 31-41.

[12]Johnson, C. S. *Growing Up in the Black Belt*, American Council on Education, 1941.

[13]Lewis, C. *Children of the Cumberland*, Columbia University Press, 1946.

[14]Merton, R. K. "Bureaucratic Structure and Personality", *Social Forces*, 1940, 18, 560-568.

[15]Powdermaker, H. *After Freedom*, Viking, 1939.

[16]Rosten, L. C. *The Washington Correspondents*, Harcourt Brace, 1937.

[17]Shaw, C. R. *The Jack Roller*, University of Chicago Press, 1930.

[18]Sutherland, E. H. *The Professional Thief*, University of Chicago Press, 1937.

[19]Waller, W. *The Sociology of Teaching*, John Wiley and Sons, Inc., 1932.

[20]Warner, W. L., Junker, B. H. and Adams, W. A. *Color and Human Nature*, American Council on Education, 1941.

[21]Whyte, W. F. (editor) *Industry and Society*, McGraw-Hill Book Co., 1946.

DISCUSSION

DR. STANSFELD SARGENT: I wish to add a few words of interpretation relevant to our paper which Dr. Komarovsky has just read, and, I hope, to other papers as well. I am somewhat concerned about the difficulty we seem to have in achieving a concept of personality which is psychologically meaningful. Sometimes we use concepts like "basic personality structure," "social character" and the like, which sound plausible but quite hypothetical, as Dr. Bateson already pointed out. On the other hand we frequently employ terms like "values," "attitudes," "traits," "habits," "sentiments," "roles" and the like, in referring to one or another aspect of personality. I believe we must do a bit of analyzing here if we are to avoid confusion.

As I see it, psychologists have not yet been able, unfortunately, to work out a definition of personality which is useful to specialists in other fields, notably anthropologists, sociologists, and psychiatrists. Hence these specialists have attempted their own interpretations and analyses. The

Kluckhohn and Mowrer article already referred to has presented one type of analysis, dividing personality into universal, communal, role and idiosyncratic components.

But such terms, it seems to me, deal with origins or casual factors rather than with psychologically meaningful dimensions of personality. I believe we have enough data about personality to attempt other kinds of analysis. For example, psychologists are pretty well agreed that temperament consists of physiologically-based characteristics such as speed, energy-level and mood or emotional tone. This is one aspect of personality. They consider personality traits as tendencies to behave in fairly consistent ways—extrovertedly, submissively, socially, neurotically—in a variety of situations. But attitudes are something else again—learned tendencies to feel and to behave in a particular way toward certain persons, groups or situations. I use attitudes here in a broad sense, to include such concepts as values and interests.

I do not mean to imply that these are *the* dimensions or components of personality. They are simply three of several possible aspects, which, by the way, are commonly differentiated by psychologists and by some social scientists, though not always explicitly. But I think such a scheme may be useful to students of culture and personality, as, for example, in suggesting which aspects of the person are greatly affected by culture and which are not. Psychological evidence already exists to indicate that environmental influences are most effective with respect to attitudes and values, and least effective at the level of temperament, with personality traits somewhere in between. I suppose anthropologists recognize this, since "attitudes," "values" and "attitude-value systems" are terms sometimes used as synonyms for "personality." To the psychologist, however, personality is both broader and deeper than values and attitudes.

A related thought—for whatever it is worth—is that some aspects of personality, like temperament and intelligence, affect primarily the quality or intensity of behavior rather than specific content or direction. A man may behave animatedly or intelligently (or the opposite) whether he is selling groceries, arguing about politics, teaching a class or managing a factory. Temperament and intelligence, in other words have to do with *how* a person behaves rather than with the nature or content of the particular act he performs. On the other hand attitudes have much to do with the specific acts of behavior—the ticket he votes, the way he treats his wife and children, the books he reads and so on. Nature bulks large in determining potentiality; nurture in determining specific content of behavior.

One final thought. We often find ourselves speaking in terms of *either* personality *or* social behavior instead of personality-in-culture, the importance of which Dr. Murphy indicated. Dr. Fromm, for example, contrasted social character and individual character; Dr. Hanks suggested a continuum of behavior running from ths idiosyncratic at one end to the institutional at the other. These treatments are somewhat similar, it seems to me, but one is angled toward personality and the other toward behavior. I believe the concept of role is of special importance here. Roles are culturally and socially defined patterns or types of behavior which come to serve as habit systems or directive tendencies or even as the individual's central conception of himself. In other words, role seems to be a concept which fits in particularly well with the personality-in-culture idea.

CHAIRMAN: All papers are open for discussion.

DR. L. K. FRANK: It has been suggested that we need more quantitative procedures. Under accepted quantitative procedures we try to measure various aspects, traits, variables which we then proceed to make anonymous so we can handle them by statistical techniques—frequency distributions, factor analysis, etc.

If we're interested in studying regularity and patterns, that is without doubt important. But if we're going to study idiosyncratic personality we've got to deal with particular individuals, with the observations and data identified so they can be seen in the context of the whole personality. That would involve what I call biological relativity, for which we have not yet worked out the techniques.

We've got the people studying regularities, which is important. We've got the people studying individual personalities, where this relativity comes in. If we can recognize that, maybe we could resolve those difficulties and say, "Look, different kinds of problems call for different kinds of methodologies." I deplore a refusal to get at the problem of personality by saying it's too difficult. Let's go back and measure separable traits and variables, because otherwise we're just avoiding the basic problem. When Dr. Klineberg says we need the quantitative—yes, we do. But is that going to help us study the problem of personality?

DR. KLINEBERG: I wasn't suggesting that the quantitative should exclude the other; I am in complete agreement with Dr. Frank.

Coming back to Bateson's point: he says he won't quantify. Well, he doesn't have to! I suggested two ways of looking at it—one within the framework of the ethnological study, in order to get the informants to give us more information about whether things are uniform or variable; and if they're not uniform, in what ways they vary. That, I think, can be done without quantification in the sense to which he objects.

I went on to say that other methods could supplement the techniques the ethnologist uses. If he doesn't like to use them, that's his decision. But it seems to me psychologists could work with anthropologists. Others, with still other techniques and interests, might combine to do work on a somewhat more quantitative level. I don't see why the ethnologist should accept or reject this as part of his own field work; it is a type of supplementation.

DR. KLUCKHOHN: It seems to me there is an unfortunate implicit assumption in what has been said—a kind of two-category business—that

158

either we quantify or we don't. *What* we should quantify is important. Certain things we can and should quantify, as Dr. Klineberg said.

An anthropologist is obligated to say not only that the Waga-waga do so-and-so, but that he has seen 20 cases where this behavior was involved: 17 cases where so-and-so happened, and 3 in which such-and-such happened. He also is obligated to quantify, when he makes a generalization, to give the reader some basis of knowing whether this is based on the statement of two informants or twenty, observation of one case, of fifty cases, etc. That type of quantification we don't have to wait for. It is simpleminded, perhaps, but we should have done it. Anthropologists have neglected it, and, in general, tend to be stubborn in continuing to neglect it.

INTEGRATION FOR FUTURE STUDIES

RALPH LINTON

Problems of Status Personality

In discussing the concept of Status Personality and the problems connected with its study, I believe that we can take as our basic postulate that the members of different societies show different personality norms. Various investigators have coined various terms to designate these norms: "National (or Tribal) Character", "Modal Personality", "Basic Personality Type" and so forth. While there may have been slight differences in the meanings of these terms when they were coined, they seem to be used interchangeably at present. Since the word "Character" has an established meaning which does not seem appropriate to the phenomenon in question, I prefer to ignore the first of these designations. "Modal Personality" and "Basic Personality Type" seem to differ mainly in stressing different aspects of the same phenomenon, as will be pointed out shortly. Actually, the choice of terms is of no great importance as long as we have a clear understanding of what we are talking about.

The "Modal Personality" for any society can be established directly and objectively by studying the frequencies of various personality configurations among a society's members. The fact that, to the best of my knowledge, it never has been so established does not invalidate the concept. My own experience, based on informal observation rather than exact tests, suggests that, given a sufficiently large sample, any personality configuration found in one society can be matched in other societies. However, there can be no question that frequencies of various personality configurations do differ markedly from one society to another. A configuration which must be considered normal for one society on purely statistical grounds may be highly aberrant for another. The Modal Personality for any society corresponds to this statistically established norm.

The term "Basic Personality" or "Basic Personality Type" reflects a dynamic approach to this phenomenon of Modal Personality. Numerous investigations have made it clear that the Modal

Personality for any society bears a close relation to the culture of that society. To put the matter in its simplest terms, the sort of people who are most numerous in any society are also the sort of people who would find its culture congenial in any case. They are the sort of people who, if they had come into the society from the outside, with their personalities already formed, would have found it easy and pleasant to learn the society's ways, to accept its values and attitudes and to become respected citizens.

This congruity between the Modal Personality and the culture of various societies seems to be quite as characteristic for groups of mixed racial ancestry as for those which are relatively pure. We may assume from this that the culture of any society plays a dominant role in shaping the personalities of most of the society's members. That there are other than cultural factors involved is indicated by the appearance of aberrant personalities in all societies. However, we still know so little of just what these factors may be that it seems best to ignore them for the present. We will limit our discussion to the interrelations of the "normal" members of a society with their culture.

The relation between "normal" individuals and the culture of their society is unquestionably a reciprocal one. It is a "feed back" phenomenon of the sort which is just now attracting the attention of workers in many other branches of science. On the one hand, the culture shapes the personalities of a society's members. On the other, the members of a society are responsible, in the long run, for shaping the society's culture. The processes involved are complicated but quite recognizable.

Societies and their associated cultures are continuums. The individuals who enter such a continuum, usually by the accident of birth, are exposed to cultural influences during the entire time they remain within it. These influences are represented concretely by what other members of the society say and do and, especially during the early part of the individual's sojourn, by what they say and do to him. Because of his complete dependence on others, the infant or small child is particularly susceptible to cultural conditioning. The findings of clinical psychology seem to indicate that most of the basic patterns present in the adult personality are established during the first few years of life. Moreover, a series of studies carried out on various non-European societies has demonstrated the existence of certain fairly constant linkages between particular techniques of child care and particular features of the Modal Personalities of these societies.

As the individual grows up, his relation to his society's culture gradually changes. When the basic patterns of his personality have become established, cultural pressures seem to operate mainly to reinforce the results of his early experience. How far such pressures may be able to alter the basic patterns is a question which we cannot settle at present. As we shall see, the systematic study of Status Personalities may throw more light on this problem than any other line of research can. However, it is safe to say that the maximum influence of culture upon personality is exerted during the individual's childhood.

In contrast to this, the individual's potentialities for influencing culture are negligible in childhood and reach maximum intensity when he is an adult. His influence may be exerted in either of two ways: (1) He may function as an active agent in culture change, operating either as an inventor or as an innovator for borrowings from other cultures. Such activities seem to be confined to small numbers of individuals in any society. (2) He may function as a more or less passive agent in culture change through his ability to accept or reject the new items introduced to the society by the inventor or innovator. Most of the members of any society maintain this role and its importance must not be underestimated. Unless a substantial number of a society's members finds a new idea or form of behavior congenial, the new thing has no chance of becoming a part of the society's culture. Even established culture patterns are liable to elimination or modification when they cease to be congenial.

All the evidence now available indicates that cultures are constantly changing although the rate of change may vary not only from one culture to another but also at different points in the same culture continuum. Human societies normally persist for many generations and are composed, at any given time, of individuals at all age levels. It follows that all types of interaction between the culture of a society and the individuals who compose it are going on simultaneously. At the very moment when the culture is shaping the personalities of young individuals and reinforcing many of the personality characteristics of their elders it is also being shaped through the activities of inventors, innovators or simple selectors.

The personality characteristics which are "normal" (in the sense of "most frequent") for the members of a society at any time will exert a strong influence on current developments within its culture. It is the organized aggregate of these characteristics which has been referred to as the "Modal Personality" or "Basic Personality" for a society. Since this configuration seems to be basic to much of culture change and to underlie most, if not all, of the variations in personality which any society recognizes and approves, "Basic Personality" seems to be the more appropriate term for it when dynamics are involved.

The members of any society are usually unconscious of their own Basic Personality, dismissing its characteristics as those of human nature in general. However, they are if anything over-conscious of certain variations in personality which their society not only permits but also encourages. Thus all societies assume that the individuals who occupy certain positions in their systems of organization will, as a group, show personality norms differing from those of individuals in certain other positions. All societies seem to assume this for such groups as men and women or chiefs and commoners while many of them extend the concept to include practitioners of certain trades. Thus less than a century ago, North Europeans assumed that all tailors were cowardly, all butchers brutal if not sadistic, and all blacksmiths men of strong character.

The study of such Status Personalities, as I have chosen to call them, can scarcely fail to produce results which will be significant for the understanding of many personality phenomena. Common status provides one of the simplest and at the same time most significant frames of reference within which groups of individuals can be observed and compared. Persons who share a common status within a society are all subject to the same sort of formal social pressures and are expected to learn and adhere to similar culturally patterned forms of overt behavior. A comparative study of how different individuals within such a group react to these common pressures and of the personality factors underlying their reactions should prove exceedingly enlightening.

Social positions, i.e., statuses, are of various sorts and each sort carries its own potentialities for personality study. Those supposedly linked with differing personality norms fall at once into two classes: (1) Those which derive from a class or caste structure within the society and (2) Those which do not involve factors of class or caste. Any society with a fully developed class structure is really an organized aggregate of sub-societies each with its own sub-culture. The class-linked status personalities in such a society correspond more closely to Basic Personalities in both genesis and characteristics than they do to the status personalities of the second type. In simple terms, the members of each class are shaped by their own culture and their personality norms derive first of all from this culture and only secondarily from the culture of the larger configuration of which their class forms a part.

The study of class-linked status personalities within a single society should throw considerable light on the dynamics of personality formation and especially on the relations between patterns of early childhood care and adult personality. One might anticipate that methods of child care would vary from class to class, but it seems that this is by no means always the case. Thus in many class organized non-European societies the patterns of infant care seem to be closely similar throughout. Even in societies where the ideal techniques of child rearing are different for different classes, the actual techniques may be very similar. There seems to be a universal tendency for upper class parents to leave the care of their children, especially infants, to lower class servants. This is easily understandable in view of the oppressiveness of the infants' physical demands. Such servants, unless kept under constant surveillance, will deal with their charges according to the culture patterns of their own class.

During the last few years, a number of investigators have attempted to account for the observed differences of Basic Personality in various societies on the basis of the differing infantile experience of persons raised in these societies. Great stress has been placed on the experience derived from patterns of nursing, swaddling, sphincter control, etc. It would seem that a crucial test of these theories could be made by comparing status groups who had received the same treatment in these respects while being required by class differences to adjust to widely different adult roles.

Among the status personalities which are not class linked, two types seem to be of particular interest for dynamic studies. One

167

of these consists of those statuses whose demands upon the individual are consistent throughout most of the life cycle. An example of this would be the assignment of different personality norms to men and to women. All societies have different personality stereotypes for the two sexes although, as Dr. Margaret Mead has delighted in pointing out, the content of these stereotypes may vary considerably from one society to another. A second example would be the assignment of a distinct status personality to eldest sons in certain societies which combine primogeniture with extended family leadership.

In both these cases the individual's adult role can be predicted from the moment of birth and steps can be taken to train him for it in terms of both techniques and value-attitude systems. As far as one can determine from simple observation, most societies have developed effective methods for doing this. While physiological differences may complicate the problem in the case of male and female status personalities, they would not enter into the other example cited. Eldest sons as a group would not differ significantly from any other sons, yet societies in which lack of aggression and fear of assuming leadership or accepting responsibility are the rule still contrive to instill these qualities into their potential family heads. It is significant to note that in neither of the cases just cited is there any recognizable difference in infantile care. Males and females, eldest and younger sons are subjected to identical patterns of nursing, swaddling, sphincter control, etc. The shaping of the individual for his or her adult role is undertaken deliberately and is delayed until after the dawn of intelligence.

Still more interesting than such life-long status personalities are those which are linked with certain periods in the individual's life cycle. There are numerous societies, including our own, in which the same individual is expected to manifest different personality characteristics at different age levels. Often he is expected to undergo a veritable psychological transformation when passing from one age group to the next, as from adolescent to adult status or from adult to old. Since our own society expects a transformation of personality between adolescence and maturity, we take it for granted that such a transformation can occur and try to account for it in terms of the changing physiology of this life period. We anticipate no change in personality between adult and aged statuses and I believe that most students of personality would doubt that any significant change could occur at this point.

In view of the foregoing, it is interesting to note that there is at least one society, the Comanche, whose patterns are diametrically opposed to our own in this respect. Comanche childhood is a careful and continuous preparation for full adult status. As soon as the child can walk he is dressed in a miniature replica of adult costume. He is given tasks which are like those of adults but carefully adjusted to his strength. Every device is employed to make him vigorous, individualistic, aggressive and competitive in order that he may become a successful warrior. The behavior which his society expects of him is consistent throughout and even the arrival of puberty passes without ceremonial recognition. However, if he survives a life of warfare until he reaches the point where his physical powers begin to wane, his personality is expected to undergo a sudden and complete transformation. As an old man he is expected to be docile, cooperative, good to women and children and willing to risk slights and offenses to his dignity by acting as mediator in quarrels between younger men. It would be interesting to know how many individuals were able to really experience such a personality transformation. Of the old men whom I knew several, after fair success in the warrior role, had sunk back into that of old men with considerable satisfaction. I gathered that they had become very bored with fire eating and honor watching and were glad to take a rest.

The first problem which confronts the investigator in any study of status personality is that of how far the overt behavior of individuals, when culturally patterned, can be used as an index of personality. It seems that given an adequate system of rewards and punishments, any individual can learn to perform any role at least insofar as the behavior expected of him is routine. Undoubtedly there are many individuals in all societies who find their social roles uncongenial; yet most of them contrive to function with moderate success and without too great psychological discomfort. They may even succeed in adjusting to two or three different roles each of which would appear to be congruous with a different sort of personality and in shifting from one to another of these according to the cues which they recognize. The petty official obsequies to superiors, a tyrant in the bosom of his family

169

and a model of good fellowship around election time would be a case in point.

Most "normal" individuals seem to have this chameleon ability fairly well developed. It appears to be weakest in certain types of neurotics and one wonders whether the slight attention paid to it by some Depth Psychologists, especially by certain Psychoanalysts, may not be related to the highly selected subjects on whom their theoretical formulations have been based. Here again the study of series of individuals within clearly defined status groups would be exceedingly informative.

As has already been said, all societies have developed conscious stereotypes for certain Status Personalities. Such stereotypes may or may not correspond to reality. Once firmly established, they themselves become culture patterns which may be transmitted verbally long after they have lost any justification which they may have originally had. An excellent case in point would be the stereotype for Negro as contrasted with White personality norms in our own society. Anyone who has come to know a number of present day Negroes as individuals knows how far the carefree, good-natured, shiftless stereotype differs from the hostile and anxiety-ridden reality. Nevertheless, in dealing with Whites, the Negro will, with few exceptions, behave in the ways that the stereotype calls for since this is the behavior which is most immediately effective.

I am ready to go a step farther and suggest that until we have more information than is now available, we cannot dismiss the possibility that Status Personalities are really cultural fictions. It is quite conceivable that we may be dealing with differences in complicated and coherently organized roles rather than in personality norms. The stereotypes for Status Personalities which all societies have developed perform important functions. On the one hand, they reconcile the society as a whole to what might otherwise seem cruelty or injustice toward particular groups within it. If most of a society's members believe that such groups differ from themselves in aims and attitudes, they will not identify with them or suffer any pangs of conscience. On the other hand, Status Personality stereotypes may do much to reconcile a society to domination by small numbers of aristocrats who are represented as having all the qualities which the society idealizes.

170

Thanks to the use of Rorschach, Thematic Apperception and an increasing battery of similar tests, the reality of different Basic Personality configurations for different societies seems to be firmly established. It remains now to apply such tests to different status groups within single societies. As far as I can discover, little or no work along these lines has been done to date. The Social Scientists who could delimit such status groups have lacked psychological interests while the Psychologists have lacked the techniques for delimiting such groups for themselves. It is to be hoped that the two disciplines can get together in the near future and pool their abilities.

DISCUSSION

DR. L. K. FRANK: It seems to me it might be worthwhile to study various aspects of professional training—the ways in which a person has to learn to become a doctor, a nurse, a teacher, and has to repress, perhaps, a lot of personality or normal emotional reactions in order to fit into the professional practice. This would give one a very close and intimate glimpse right in our own society of how status confers upon the individual certain obligations and how the personality may then use that in a selective fashion, so you get it both coming and going.

DR. RALPH LINTON: There is no question that in all societies you get very definite stereotypes, not only for behavior but for assumption of deeper levels in the personality, attitude-value systems, and patterns of conventional response, etc., which are taken for granted for individuals in particular statuses.

DR. DAVID BIDNEY: I wonder if Dr. Linton would care to comment further upon the relations between basic personality structure and the status personality, especially with reference to the distinction between the ideal and the actual.

DR. LINTON: I would say that the basic personality, representing the particular collection of attitudes, values, and conditioned emotional responses, would normally underlie the status personalities. The various status personalities would be more in the nature of the various possible implementations of this general fundamental value system.

DR. BIDNEY: Would there ever be a conflict?

DR. LINTON: I think that there might very well be, especially under conditions where a culture was in fairly rapid process of change. I believe, however, that if you have a reasonably stable situation, where there are no strong external pressures upon the society, that the difficulties would

171

tend to iron themselves out. That is, the distinctions between the status configurations would still be perfectly clear but they would, by gradual modification and adjustment, be reduced to terms that would make them congenial with the basic personality system. However, I have had the disadvantage to work largely with cultures which were subject to some degree of acculturation, where you don't know how much more rapidly they were changing than cultures might in a situation where the European hadn't come in. But I must say my own experience has made me feel terribly doubtful about pictures of fairly consistent cultures. In any culture I have had anything to do with there have been certain factors you simply couldn't account for in psychological terms, and I couldn't see why they were there. In many cases they seem actually to lie not in head-on collision, but more or less in idealogical conflicts with some of the other patterns.

Dr. Gregory Bateson: I would like to raise the question whether these status personality differences are always really as profound as they appear to be. First, consider the status differences between parent and child. What you typically have, as far as we know, is a setup in which the child tries performing roles which we usually say are complementary to those of the parents. He acquires certain characteristics, a basic personality structure, if you will, which fits him to be a parent, and performs those acts which are complementary to those he has learned in childhood. So that a lot of these status shifts can be described much more simply as some sort of obverse-reverse changes. Second, status differences could arise, as Dr. Linton mentioned, in cases where you have a lower class nurse bringing up the children of an upper class, aristocratic family. I would question whether she does in fact treat those children exactly as lower class children are treated by lower class mothers. I suspect that she would treat those children warmly, as she has grown up to believe children are treated, but with this difference running consistently through her behavior—the knowledge that they are upper class children. So that your status difference between upper class and lower class is capable again of simpler phrasing.

Dr. Linton: I quite agree. Having been brought up by an old colored woman who had also reared my mother, I have early memories of a large number of things that were "not fittin" for white children that would be for colored children. At the same time I suspect that in feeding habits, anal control and other functions at the physiological level you would find the patterns the nurse applied were pretty much the ones that would be applied in her own society. In other words, the basic question here is: how far is the personality formed by these factors which operate on the child without the child really understanding what is happening, and how far is it formed by actual instruction. I think this is a question we have not solved at all at the present time.

Dr. Otto Klineberg: Professor Linton, would you say a word about conflicts of status? After all, an individual has a lot of different kinds of status at the same time and plays a lot of different roles in society. What happens to the conflicts which occur?

DR. LINTON: I think that this reflects very accurately the loose nexus which ordinarily exists between the core of the personality, or fundamental value system, and the superficial behavioral adjustments. While we know that an individual can occupy any number of statuses, at a particular moment in time you may say that he has activated such and such a status, and that he is behaving in terms of this status while the others are latent. He knows the cues and the proper responses. We might say that he is still occupying these various status positions within the social structure. But he is not, *pro tem,* operating within them. The classical example of this sort of thing is the old story of the famous Highlander who has killed a member of another clan. He knows he will be hunted down; so he immediately goes to the clansman's brother and says: "There is blood on my head. I claim protection." According to the story, this conflict is solved in a very simple fashion. The brother operates first as host. He protects the murderer until he gets him out of clan territory. Then he shifts and behaves as brother of the murdered man, and fights the murderer to the death. You must remember that all social and cultural operations take place in a time field. One can operate in terms of different statuses at different times without real conflict, although these different status behaviors may actually negate each other in terms of results.

DR. KLINEBERG: In other words, status personality would be "status-in-the-plural" personality.

DR. LINTON: For the individual, yes. Where a number of statuses normally converge on the same individual you will find that they are lumped together and are treated more or less as a unit, and usually have congruous requirements, in terms of personality.

DR. HORTENSE POWDERMAKER: I should like to point out that unless one takes into consideration some of the points Dr. Linton has raised, both the problem of status in terms of personality and the temporary personality role (which is not at all the real personality), one is in danger of studying abstractions which have little relation to reality.

DR. LINTON: In connection with the basic personality and culture pattern, the thing to remember is that there are always individuals in every society who do not exhibit the basic personality of that society, whatever the reasons are. But as far as the development of the culture goes, it is a sort of majority rule proposition. If most of the people in a society—in the controlling group within a society—have certain personality configurations, the culture will then tend to be organized in congruity with them.

173

*HARRY STACK SULLIVAN

Multidisciplined Coordination of Interpersonal Data

When I was asked to take part in this two-day conference, it occurred to me this was an ideal occasion for attempting to show something of the psychiatrists' possible contributions to this sort of teamwork. Dr. Linton's remarks could scarcely be improved upon to accent the central thesis which I hope to communicate; namely, that psychiatry, defined as the study of interpersonal relations, has moved in the direction of extremely useful schematizations of actual living and has evolved some techniques for its investigation which are of real importance to the social scientist, even as the social scientists' current schematizations and newer techniques for investigation become more and more useful to the psychiatrist.

Whether the series of hints and indications I shall throw at you succeed in communicating much about this current position in a twenty-five-year effort to make sense of my experience is a question. There is no question about the value to me of any comments you will be good enough to make after you have undergone what I am about to do with a series of summary statements, and perhaps ill-conceived attempts at a diagram.

In any discussion about personality considered as an entity, we must use the term, *experience*. Whatever else may be said about experience, it is in final analysis experience of *tensions* and experience of *energy transformations*. I use these two terms in exactly the same sense as I would in talking about physics; there is no need to add adjectives such as 'mental'—however "mental" experience itself may be conceived to be.[1]

In the realm of personality and culture, tensions may be considered to have two important aspects: that of tension as a poten-

*Deceased Jan. 15, 1949.

[1]For a discussion of the philosophical aspects of the concept of *tension*, see Dunham, Albert. PSYCHIATRY 1:179-119, 1938.

175

tiality for action, for the transformation of energy; and that of a *felt* or wittingly noted state of being. The former is intrinsic; the latter is not. In other words, tension *is* potentiality for action, and tension *may* have a felt or representational component. There is no reason for doubting that this contingent rather than intrinsic factor is a function of experience rather than of tension *per se,* for it applies in the same way to energy transformations. They, too, *may* have felt or representational components, or transpire without any witting awareness.

TABLE I[2]

$$
\text{EXPERIENCE is of} \begin{cases} \text{tensions} \\ \text{energy transformations} \end{cases}
$$

$$
\text{occurs in 3 modes} \begin{cases} \text{prototaxic} \\ \text{parataxic} \\ \text{syntaxic} \end{cases}
$$

$$
\text{TENSIONS are those of} \begin{cases} \text{needs} \begin{cases} \text{general} \\ \text{zonal} \end{cases} \\ \text{anxiety} \end{cases}
$$

$$
\text{ENERGY TRANSFORMATIONS are} \begin{cases} \text{overt} \\ \text{covert} \end{cases}
$$

Yet the undergoing of tensions and of energy transformations, however free the events may have been from any representative component, is never exterior to the sum total of *living* and in many instances not beyond the possibility of some kind of *recall*— indication as of the dynamically surviving, actual past, with detectable influence on the character of the foreseen and dynamically significant neighboring future.

These observations have required the hypothesis that *experience occurs in three modes:* the *prototaxic,* the *parataxic,* and the *syntaxic*—of which the last mentioned is by far the easiest to discuss, though the least frequently encountered. All the experience of the first months of postnatal life is in the prototaxic mode; much of anyone's life experience is in the parataxic mode; and some widely varied part of one's experience from say around age three years is in the syntaxic mode.

[2]The Tables and Figures are reproduced by courtesy of PSYCHIATRY: Journal for the Operational Statement of Interpersonal Relations, published by the William Alanson White Psychiatric Foundation, Washington, D. C.

A person's experience in the prototaxic mode is quite probably a discrete series of significantly different momentary states of the psychophysical organism extending from an indeterminately early time to the present. It cannot be a continuum. The factor of significant difference in momentary states is doubtless both a function of biological developmental emergents and a function of past experience. Prototaxic experience of the most elaborated kind may be the wholly unformulable—and, therefore, wholly uncommunicable—part of some mystical experiences of "cosmic identification" and the like, and of some dreams. The one *relationship* which certainly exists between items of experience in the prototaxic mode is succession, place in organismic or biological time.

As one's capacity to adduce relations among the events of one's experience grows, many of these experiences come to show an increasingly *general* character; they "take on personal meaning" —are organized into one or another of the *personifications* of *'myself'* which centers around increasing acquaintance with *'my body,'* and into personifications of sundry other people in the case of the more significant of whom the personifications grow to be and function as *eidetic* people.

To the extent that observation, analysis, and the eduction of relations is subjected to *consensual validation* 'with' others, it ensues in experience in the syntaxic mode. All the rest is experience in the parataxic mode.

Needless to say consensual validation does not mean the establishment of correctness in some absolute sense; it means only that degree of approximate agreement with a significant other person or persons which permits fairly exact communication by speech or otherwise, and the drawing of generally useful inferences about the action and thought of the other. A great deal of most people's syntaxic experience is bound by the prescriptions and limitations of the culture; the exceptions to this being the results of rigorous "thinking" from actually adequate premises, and testing by crucial experiments.

I trust that this condensed statement has not obscured to you the fact that most of the experience which enters into our living occurs in and remains in the parataxic mode. Some of it occurs in, or is subsequently elaborated into, the syntaxic mode. I have put *thinking,* above, in quotation marks because, so far as I can discover, *known* thought—referential processes within awareness —is but a perhaps small part of the covert processes that are concerned in any thinking. For all I know, experience in the proto-taxic and parataxic mode is always or very frequently involved in the unknown processes which underlie or culminate in known reveries and logically formulated ideas in the 'contents of consciousness.'

Referring back to Table I, it is to be noted that tensions are subdivided into those of *needs*—with two subdivisions, general and zonal—and those of anxiety. The tensions of *general* needs have, one might say, physiological basis; they reflect, for example, the biological requirements of the human animal, for metabolic activities, for other factors in survival, and for reproduction. The *zonal* needs are additional to these general needs, however closely the totality of zonal needs may be related to that of general needs. They arise from, or as a specific manifestation of, what we conceptualize as the *zones of interaction* with the environment; the specifically characterized organizations of *experience and* biological factors which constitute the discriminable loci of other events with events of "my body" at the conscious or witting level, and with the totality of the human being. Let me hint at the meaning of this by mentioning some of these zones: the oral zone, the manual zone, the anal zone, the genital zone; and, in a somewhat different category, the general tactile zone, the temperature zone, the aural zone, and visual zone.

Tensions of anxiety are of a quite different nature. Let me quote here from a study in the course of preparation for another purpose:[3] "Like any mammalian creature, man is endowed with the potentialities for undergoing *fear,* but in almost complete contradistinction to infrahuman creatures, man in the process of becoming a person always develops a great variety of processes directly related to the undergoing of *anxiety.*

"As felt experience, marked fear and uncomplicated anxiety are identical; that is, there is nothing in one's awareness of the discomfort which distinguishes the one from the other. Fear, as

[3]Since published as "The Meaning of Anxiety in Psychiatry and in Life", PSYCHIATRY, 1948, 11:1-13.

a significant factor in any situation, is often unequivocal. Anxiety, on the other hand, in anything like the accustomed circumstances of one's life is seldom clearly represented as such in awareness. Instances of fear in the course of accustomed peacetime living are not numerous while instances of—generally unrecognized—anxiety are very frequent in the waking life of a great many people.

"The significant pattern of situations characterized by the tension of fear is not recondite and is roughly the same for all people, excepting for the effects of habituation. The significant pattern of situations which arouse anxiety is generally obscure; can be almost infinitely varied among people; and shows much less, and very much less obvious, effects of habituation.

". . . Anxiety from its mildest to its most extreme manifestation interferes with effective alertness to the factors in the current situation that are immediately relevant to its occurrence, and thus with the refinement and precision of action related to its relief or reduction.

". . . Anxiety as a factor in behavior is first manifested in early infancy . . . Very young infants show grossly identical patterns of behavior when they are subjected to 'frightening' situations and when they are in contact with the person who mothers them *and that person is anxious, angry, or otherwise disquieted.* Something which develops without a break into the tension state which we have discriminated on the basis of its specific differences from fear can be *induced* in the infant by *interpersonal influence,* in contrast to the evocation of primitive fear by sundry violent influences from 'outside' or 'inside' the infant's body.

"This *interpersonal induction* of anxiety, and the exclusively interpersonal origin of every instance of its manifestations, is the unique characteristic of anxiety and of the congeries of more complex tensions in later life to which it contributes . . ."

Table I finally contrasts the energy transformations which are "objectively" manifest with those the occurrence of which may only be inferred—"introspective accounts" notwithstanding, for these accounts are overt energy transformations often by no means simply related to the covert processes to which they are presumed to be related.

"The next Table carries us somewhat further. The term,

euphoria, refers to a polar construct, an abstract ideal, in which there is *no* tension, therefore no action—tantamount in fact perhaps to something like an empty state of bliss. The level of euphoria and the level of tension are inversely related. There is no zero or utter degree of either. Terror is perhaps the most extreme degree of tension ordinarily observable; the deepest levels of sleep, perhaps the nearest approach to euphoria."

TABLE II

EXPERIENCE

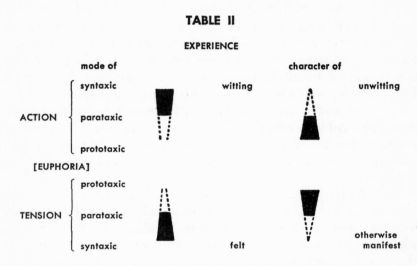

By the device of this Table, I hope to suggest that no experience of tension or action in the prototaxic mode is witting. It is all, in the jargon of some years since, "unconscious." On the other hand fully consensually validated action and "thought" may also be wholly unwitting, as we see in instances of what are called the manifestations of *dissociated* motivation. Tensions, to repeat myself, may be felt tensions; but, particularly for those experienced in the parataxic and the prototaxic mode, may have no representation in focal awareness but are otherwise manifested—as in the case of a person whose skeletal musculature shows a high oppositional postural tone, without his being aware that he is "tense."

You may have noticed a certain clumsiness in the expression "human being considered as a substantive unit" used earlier, and wonder if this is equivalent to the term "person" and to the term "personality."

Person is a relatively non-specific general reference to unques-

180

tionably extant, "purely imaginary," or—the usual—blend of demonstrable biological reality and imposed personification to which many people refer as human individuals. Table III reflects the precise meaning of the term "personality." At first glance, this may seem to be a great come-down from the conviction of unique individuality which each of you entertains about yourself.

TABLE III

PERSONALITY: the relatively enduring pattern of recurring interpersonal situations which characterize a human life.

PATTERN: the envelope of all insignificant differences.

Much depends on grasping the particular denotation of the term, "pattern." Insignificant differences are included in any particular pattern. As soon as a difference becomes significant, the pattern is not the same but a different one. The realm of perceived articulated sound—whether speech, music, or another—is, so to say, nothing but patterns. Take, for example, Mozart's Quartet in F Major (K. 370). Any member of a quartet which performs it can make a number of mistakes; and any but the most remarkable of oboists, truly disconcerting noises; yet these differences do not obscure the pattern of the Quartet. It can even be "swung," by a dance orchestra and still, if one's irritation is not too great, be recognized as a systematic distortion of the wonderfully complex pattern of sounds and relations which is the Quartet.

The study of personality cannot, then, deal with individual transient phenomena or with unique episodes, but only with delineable patterns of recurrent processes in interpersonal fields, except when a transient phenomenon or unique episode is recognized as a significant difference from a delineated pattern—and, as such, either *a chance occurrence* or an item in some other pattern of presumptively recurrent interpersonal field.

The determination of the probability that an observed significant difference in the shape of a transient phenomenon or incongruous episode *is* a (mathematically) chance occurrence or the sign of a usefully meaningful change of pattern is a recurrent task in the earlier phases of any adequate intensive study of personality. The difficulty of this task is somewhat reduced by the use of a heuristic frame of reference, the stages of development

181

of potentialities for interpersonal relatedness, and the history of corresponding patterns of relations which the subject-person can be led to reveal.

TABLE IV[4]

Stages in the development of potentialities which may be manifested in interpersonal fields [from mostly West European data]

1. INFANCY to the maturation of the capacity for language behavior

2. CHILDHOOD to the maturation of the capacity for living with compeers

3. JUVENILE ERA to the maturation of the capacity for isophilic intimacy

4. PREADOLESCENCE to the maturation of the genital lust dynamism

5. EARLY ADOLESCENCE to the patterning of lustful behavior

6. LATE ADOLESCENCE to maturity

------

[4]Since the occasion of this Conference, I have changed the statement of criteria of Stages 4 and 5—the above statements of which had survived unchecked from an earlier formulation. I now consider that Preadolescence ends and Early Adolescence is ushered in by maturation of capacity for intimacy with a member of the other sex—which, so far as I know always occurs, if at all, after the physiological puberty change. Late Adolescence occurs upon the patterning of lustful, heterosexual behavior. These revised criteria take better account of the many deviations which are lumped under "sexual peculiarities."

A rigorous analysis of lustful integrations (1943) shows that three factors are concerned: the intimacy need and precautions concerned; the preference as to partner or substitute therefor; and the form of genital participation or substitution. There are 54 meaningfully possible patterns arising from combinations of these factors; overt manifestation by the male of 6 of which is improbable; of 3 others, certainly infrequent. Forty-five different patterns of *sexual behavior* and 54 patterns of sexual *revery processes* have to be recognized in characterizing a person's dynamic participation in such a field. Twenty-three of the 54 are confused in "homosexual behavior or tendencies;" 25 of the 54, in "heterosexual behavior or tendencies." It is not strange, therefore, that many previous discussions of Sex have been rather unhelpful.

182

However infrequently the fact may have been noticed, nothing is clearer than that personality undergoes rather striking changes at comparatively well-marked times in the progression from birth towards maturity, as well as in certain critical circumstances, such as those of the eruption of acute mental disorder, or recovery therefrom, or when one has had an exceedingly fortunate or unfortunate experience. From the more biologically timed of these changes, it is evident that the maturation of the more significant capabilities of the underlying human animal takes from 10 to 17 or more years of life-time. Obviously, infantile experience, and the experience of childhood, as here defined, is far from an adequate explanation of the potentialities for and characteristics of interpersonal relations at later stages, although I can go with Freudian and related approaches to human development to the extent of saying that sufficiently unfortunate experience at stage one or two can make a desirable progression through subsequent stages less probable. Whenever great warp has been incorporated in personality, it takes very fortunate experience in a later stage to eliminate serious deviation as a permanent result. But, in complete contradistinction to the ordinarily accepted Freudian and related views I will assert that it is adequate experience in stage 4 that determines one's automatic ease or unvarying stress in dealing with any significant member of one's own sex; as adequate experience in stage 5 determines one's ease or discomfort in dealing with significant members of the other sex—regardless of anything that has gone before.

Let me now pass on to the most dubious part of this talk, a discussion of interpersonal fields with the aid of some merely suggestive diagrams.[5] Fig. 1 shows a way of depicting "a personality," the hypothetical entity which we posit to account for interpersonal fields.

"Looking first at the upper figure, note that there is a complete central disc—representing the serially matured inborn capabilities; half of which have been developed by experience as shown in the sectors; half of which, in this instance, have not been

[5]The following several paragraphs are mostly quoted from the paper cited in reference footnote 3, which used the herewith black-and-white reproductions instead of the colored diagrams actually utilized in the course of this presentation.

realized because no related experience has occurred—this being
indicated by the semicircle of dashes.

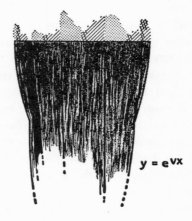

$$y = e^{vx}$$

Fig. 1

"Each of these sectors in itself indicates a major motivational
system. Please do not think that there are but six major motivational systems; it is convenient to draw six sectors. In each of
these sectors, you will note that in their periphery, there are three
types of shading. The dotted shading is that part of experience
organized in the particular motivational system which is in the
self-system—which ordinarily means that it is readily accessible
to awareness, recall, and so on. The cross-hatched section next

to it represents the experience which is fraught with anxiety. The single-hatched area beyond represents the part of experience related to that particular motivational system which is not in the self-system and, under all ordinary circumstances, is quite difficult or impossible of access to awareness.

"The drawing below this represents an extension in time of the more recent phases of the personality under discussion up to the immediate present. The formula indicates that the boundaries of each of the sectors will be instances of the so-called snowball law, the law of growth—$y = e^x$—the v in the formula represents a complex variable about which I will content myself by observing that it increases rapidly in the immediate neighborhood of each of the developmental thresholds indicated in Table IV, and diminishes thereafter to the proximity of the next threshold."

The near future is just as real an element in interpersonal relations as is the near past. The dynamic importance of both may be low, as in the case of a so-called *psychopathic personality*. On the other hand, foresight may be a very important factor in determining the character and course of the field processes. A great deal of living that is said to manifest "good judgment," "strong will," "steadfast determination," and the like—all with a rosy ethical connotation—can be explained by appeal to this factor of foresight. Decision and choice are mostly a function of foreseeing 'hypothetical' courses of events, but foreseeing them as forward-looking functions of both easily recollectable and ordinarily inaccessible experience, and with full play of the anxiety factor. In other words, foresight is no more entirely a witting process wholly within awareness than is observation and analysis of the momentary present or the past. In some people, many steps in the process can be recalled and formulated; in others; few or even none of them but the end result—the "choice."

Figure 2 and the discussion following are quoted from or based upon the treatment of 'a schizophrenic episode' which appears in "The Study of Psychiatry," (PSYCHIATRY, 1947, 10:355-371), which may well be read as a supplement to this lecture. Be warned that the same devices of shading are used in depicting durable personality organizations and in indicating shifting field forces.

"In Fig. 2 we are no longer concerned with the representation of a hypothetical personality but with depicting an instance of an interpersonal situation, the sort of thing that can be studied by a psychiatrist. I attempt to show a simplification of the early stage in a relatively durable relationship of two people, one of whom you will observe is more nearly a 'well-rounded' or more developed personality than the other. Let me for brevity call the six-sectored representation, Johnnie Jones, and the other, Richard Roe.

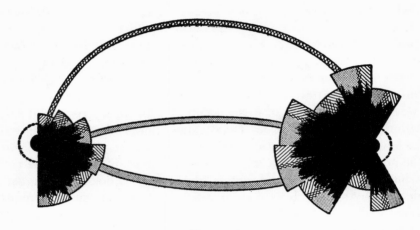

Fig. 2

"You will note that the uppermost line representing a field force is cross-hatched. This is intended to represent force which tends to keep these two people from growing more intimate, what may be called disjunctive force, and *the* great disjunctive force in interpersonal relations is anxiety. Below that there are shown two dotted lines of force which represent conjunctive forces, forces tending to improve the relationship, or in ordinary discourse, to draw the two people closer together.

"Let us notice that the uppermost sector of the left-hand figure, Mr. Jones, is very much smaller in area than is the corresponding sector in Mr. Roe to which it is linked by "Jones' anxiety." At the risk of adding confounding to confusion, let us make these sectors 'heterosexual motivation.' The disjunctive force arises from the anxiety-laden part of Mr. Jones' very limited development of heterosexual motivation. This means that Johnnie Jones

186

cannot discuss comfortably with his friend, Mr. Roe, matters pertaining to this phase of living. Mr. Roe readily becomes aware of the embarrassment and avoidances that ensue after any remarks which touch upon Jones' deficiencies in this area.

Other diagrams can be used to depict both disjunctive and conjunctive forces representing later stages of the relationship.[6] For example, a dotted line drawn between the non-self areas of two other sectors reflects a situation often observed in interpersonal relationship; namely, that powerful conjunctive force can arise from congruent motivational systems and exert influence in the interpersonal field wholly exterior to the awareness of the persons concerned.

Further elaboration and modification of Fig. 2 may be used to depict onset of the schizophrenic episode in the relationship of Jones with his friend. One can see how contact becomes relatively fixed through an eidetic personification forcibly shutting off further acquaintance with Mr. Roe. A new disjunctive force may appear, *uncanny* emotion, reflecting an important aspect of personality development; namely, the interlocking connection of past experience not only in, as it were, the sub-sections of personality currently manifested, but also throughout the historic past of personality.

A "surface" pattern modification of Figs. 1 and 2 may be used to show all Mr. Jones' experience from his initial meaningful contact with Mr. Roe to the point where actual contact with Mr. Roe has yielded to a relative equilibrium with an eidetic Mr. Roe after the onset of the psychotic relationship.

"In the study of any anxiety-fraught experience one discovers that the particular pattern of the situation which provokes anxiety can be traced to a past relationship with particular significant people in the course of which one experienced anxiety that was more or less clearly observed to relate to particular interaction with them.

"The complement of eidetic people which each of us carries with us and lives with reaches back in every instance to the first pair of our personifications: the *good mother associated* with the

[6]The reference cited in footnote 3 contains three additional diagrams not included here because of space limitations.

relaxation of the tensions of recurrent needs, and the bad or *evil mother* associated with the undergoing of anxiety.

"The next link in the inevitable developmental chain is the triple personifications of Good Me, Bad Me, and the always rather shadowy but dreadful Not-me. Bad Me is constructed from experience with anxiety-fraught situations *in which the anxiety was not severe enough to preclude observation and analysis*. Not-me grows out of mostly retrospective analysis of observed precursors to the paralysis of referential processes which is always associated with sudden severe anxiety.

"Anxiety as a functionally effective element in interpersonal relations has to be mild in degree or gradual in its increasing severity. Sudden severe anxiety, or anxiety which increases very swiftly in severity is undergone in later life as what I call *uncanny emotion*, chilly crawling sensations, and the like, often meant by the words 'awe,' 'dread,' 'loathing,' and 'horror.' Uncanny emotion is an all but functionally ineffective element in interpersonal relations; it arrests useful transformations of energy other than (1) certain obscure covert processes which, if they occur, may be called "adjustment to the uncanny" with escape into more refined and less paralyzing anxious states, (2) those which make up the schizophrenic disturbance of awareness with its varying influence of the Not-me components, or (3) apathy—which I shall not here discuss."

In case my comments on eidetic people are not clearly communicative, let me attack the problem from another standpoint. All of you must occasionally be afflicted by the necessity of writing "papers" or books, as well as by the necessity of giving "talks." I have far more trouble with the former than with the latter. While I talk to you, I vocalize a series of sentences which present themselves for utterance; but, as I utter each statement, a "part" of me, a characterizable subpersonality of mine, *listens*. This listener is a more or less adequate representation of those of my auditors to whom I "hope to be able to communicate something of my meaning." If a particular sentence impresses my private listener as equivocal, ambiguous, subject to misinterpretation on the basis of a probable preconception, or otherwise probably unsuccessful of communicative function, supplementary sentences are produced for utterance in that connection, before the particular topic is left. This private listener has grown as a complex function of information I have picked up over the years, of experience I have undergone and more or less formulated, in the activity of vocal exchange of ideas. The way "he" intervenes on a particular occasion is more or less adjusted to presumed characteristics of the particular "real" audience to whom I am speaking— or rather to the part of it above specified, made up of those I can foresee as learning something of my views if "he" does a good job of running correction.

This may seem to be a tedious process but it is as nothing to the trouble I have with my private "reader." My "listener" can use my eyes and ears, and adjust "himself" to signs from the 'real' audience *in medias res*. Not so, my "reader," who has to represent a mediate public. "He" is so troublesome that I have had to make a study of the patterns characterizing "his" activity. I conclude that "he" is a queer combination of a high-grade imbecile and a bitterly paranoid critic. Every sentence has to be tortured into such shape that it cannot be misunderstood by the stupid or savagely misconstrued by an intelligent but bitterly hostile critic. My dealings with "him" are simply exhausting, and my writings reflect this—and a perhaps erratic recourse to his 'alternate' whom I built up by borrowing from the late W. I. Thomas the idea that one writes books for a very small audience of respected colleagues, any and all other readers being "gravy."

This is the more difficult element in the field theory of interpersonal relations. It requires attention to the surviving influence and foresightful impact of unembodied but none the less characterizable personified existents, these eidetic[7] people historically related to 'real' people of one's past experience, but related to them in a dynamic rather than a mere static survival way. I mean here that eidetic people, these potent personifications, change, however slowly; they too are altered by experience subsequent to the occasions on which their particular prototypes exerted their effect on one. Under effective psychotherapy, some of them may change very greatly, quite swiftly, and particularly fortunate experience unrelated to intentional therapeutic interventions may be equally effective.

[7]This word, I have borrowed from Jaensch, but without any of the context of meaning in which he used it as a term.

Personality, then, is to be observed in interpersonal relations, in field processes including two or more loci. It is the abstract of relatively durable patterns of such fields, considered from the standpoint of *one* of these loci. These patterns, however, on scrutiny show the coincidence and dynamic interaction of other fields, all but one of the loci of which are of the eidetic kind. These latter, unrealistic loci are in equilibrium with the "real" personal locus; which, however, does not mean that they are inert. Quite the contrary, they and their equilibrium relations constitute a large part of the personality system which is the "real" person under consideration. This accounts for much of the inadequacy and inappropriateness of the field processes in which the particular person gets himself involved, for the eidetic personalities which are also involved limit or restrict the freedom of the situation through *self-system effects* and the disjunctive force experienced as anxiety.

To make the point of this whole presentation, let me first say, for example, that I believe *status personality* as discussed by Professor Linton can be reformulated in terms of this field theory in a way that would shed light helpful to him and to me.[8] The data and hypotheses with which psychiatrists and social scientists have to deal require this sort of reformulation if new and more adequate concepts are to be evolved and more useful types of investigations called into being. My effort today gives you at

[8]In "Towards a Psychiatry of Peoples," PSYCHIATRY, 1948, 11:105-116, I say "Progress towards a psychiatry of peoples is to be expected from efforts expended along two lines of investigation: (1) improving grasp on the significant patterns—and pattern of patterns—of living around the world; and (2) the uncovering of significant details in the sundry courses of personality development by which the people of each different social organization come to manifest more or less adequate and appropriate behavior in their given social setting.

"Each of these lines of investigation is a necessary supplement to the other. The first, which may be taken to pertain more to the interests and techniques of the cultural anthropologist, cannot be pushed very far, very securely, without data from the second. The second can scarcely produce meaningful data except it be informed by the provisional hypotheses of the former. The two provide indispensable checks upon each other, without which neither can proceed noticeably without running into increasing uncertainty."

least an idea of the difficulty of preliminary communication in building up the multidisciplined thinking which I bespeak. It is certainly difficult but I do not believe that it is by any means impossible. If you have seized anything useful in your thinking from this blend of words and visual hints, I have, in fact, demonstrated the possibility of the approach.

DISCUSSION

DR. JOSEPH BRAM: Several years ago when I studied juvenile delinquents in a reform school, it was brought to my attention that if a boy who has committed violent delinquency is not brought to court and investigated, he is very likely to show an ordinary boy's behavior and personality pattern. However, when he is forced to stand for some time under the eyes of various examining representatives of justice—pychiatrists and others —he is likely to become delinquent, that is, to assume a behavior pattern characteristic of a delinquent boy. He begins to swing his arms. He talks freshly. He talks back to the judge. And he begins to see himself in a different light. As a result of it he acts with regard to the world, not as before, but as a delinquent.

An example is provided by Nehru in one of his books. He says that a non-Hindu can hardly imagine how close the ideal of saintliness is to every average Hindu. Under the pressure of personal loss or tragic experience, any Hindu may, at the drop of the hat, decide to become a saint, retire from life, and follow certain traditional established patterns of saintly behavior and practices.

Now I want to ask the speaker: are eidetic personalities necessarily people who lived, who existed, whom we may have distorted and simplified in our imagination? Or could they be a product of our tradition, that is, stetreotyped images of a saint, a delinquent, or any other character of this kind? If the second is true, then our interpersonal relations may be affected by our identification with such imaginary but culturally known characters.

DR. SULLIVAN: The hypothesis assumes that. One of the most astonishing demonstrations of it is shown by people of very limited experience attempting to be a stereotype. One that all of you somewhere in life have encountered is the person being a great man. He has synthesized himself as a great man, but his experience just isn't equal to the strain. It doesn't come off; it's a bad show. But here is one of the several eidetic me's: "I am a great man."

Without a doubt stereotypes are to be interpreted in that sense. Culture heroes, for example, have very real existence. I remember that one investigator got accounts of the stories of a certain Indian culture hero from several informants and noticed individual differences. I think it is a quite interesting instance of the reality of these mythological figures as governors of behavior.

DR. MUZAFER SHERIF: As a social psychologist I am much interested in the genesis of the ego system and its connection with anxiety as contrasted with fear. I wonder if you'd comment on the ego system and relate it to the conception of the genesis of the ego in orthodox psychoanalysis, because the ego and superego are becoming very important in culture studies.

DR. SULLIVAN: I am enormously indebted to Freud for his initial formulations, but diverge from the formulations by his followers. I have found that this conception of the superego served no useful purpose in my work, which advances a simpler hypothesis. I can't care for anyone's grasping anything except that a significant person has been experienced as disapproving, whereupon it becomes necessary to develop special machinery in that area of the field relationships.

Anxiety is the only thing on earth that no one wants. Anxiety is induced by negative, hostile feelings on the part of the significant environment, and tends to survive as such. To separate ego and superego seems no longer to be profitable. The notion of the unconscious component in this seems to me wholly confusing. The work of the psychiatrist is to map out the points where anxiety is encountered in the field of the patient (including the eidetic field), which sounds very strange if one thinks of an unconscious superego. It is a much better hypothesis, for producing collaboration between social scientist and psychiatrist, if we avoid this tripartite division and remain clear on the enormous importance of anxiety as literally an oppositional or disjunctive influence. It always has an interpersonal source, always rests historically on interpersonal experience.

QUESTION: Don't peoples differ in their potentialities for experiencing anxiety?

DR. SULLIVAN: I wouldn't know. Undoubtedly there are differences in annate susceptibility to anxiety, but they are irrelevant to formulating a hypothesis of interpersonal relations. We can not deal with insignificant differences without getting utterly lost.

DR. DAVID LEVY: I'm interested in anxiety having its origin in interpersonal relations. I want to propose a problem—to understand the differentiation of anxiety from other types of tension.

I think of a case like this: a child sees his father in pajama trousers and has a definite anxiety, just as a dog sees his master for the first time in a different suit and barks at him as at a stranger. That's anxiety; a formation pattern is changed. When a child, coming home, finds that a painting has been removed from the wall, he has a definite feeling of anxiety. Can you distinguish this from anxiety growing out of interpersonal relationships?

192

DR. SULLIVAN: I once found young skunks could experience fear in a sufficiently new and unfamiliar environment. Novelty could produce fear, as with the child who sees his father without a pajama coat. But anxiety always is produced by a disturbed state in another person; it is not connected with the world other than persons. Fear provoked by novelty wears out fairly soon as one becomes accustomed to them, but you don't become accustomed to anxiety-provoking situations. Anxiety interferes with the very things that eliminate fear. Anxiety always is opposed to the satisfaction of any need and tends to block it. The approach to anxiety situations has to be tangential, dealing with eidetic people who are still extent. With fear, however, experience can have a rectifying effect very quickly.

DR. LUCIEN HANKS: Please clarify the notion of equilibrium a little more. Does it imply that interpersonal relations are determined by anxiety-producing situations?

DR. SULLIVAN: People's resistance to learning anything in certain fields is amazing; we might call it "selective inattention." Time and again something will happen which anyone would interpret as making a change desirable, but a person can go on as if nothing impinged on him. His relation with eidetic people is such that, if he attended to these experiences we all see happen to him, it would involve shifts in the equilibrium to which he is accustomed. Equilibrium resists experience and keeps one from being reachable by what goes on around him.

QUESTION: The picture missing from the wall might be either a fear or anxiety situation, might it not?

DR. SULLIVAN: Yes, I have no way of knowing the extent to which it has personal reference, which will have to be discovered in each instance. But Dr. Levy emphasized novelty, and I have found that a sufficient degree of novelty will frighten anything. In some marginal situations it is hard to distinguish fear from anxiety. And sometimes one is anxious about being afraid, as in military service.

DR. L. K. FRANK: Is it anxiety about fear, or about other persons' reactions to manifestations of fear?

DR. SULLIVAN: The anxiety mechanisms as it is ordinarily manifested anticipates the other fellow's reaction. Sometimes, in an interview with a naive person, you may say, "What would I have thought, had you said what was in your mind?" Then you hear a statement of the anxiety—not *complete*, but very predictive. As the patient was about to say something he anticipated a conventional reaction on your part, which blocked it.

DR. FRANK: Wouldn't the reality of interpersonal relations become clearer if we reemphasize that the child has to grow up to live in a symbolic cultural world of meanings and values defined by other people? Therefore the whole problem of conduct is one in terms of what other people have said or will say about you, as they approve or disapprove. This relates to things we said before—namely, how the cultural agents—

family and others—transmit these definitions. Then the child takes them over and tries to approximate them. There's always a personal intervention in the definition.

DR. SULLIVAN: Something tangential to Dr. Frank's comment ought to be said here. So simple a thing as educational training can have the most disastrous consequences. For example, too much emphasis on toilet training may interfere with speech learning, as they are linked fairly closely. Where educational effort is applied before maturation justifies it, interpersonal interaction becomes vitally important to avoid anxiety. Otherwise a peculiarity of personality results which only fortunate later experience will correct.

QUESTION: Could we go back to the discussion about the Japanese who doesn't do something because he's afraid of being ridiculed, and who carries this around as an impulsion within himself?

DR. SULLIVAN: As I said in commenting on Dr. Benedict's book, shame is a derivative of anxiety, as guilt is an earlier inculcated derivative of anxiety. But anxiety is the mortar, you might say, that makes them both work.

Shame problems are more amenable to psychotherapy than guilt problems. Dr. Hanks' Area 1 consists of things that are impressed so early and so consistently that they act with that automatic character of the purely unconscious; whereas shame always has components that reach into the consciously accessible. Therefore, you might say that guilt enforces its dictates by shame. Both, of course, involve learning, as does all cultural evolution of personality. I regard this conception of anxiety as of profound importance.

QUESTION: Is the timing of habit training of most importance, or the attitudes of the parents administering it?

DR. SULLIVAN: Much habit training is impossible before a certain time. Anxiety-driven efforts to train habits before that time lend to complex deviations of personality which may never be studied by anthropologists.

Now as to methods: the crudest of all is education by anxiety, and the next crudest is education by avoidance of anxiety. A great deal of our socialization is moving from highly to less highly anxiety-laden things. In between is the educational effect of trial and success. You can't train a person to love anybody before he's pre-adolescent. You can get him to sound like it, to act so you can believe it. But there is no real basis, and if you stress it you get queer results, many of which become neuroses.

Then there's the effect of the method—what is the enforcing agency? If it's crude anxiety, learning is almost certain to be bad, because anxiety always opposes the satisfaction of needs. Anxiety is the least hygienic method of education, but it is an inevitable one. There is no parent who can escape the social pressure. They've got to produce children who can get by with other children—that's their anxiety. And the children take over anxiety in this field.

194

HENRY A. MURRAY

Research Planning: A Few Proposals

One recurrent strand in the long braided chronicle of science is the story of struggles for agreement among champions of incompatible conceptions. Although the courses of these struggles are marked by frequent failures, some partial, some complete, the enduring need for consensus has responded to failure by generating ever more effective rules of procedure—rules of observation, experimentation, conceptualization, validation, and communication —and today a vast amount of experience goes to show that loyalty to these methodological principles is very likely—more likely than disloyalty—to lead on to collectively satisfying goals.

Let us not forget that science is a cutural institution, a highly differentiated social enterprise, and that a would-be contributor has two tasks: 1, to construct the best possible formulations of accurately observed events, and 2, to convince his fellow architects that these formulations should be incorporated in the existing edifice of postulates and theories. The rules of procedure which have proved most successful in fulfilling these two tasks constitute the intellectual superego which scientific education is designed to inculcate. Just as the best type of moral superego consists of rules which are most conducive to mutually enjoyed and productive human relationships on the behavioral level, the best intellectual superego, one might say, is composed of rules which conduce to the most productive and mentally satisfying collaborations on the conceptual level.

Now, I propose, granted your forbearance, to masquerade for the next few minutes as an itinerant representative of this species of intellectual superego, not, let me hasten to say, because I have scrupulously obeyed its dictates and been rewarded, but because I have suffered from defying them. Thus I take after the man or, more commonly, the woman who, after two or three cacophonous marriages which terminated in divorce, elects the role of counselor in marital affairs. My object is merely to pour into the new bottles of basic social science some old wine from the vineyards of the more experienced and exact sciences, in the hope that small

195

doses of this heady distillate will serve to speed the maturation of our discipline.

Before attempting this exercise, let me forestall misunderstanding with an explicit statement of opinion on one issue. I believe that although there are a few general principles common to all intellectual superegos, every science requires a special type of superego, one that is suited to the peculiar nature of the objects and events that must be represented and explained. I believe, furthermore, that the structure of each superego should vary with the degree of development of the science which it governs. In the early stages of a discipline, or whenever phenomena of a novel sort are to be examined, an overall survey resulting in a few vaguely orienting ideas—such as might be produced by an imaginative mind with a loose and lenient superego—is often more useful than a meticulously precise study of a small segment of the field. My guess is that we would have no more than a fraction of the clarifying psychoanalytic concepts which are available today if Freud had had a highly developed scientific superego. Consequently, I am not inclined to favor the indoctrination of men of our profession with the methodological principles of physics, not only because these are not appropriate to the analysis and reconstruction of social events, but because the quantitative precision which they demand is likely to persuade a man to restrict his attention to some measurable—usually small and unimportant—part of a field of interaction, and so to step into the trap of misplaced concreteness.

Thus the intellectual superego I am partially and provisionally representing is not a high and mighty creed, but a rather primitive code, suited, I trust, to the present capacities of basic social scientists—psychologists, cultural anthropologists, and sociologists.

The title of this conference is sufficient designation of the kind of occurrences I have in mind as topic for research. I take it that we are interested not only in different forms of culture and how they are conserved by socialization and repetition, but also in the sudden or gradual abandonment, the creation and the integration of common forms of feeling and behavior. We are intent on studying the modes and products of interactions between unconventional individuals and the conventional majority. Finally we want to know the effect of the whole cultural system of each society on the health, happiness, and development of its members.

Since studies of this sort call for the estimation of a multiplicity of variables and the observation of many interrelated patterns, I shall confine my remarks to multiform, multidisciplinary, collaborative researches.

The random proposals I have to offer will be arranged under four headings: conceptual scheme, strategic hypotheses, tactics, and research staff.

Conceptual Scheme. The aim of a scientist is to fashion the conceptual and technical tools which will enable him to analyze any event or any coherent sequence of events into its constituent elements and, then, to recombine these elements into a sufficient representation of the observed phenomena. In an ideal model nothing essential to an understanding of the occurrence is omitted, nothing that is not strictly relevant is included.

Having learned how to divide the incessant flow of human events into natural units of interaction, to circumscribe space-time fields (Lewin's ovals) that are susceptible of thorough and accurate observation, the social scientist's first task is to find the best way of analyzing these fields, that is, to decide which elements should be abstracted from each concrete totality. Just as a mapmaker, before traversing a given region, will list each kind of object—lake, river, mountain, road, town, church, historic site—which he thinks should be portrayed symbolically in his map, so should the social scientist built a conceptual scheme which includes all the elements (and their attributes) that require discrimination in observing and interpreting human behavior.

Whether aware of it or not, every man has floating in his head a miscellany of woolly, fuzzy-edged notions which are influential in determining what he will involuntarily notice, what he will intentionally look for, and what he will remember and report. The scientist's office is to screen these determinants, reject some, accept others, to create and to refine, and finally to bring forth a cluster of clearly defined variables. Thus will he provide himself with the best obtainable guaranty that in performing his primary function —that of observation—his perceptions will be sharply focussed on the significant features of behavior and not distracted by irrelevant details.

Which variables are selected for definition will depend not only on the topic and purpose of the research, but on the investigator's assumptions, on the conception of reality which comes natural to him or which he has consciously and explicitly adopted. It is a man's basic conception of reality which determines his mode of analysis and hence its end-products, the elements with which he deals. Today we are fortunate in having at our disposal a number of abstracting systems—magnificent constructions which are still in progress—and we should not complain overmuch if these systems are in certain respects discordant with each other, and taken individually are either vague and unrefined, or applicable to only a limited range of situations. Hull's admirable achievement stands out as the most finely differentiated, the most logically constructed, the most self-consistent, and very probably the most adequate for the kind of rigidly controlled phenomena with which it deals; but, as far as I can judge, it is still deficient in comprehensiveness: a large variety of important human experiences has yet to be embraced by its net of concepts.

The sensational Freudian system, on the other hand, is notable for the significance and strangeness of the occurrences which it is capable of interpreting, its range of application, the universality of its concepts, its often relevant mode of dividing the personality into id, ego, and superego, its detailed account of the transmutations of the ever-restive sex drive. No doubt it is the most adequate set of theories we possess for the understanding of many critical human states and symptoms. Its formulations, however, never approximate completeness. Much of what is obvious, healthy, and creative is disregarded. It provides no place for a number of environmental determinants and distinguishes only two drives—sex and aggression. In Freud's system there is no formal recognition of hunger, envy, and ambition, of the drives for money and possessions, for friendship and association, for dominance and power, for appreciation and prestige. Most analysts, however, have noticed that aggression is as commonly aroused by the frustration of one of these motivating forces as it is by the frustration of the sex instinct. Despite steady progress by Hartmann, Kris, Loewenstein,[1] and others, psychoanalytic theory

[1]See, for example, Hartmann, H., and Kris, E., "The Genetic Approach in Psychoanalysis," in *The Psychoanalytic Study of the Child*, Vol. 1, New

is still largely undifferentiated.

Neither the Hullian nor the Freudian scheme is suitable for representing complex social situations such as this conference, the field which has been created by the present gathering. For this we must turn to Lewin, whose system is comprehensive, fairly coherent, susceptible of differentiation, and reasonably successful in exhibiting the chief components of overt human interactions. It is weak where the Freudian scheme is strong—in explaining the internal proceedings of personality—and it is vague where the Hullian scheme is rigorous—in accounting for the details of tactical learning—but, taken in conjunction with these other two, Lewin's mode of thought provides a very promising foundation for further speculative developments.

I have diverged from the appointed path. It was not my intention to discuss the pros and cons of this or that cluster of abstractions, but, first, to draw attention to the confusion of tongues, to the disorder—I shall not say chaos—among our symbols of discourse, and, second, to prescribe an old family remedy.

On the theoretical level we are living in a land of plenty but are unnecessarily embarrassed by the circulation of different terms for approximately the same concept (*cf.* instinct, drive, need, purpose, desire, wish, intention, and motive; sentiment and attitude; value, cathexis, and valence), by the use of one term for different concepts (ego, status, institution), by numerous overlapping concepts (status and role, superego and ego ideal, purpose and goal, dependence and need for security), and, more generally, by the elusiveness of almost all our notions. Let one illustration suffice: the word "ego" is most commonly used to refer to a slowly developing governmental structure of the personality, which is characterized by the attribute of consciousness, and by the capacity for objectivity (reality sense), rationality, emotional control, foresight, systematic planning, persistence of effort, the fulfillment of verbal commitments, and so forth. But "ego" is also used by psychoanalysts and psychologists alike as synonymous with "self", and in various hyphenated words has such connotations as self-

York, 1945; and Hartmann, H., Kris, E., and Loewenstein, R. M., "Comments on the Formation of Psychic Structure", in *The Psychoanalytic Study of the Child*, Vol. 2, New York, 1946.

interest, self-centeredness, and self-esteem. Ego-centrism, scarcely distinguishable from narcism, is considered to be maximal in infancy, that is, at the time when the ego (in the first sense), is minimal. "Ego instincts" has been used to denote a shadowy fellowship of drives that includes hunger and ambition (craving for omnipotence). More recently, psychologists have been speaking of "ego-involvement" when they wished to describe the state of a man who is emotionally committed to a task because his prestige or self-esteem will be affected by the outcome of his effort.

Surely without taxing our brains we could list many other specific sources of recurrent failures to communicate, and yet we have been content—and I am no exception—to converse in this Tower of Babel as if we were ignorant of the fact that the solution of our difficulties lay near at hand.

My first proposal, then, is that social scientists—those with the requisite disposition and talent—devote themselves, more resolutely than they have so far, to the building of a comprehensive system of concepts which are defined not only operationally but in relation to each other. The latter is essential to a complete exposition because, since none of the entities which we isolate in thought is isolated in nature, the manifestations of each entity vary with the character, strength, and position of the associated entities.

A more modest proposal would be that planners of researches take pains to define operationally and relationally variables which are pertinent to the topic of their investigation.

Although knowledge of operational definitions is now widespread, the number of social scientists who are scrupulously putting this knowledge into practice is astonishingly small. No wonder that psychoanalytic theory is still a vague and ambiguous mythology.

Except when experimenting in a strictly controlled field, we do not require rigorous operational definitions such as are necessary in the physical sciences, but if we purpose to grow beyond puberty we must bring our concepts much closer to the subjective and objective realities which we are capable of distinguishing. For us the definition of a variable is perhaps sufficiently operational if it includes 1, a list of its different manifestations, and 2, a description of the ways in which these manifestations are discriminated or measured. The first (1) might be called a "criterial" definition since it consists of the various criteria (signs, symptoms, indices) by which the activity of the given variable, or the occurrence of the designated condition, may be inferred, and in terms of which, if possible, its intensity or strength can be roughly estimated. Such a definition is tantamount to specifying—for the sake of clarity of thought and communication—the permissible grounds for every interpretation or judgment. It describes the subjective and objective facts which justify the diagnosis, say, of anxiety, of superego activity, of emotional stability, of introversion, or of high intelligence. If one scientist assesses intelligence in terms of the *difficulty* of the problems which can be solved regardless of time, and another scientist measures it in terms of the speed and accuracy of solving *simple* problems, the two men will not infrequently disagree in their estimates and this may give rise to futile, and perhaps bitter, arguments. The standard cure, as you all know, is to call for statements of criteria and thus very simply to reveal that each man has been measuring correctly a different manifestation of the variable or, if you will, a different variable. A hundred current misunderstandings could be resolved by the application of this remedy. Will we persist in shunning it?

An operational definition of an entity also includes a description of the situations and techniques by which it is elicited and, if possible, measured. This applies particularly to the use of various diagnostic instruments. Introversion as discriminated by the Rorschach will not correspond exactly to introversion as estimated by listening to free associations or by administering and scoring a given questionnaire. Although such technical devices are being used more and more, simple observation of behavior and interpretation of subjective reports are still, and will no doubt always be, the most common social scientific operation (supplemented when possible by a moving picture camera with sound track). Hence, for most work, the recording instrument will be the scientist himself, a complex organization of needs, beliefs, presuppositions, and prejudices. Although the ideal aim of operational definitions is to eliminate unknown and distorting processes in the scientist's mind, this is unattainable in practice, and so, theoretically, a complete definition of an entity should include an account of how it is appraised by different types of scientific personalities.

201

This point will be mentioned later in connection with the problem of assessing members of the research staff.

The task of defining each entity in relation to other entities is tantamount to the formulation of the fundamental postulates which transform a mere aggregate of concepts into a theoretical system. This matter is too complicated to be discussed here but the mere mention of it at this point serves as a bridge of thought to my next topic.

Strategic Hypotheses. In recommending that we social scientists refrain from undertaking any research project until we have formulated one or more hypotheses to be verified, I am merely proposing a wider adoption of the policy which Newton introduced to replace the laborious method of indiscriminate observation and induction set forth in Bacon's *Novum Organum*, "a method which, if consistently pursued," Whitehead assures us, "would have left science where it found it." Newton's practice has been followed with conspicuous success by a long procession of experimentalists in the physical and biological sciences, and in certain special fields of psychology, but it has yet to be accepted on a broad front by social scientists. Most of our investigations have been of the exploratory, fact-collecting type, and of these not many have yielded generalizations of high subsuming power. Conspicuous exceptions might be mentioned: Lewin's architectonic researches, the Hull-inspired work of Dollard and Miller (and associates) on frustration and aggression and on learning, and, in sociology, the recent attempts of Leighton,[2] Kluckhohn,[3] and others to crystallize their observations in the form of definite principles, postulates, or theorems.

To formulate an hypothesis which can be tested is to make a direct, though tentative, contribution to the development of science, to offer a stone for the building of the temple, the edifice of concepts and theories which we envisage as the ultimate desideratum of our vocation.

Composing a set of hypotheses amounts to no less than the erec-

[2]Leighton, A. H., *The Governing of Men*, Princeton, 1945.

[3]Kluckhohn, C., "Group Tensions: Analysis of a Case History," Ch. XIV in *Approaches to National Unity*, ed. by Bryson, L., Finkelstein, L., MacIver, R. M., New York, 1945.

202

tion of a clearly defined goal and hence of a focus for orientation, a point of reference for judging the suitability of available or devisable techniques. Such a goal is the best assurance that science will be advanced through proofs of one or more significant propositions.

Too many researches are undertaken, I submit, with no expectation in mind except that it would be "interesting" to study this or that group of people, or that it would be "interesting" to administer this or that battery of tests to some complaint population. It may, of course, be advisable, in dealing with a society or with a class of phenomena about which little is known, to perform a preliminary survey in order to acquire enough data for constructing verifiable hypotheses; but in most cases, I would suppose, present knowledge provides ample ground for tentative generalizations. Today we are surfeited with facts; what we need are the saving modes of analysis and reconstruction.

Another advantage of hypothesis-making is that verified deductions are deservedly accorded a higher scientific status than logical inductions. One feels more certain of a theory which leads to a correct prediction of behavior in a specified situation than of a theory which provides a plausible explanation of behavior after it has occurred. The slightest acquaintance with the childhood history of science will convince us of the almost limitless power of the human mind to produce explanations of events and rationalizations to support them, which, though almost wholly defective or meaningless, satisfy educated people and survive uncontradicted for generations. As an illustration of the capability of reason, recall the prodigious feat of Goropius Bacanus, a learned Jesuit of Antwerp, who succeeded in proving that Adam and Eve spoke Dutch in Paradise. And as one of many examples of the enduring power of error take, in the field of medicine, the fourteen hundred years' reign of Galen's misconceptions. The best safeguard against the wiles of imaginative thought and against intellectual inflation is the scientific ritual of prediction and validation.

If, before planning a research project, we spend whatever time is necessary defining and evaluating alternative hypotheses, there will be less likelihood of our committing ourselves for a long season to a relatively trivial investigation. The secret of success is a *strategic* hypothesis, that is, an hypothesis which, if verified, will stand as a basic proposition or will constitute the logically next step in the systematic development or validation of a theoretical system, or which will open up new fields for significant research and discovery.

There is unanimity, I trust, in our evaluations of the peril of the present human situation, a worldwide condition of mounting resentment and belligerency that is moving towards explosion, an explosion which will almost certainly inaugurate a course of unexampled regression and destruction. Thus among several possible futures is the disintegration of the social structure on which the very existence of science depends, and, if we are devoted to humanity or to our vocation, it is imperative that we apply, as physicians do, whatever wisdom, knowledge, and skills we have or can acquire to the task of preventing this fatality, of checking, if not curing, the present ominous epidemic of antagonisms. Consequently, for our time, a "strategic hypothesis" might well be defined as one which is strategic not only in respect to the advancement of knowledge and theory, but in respect to the advancement of fellowship, social integration, and ideological synthesis.

As Yeats has written: "Things fall apart; the center cannot hold; mere anarchy is loosed upon the world . . . The best lack all conviction, while the worst are full of passionate intensity." Things are held together by mutual affection and moral conduct—social morality being nothing more or less than the principles governing the creation and preservation of the most harmonious and rewarding human relations, interpersonal and international. Hence, the crucial task today is the formulation and pragmatic validation of a regenerated system of morality and the discovery of the means by which the system can be represented to the growing child so that it becomes exemplified in action. Scientists who have been disposed to live in order to find truth must now find truth in order to live: the problems to which they dedicate their energies should, as far as possible, be relevant to the supreme goal—social reconstruction. Not only is this direction of effort necessary for mere survival, but, we can safely predict, it will elicit and be furthered by more zest in the investigator and more social encouragement and financial backing than will any enterprise which is irresponsible in respect to humanity's most terrible predicament.

Tactics. Research planning calls for the settlement of many questions which will not be discussed here. There is the question of the locus of the enterprise, whether it is to be Siam, Sicily, or Sioux City. This is commonly decided by some extraneous factor such as the location of the organization or unit to which the investigator belongs. Then there is the matter of the subjects to be studied, whether they should be representative members of the whole community, children of a certain age range, students at a college, or juvenile delinquents. Also, there is the closely related problem of the type of fields, the class of actions and interactions, which will constitute the focus of attention. All these decisions will be influenced, if not wholly determined, by the hypotheses to be tested; and, vice versa, the subjects and situations that are accessible to investigation within the sphere of the scientist's job or function will dictate to some extent the selection of hypotheses.

Here perhaps is the best place to introduce another suggestion, namely, that good objects for study at the present time are small groups evolving modes of procedure (transitory sub-cultures) as they carry on, in a series of sessions, cooperative or competitive undertakings. One advantage of a small group is that *every* member of it can be studied separately and intensively until enough understanding has been acquired to allow for predictions of the behavior of each man when called upon to join with the others in accomplishing a common task.

Another important question for decision is the time-scope of the research. Shall we study the present structures of personalities and groups, or shall we study records and memories of the past in order to understand the present, or shall we attempt to validate predictions of things to come?

Strictly speaking, the present does not exist; it is always being devoured by the past. Nevertheless, as Carl L. Becker[4] has remarked, "we must have a present; and so we get one by robbing the past, by holding on to the most recent events and pretending that they all belong to our immediate perceptions." This is especially true for a social scientist, who is not chiefly interested in the more stable features of the environment—the structure of cities, machines and tools, the anatomical characteristics of people,

[4]Becker, C. L., *The Heavenly City of the Eighteenth Century Philosophers*, New Haven, 1932, p. 119.

etc.—but rather in processes, patterns of processes, and interactions of patterns of processes, none of which exists in the flash of a moment, but each takes time, as does a melody, to exhibit itself; and so the tiniest bit of reality is an occurrence which spreads over at least a fraction of a second and the beginning of it has perished before the end is reached. Social scientists are in the habit of telescoping a long sequence of organizations of such minute processes into a single and so-called "present" event, or proceeding. The duration of one of these proceedings, or units of interaction, is what a philosopher would term the "specious present." By tacit consent the specious present is often extended to cover a time-span of months or even years. For example, a social scientist who spends several weeks or months studying an individual or several months or years studying a community may, after ordering his findings into a formulation, refer to it as the subject's *present* personality or as the community's *present* structure, despite the fact that during the period of examination more or less discernible transformations have been taking place.

Necessarily, every research will start with an examination of the specious present, of the present structure of selected personalities and/or of the present structure of some group of which these personalities are members. Besides the observation of interactions under controlled and uncontrolled conditions and the collection of subjective reports of the covert processes (feelings and thoughts) that occurred during these interactions, we have, as technical methods, numerous tests of knowledge, ability and aptitude, projective tests which reveal structural properties as well as a few imaginal elements and forms, and questionnaires which elicit information about beliefs, sentiments, and attitudes. In addition, there is the interview, which in any form, directed or undirected, is generally accorded first place among clinical procedures. Under the rubric "interview" we could include the questioning of informants with the aim of acquiring more knowledge either about the particular personalities that are being studied or about the standards and common practices of their community.

I am assuming that a thorough study of selected individuals will necessarily constitute a good part not only of any research that is concerned with the relationships of personality and culture, but also of any research concerned primarily with culture, since the stuff that conserves and develops culture is embedded in human heads and one must seek it there. The observation of behavior is essential but not sufficient; it is necessary to discover how culture-carriers define different common situations, and what are their cherished expectations and satisfactions, and what mythology controls their thoughts and feelings. Generally the best plan is to examine many people superficially and a few with penetration, remembering that most anti-cultural forces are not only covert but largely unconscious.

I would propose that in studying personality the multiform system of diagnosis and assessment be used whenever possible. Any system may be called "multiform" which includes several different types of procedures and several procedures of the same type for detecting the presence—and, if possible, for estimating the strength—of each major variable of personality. This does not call for ten times as many procedures as there are variables, because many procedures are capable of eliciting a multiplicity of variables.

Mention of the interview carries us, by an habitual association of ideas, to the topic of the past history—the past history of the person interviewed or the past history of his group—because it is chiefly through interviewing (supplemented, when feasible, by an autobiography) that one obtains the chronicle of development which is so relevant to an understanding of current patterns of activity. Very rarely are the topics of an interview limited to the specious present. Although, as Lewin argued, every factor which is required for a complete formulation of an event is operating in the field at the moment—it belongs to the present rather than to the past—some of these present components are neither conscious to the subject nor manifest to the observer, and hence must be inferred, and for inferences of this sort the most substantially supporting facts are obtainable from the past history. Biographical data, in short, is frequently very helpful in interpreting an observed proceeding.

Since the psychoanalysts, by elaborating a long, devious, and difficult technique for resurrecting traces of buried experiences, have acquired a monopoly, one might say, of this most successful mode of explanatory research, I would suggest that most workers in the area of personality and culture use only so much of the

207

psychoanalytic technique as is necessary to formulate the specious present, and devote themselves largely to the refinement of various modes of prediction research, less treacherous than explanatory research. Predictive research includes, at one extreme, studies of the reactions of different subjects to the same situation, and, at the other, studies of changes of reaction during a long series of efforts to cope with a certain type of situation.

Researches of the first sort are limited to the observation of one or two proceedings, with the environment controlled or uncontrolled; and for this an almost ideal technique is the repeated examination of projections of a moving picture reel—say, of a partially controlled psychodrama or of a partially controlled operating group. In conceptualizing an occurrence of this sort we have Lewin to help us, even though he himself never studied the personalities or the current covert processes of his subjects as required by the field theory which he expounded.

Instead of predicting a subject's actions during one exposure to a situation, we can predict his actions at stated times over a period of recurrent exposures. In short, we can investigate the developmental process—conditioning, canalization, learning, socialization, the acquisition of culture—as it occurs under different conditions. We can study the genesis of complexes, the gradual achievement of self-control, the stages in the construction of some complex object, the waxing and waning of a friendship. We can attempt to predict what effect culture will have on a growing personality and what effect he will have on it.

Now, before bringing the topic of tactics to a close, let me add two further proposals; one, that we organize the procedures of each investigation according to an experimental design which will permit us at the end to treat our data, so far as feasible, in an approved statistical fashion, and two, that we include in our system of procedures, techniques for measuring the typical misperceptions and misapperceptions of each member of the staff. It is standard practice in science to determine the relative accuracy of each instrument of precision. In our discipline the instrument in most cases is the scientist himself.

Research Staff. The title of this conference is evidence of a shared realization that personality abstracted from cultural forms and cultural forms abstracted from personality are errors of mis-

208

placed concreteness. The plain truth is that we are in process of forming a new discipline, basic social science. Because the different viewpoints and techniques which are relevant to this emerging science had different origins and were reared in isolation, the present enterprise calls for a multidisciplinary approach, the collaboration of sociologists, cultural anthropologists, clinical psychologists, and psychoanalysts. But the time is not far distant when these terms will designate not members of different disciplines, but specialists working within one discipline, that is to say, within the frame of a common theoretical system.

In any event, the carrying forward of a substantial piece of research in the area of personality and culture, either now or in the more distant future, will call for a staff of diverse specialists; because, even if basic social scientists should become equally proficient with all techniques, the adoption of a multiform system of procedures will require that each worker be assigned a special function, at least for the duration of a given research project.

I should like to make a plea for a staff that is not only diverse in skills but diverse in respect to theoretical convictions. For, not only do we want to bring all available truth to bear upon our problems, but we want to contribute as much as possible to the rearing of a conceptual system which integrates all valid theories, and it is easier for men of different persuasions to achieve unity when engaged in a common task than when working independently.

I am not oblivious of the possible unhappy consequences of clashes on the theoretical level, nor am I insensible to the advantages enjoyed by a conceptually homogeneous unit. If harmony of thought and coordination of action throughout the course of a single research project were superordinate aims, all of us would favor homogeneity—a group composed entirely of Lewinians, of orthodox Freudians, of Radians, of Rankians, of Reikians, or of Reichians—but such a policy could serve only as an encouragement to ever greater differentiation, if not to fanatical sectarianism, at a time when integration and synthesis are most needed. Therefore, in selecting the professional staff, I suggest that we embrace as much diversity as is compatible with effectiveness and resolve to create order out of chaos.

A good deal of current discord is the inevitable result of the fact that scientists, separated from one another, have been looking with different aims at different subjects in different situations. Concepts designed by an anthropologist to interpret the religious beliefs and rites of Tahitians, concepts proposed by a psychologist to account for the political sentiments of the American people, and concepts invented by a psychoanalyst to explain and cure neurotic illness, are not likely to be concordant. One obvious remedy is to organize research projects in which three or four able exponents of pertinent theories will collaborate in studying the same subjects with a shared aim in mind.

Another impediment to the achievement of a common theoretical system are the diverse conceptual fixations which bind our thoughts. Some of these divergences can be ascribed to deep-rooted temperamental differences, but others have been determined by circumstances and they should be susceptible of modification by circumstances. Rigidity, for instance, is a property of one's intellections which can often be diminished in degree by working as a member of a congenial group. The chief hindrance perhaps is the scientist's self-esteem cleaving to the concepts which he himself has invented. This, in some measure, is a consequence of the overvaluation of individuality and self-sufficiency in our western world. Many a scientist has been led to the fateful conviction that he must win fame as the creator of an original theory or distinguish himself as the leader of a new sect. In contrast to such men are those of a less adventurous cast who are disposed to cling to a theory out of loyalty to its admired founder. Some of my psychoanalytical friends have yet to realize that they are doing a most un-Freudian thing in conforming to Freud; for Freud, assuredly, was no conformist.

The great thing for each of us to appreciate today is that our objective is a common language. With this firmly in mind a company of dedicated workers, no matter how divergent at the start, has a fair chance of achieving unanimity, at least in respect to the concepts which are applicable to the phenomena they are studying.

It is harder for social scientists to do this than for physical scientists, and harder still if they invade, as I have recommended, the realm of values, expecting to serve as physicians to society. Here, the essential requirement is the ability to distinguish a sentiment from a fact and the practice of announcing one's sentiments

210

at the very start. This calls for integrity of a degree not yet attained by American social scientists. In the last decade all of us deplored the corruption of the German psychologists whose researches were set up to prove the superiority of the Aryan race, but it is salutary to note that all our own findings have unanimously confirmed the American system of values. It was shown, for instance, that democratic is superior to autocratic leadership, and that people with anti-Semitic tendencies have despicably distorted personalities. Pro-Semitism was not studied, partly, I suspect, because any analysis of personality as conducted today, and this is worth considering very seriously, represents a man as less balanced and less estimable than he really is. Anyhow, it is obvious that the outcome of many research projects has been determined in a critical fashion by the sentiments of the men who conducted them, and if we social scientists want to be respected as impartial observers and interpreters we must estimate the influence of our own sentiments by appropriate techniques and make whatever corrections are required. A scientist who is incapable of doing this is not fitted to engage, except as a minor technician, in an evaluative study of culture.

Almost everything I have said so far—stale ale to most of you —bears upon the problem of the effective collaboration of specialists of diverse skills and convictions, scientific and ideological. For example, one of the chief purposes of operational definitions is intelligibility of communications among members of the staff. This happens to be one of the best ways of preventing the waste of time, the countless confusions and disagreements which inevitably arise in the course of any investigation that has been hurriedly undertaken with nothing more than a fragmentary misshapen conceptual scheme.

Since there are many other determinants, besides those mentioned in this paper, of effectiveness and ineffectiveness of cooperative activity, some of which are only vaguely understood, and since human relations stand first among the objects of our professional concern, I should like to make one further and final proposal: that members of the research staff, during the preliminary formulating period, join in a systematic study of themselves in the process of working towards agreement. The purpose of this piece of action research would be not only to bring conceptual

211

order out of disorder and so to facilitate the harmonious progress of the common enterprise, but to contribute to the solution of World Problem No. 1, the harmonization of conflicting ideologies. By definition we are experts in social relations, and yet the record of our own relations as scientists—more particularly as fellow psychoanalysts—over the last twenty years looks as if our expert knowledge had been a dangerous thing. Mr. Anybody might say: social relationist cure thyself. I am not speaking from the pulpit —for my own relationships have been abominable—but from the saw-dust trail that I am walking, intent on reformation. Probably I have progressed no further than the young fellow who said, "if I have done anything I am sorry for, I am willing to be forgiven."

A BRIEF EPILOGUE

By way of brief epilogue, the editors offer a few comments on problems and issues touched upon in the foregoing papers.

The contributors, representing anthropology, social psychology, psychiatry and sociology, seem agreed upon the value of interdisciplinary approaches. At the same time, as they would be the first to admit, interdisciplinary cooperation is hampered by the particular interests and viewpoints, by the differing sets of lenses, furnished by each person's more or less specialized training.

Some of these differences are reflected in Dr. Bidney's paper on definitions and in the discussion following it. Yet all the participants apparently agree with Dr. Murphy that a reciprocal interplay exists between culture and personality, and that terms like "psychocultural" are useful in indicating this reciprocity, as Dr. Frank suggests.

On the other hand they seem less enthusiastic about Dr. Murphy's insistence that culture and personality are "two aspects of one phenomenon." Perhaps such a phenomenon is too hard to conceptualize. At any rate most investigators proceed on the assumption that culture and personality are differentiable. This is suggested by frequent concern with the problem of discerning which determinants in a given situation are attributable to personality and which to culture. In general, as shown by the interest in Dr. Hanks' paper, the participants seem to agree that institutionalized behavior, showing little intra-group variation, mirrors the culture while the more variable, individualized behavior reflects personality rather than the culture pattern.

Almost inevitably, the psychologist and anthropologist employ different frames of reference with respect to culture-personality relationships. The former addresses himself to the individual and thinks in terms of a single life span; he seeks to discover which aspects of personality are affected by which aspects of culture. The anthropologist, by contrast, operates within a larger framework; he focuses on the group rather than the individual

213

and upon several generations rather than a single life span. He shows relatively little interest in analyzing either personality or culture since his gaze is fixed primarily upon the relationship between uniformities of personality and the culture pattern as a whole—and upon cross-cultural comparisons. However, this distinction in approach must not be overdrawn; there are many exceptions. For example, Dr. Linton's paper on status personality and social role harmonizes well with the social psychological treatment of subcultural influences by Drs. Komarovsky and Sargent.

The greatest bone of contention between anthropologists and psychologists appears to be quantification. Speaking for many psychologists Dr. Klineberg makes a stirring plea for the introduction of more exact methods into field studies lest, without sampling methods and some degree of quantification, all sorts of overgeneralized and erroneous interpretations may be made. Anthropologists, notably Dr. Bateson, answer that quantification and exactness are not synonymous, and that statistical treatment of anthropological data is well nigh impossible. The psychologist, trained in the use of rigorous scientific methods, has had some success in using experimental and quantitative procedures for studying personality and social behavior. On the other hand, the anthropologist doubts that such techniques can be applied to the study of whole cultures, whether literate or non-literate. The issue is far from settled; it can be clarified only by careful comparisons of the value of different techniques used in actual field study, as the papers of Drs. Kluckhohn and Murray suggest.

Without doubt all participants in the conference are interested in dynamic interpretations of the culture-personality relationship. The three psychiatric papers present somewhat different views. Dr. Kardiner's "psychodynamics" is more Freudian than the others and stresses the extreme importance of child care disciplines in determining "basic personality structure." Dr. Fromm includes a wider variety of cultural and social influences as determinants of "social character." Dr. Sullivan's chief concern is with social rather than cultural influences, as shown by his stress upon interpersonal relations. Few of the conference participants seem willing to express a preference for one or another of these interpretations, possibly because of a lack of psychiatric training.

However, the discussions reveal frequent use of psychiatric concepts such as frustration, anxiety, and defense mechanisms, and a growing acquaintance with psychiatric literature. This is probably the greatest single change in the studies and interpretations of today compared with those of ten or fifteen years ago.

The papers and discussions alike reveal ever-increasing acceptance of new methods and research tools. One senses general agreement as to the value of biographical and linguistic approaches, of projective techniques, and of aids such as photography, moving pictures and sound-recording devices. Some though not all of the participants in the conference would follow Drs. Kluckhohn and Klineberg in their advocacy of time- and behavior-sampling and of certain psychometric tests. Best of all, perhaps, one notes a growing interest in validating these and other techniques by such standards as practicability and usefulness of insights provided.

Proposals for future interdisciplinary research are summarized in Dr. Murray's paper, in which he discusses current needs ranging from conceptualizations and hypotheses all the way to tactics and practices on field trips. The conference, in effect, made a beginning of implementing Dr. Murray's proposals. It showed that students of culture and personality, despite differing backgrounds and viewpoints, can learn from each other and can look forward to an increasing degree of mutual respect and cooperation.

THE CONTRIBUTORS

David Bidney is Research Associate of the Viking Fund. He has taught the Philosophy of Science in the Graduate School of Yale University and has delivered seminar lectures on Theoretical Anthropology at Stanford University, the University of California at Berkeley and Columbia University. His publications include: *The Psychology and Ethics of Spinoza*, 1940, and contributions on culture theory to the symposia of the Conference on Science, Philosophy and Religion, 1946, 1947 and 1948.

Erich Fromm is chairman of the faculty at the William Alanson White Institute of Psychiatry, and teaches also at Yale University and Bennington College. He received his Ph.D. at Heidelberg, and later studied at the Berlin Psychoanalytic Institute and lectured at the University of Frankfort. He is the author of *The Dogma of Christ*, 1930, *Escape from Freedom*, 1941, *Man for Himself*, 1947, and co-author of *Authority and Family*, 1934.

Lucien M. Hanks, Jr., is Associate Professor of Psychology at Bennington College. He has done field studies of the Blackfoot Indians with his anthropologist wife, Jane Richardson Hanks. During the war he did psychological work in Ceylon and Burma with the Office of Strategic Services. He edited a 1947 number of the Journal of Social Issues, entitled "Social Research in Political Decision", and is preparing a volume on governmental relations with the Blackfoot Indians.

George Herzog is Professor of Anthropology at Indiana University; previously he was for many years in the department of Anthropology at Columbia University. His major interests are linguistics, music and folklore. He has published *Jabo Proverbs from Liberia*, 1936, and is co-author of *The Cow-Tail Switch—West African Native Stories*, 1947.

Abram Kardiner is a practicing psychoanalyst and Associate Clinical Professor of Psychiatry in the Columbia University School of Medicine. He has for many years conducted seminars on culture and personality at Columbia University. His publications include *The Individual and His Society*, 1939, *The Traumatic Neuroses of War*, 1941, and *Psychological Frontiers of Society*, 1945; he is co-author of *War Stress and Neurotic Illness*, 1947.

Otto Klineberg is Associate Professor of Psychology at Columbia University, at present on leave as Director of the UNESCO project on tensions affecting international understanding. During the recent war he

217

served with the Federal Communications Commission, the Office of War Information and the U. S. War Department. He was Visiting Professor of Psychology at the University of Sao Paulo, Brazil, 1945-1947. His publications include *Race Differences*, 1935, *Negro Intelligence and Selective Migration*, 1935, and *Social Psychology*, 1940; he edited *Characteristics of the American Negro*, 1944.

Clyde Kluckhohn is Professor of Anthropology and Director of the Russian Research Center at Harvard University. He has worked in psychology and psychiatry, and has served as a consultant to the U. S. Indian Service, as co-chief of the Joint Morale Survey of O.W.I. and Military Intelligence Service. He was elected President of the American Anthropological Association in 1947. He is co-author of *The Navaho*, 1946, *Children of the People*, 1947, and *Personality in Nature, Society and Culture*, 1948, and author of *Mirror for Man*, 1948.

Mirra Komarovsky is Associate Professor of Sociology at Barnard College, Columbia University. She was formerly Research Associate of the Columbia Council for Research in the Social Sciences. She is co-author of *Leisure, a Suburban Study*, 1936, and *The Unemployed Man and His Family*, 1940.

Ralph Linton is Sterling Professor of Anthropology at Yale University and Chairman of the Division of Anthropology of the National Academy of Sciences. His publications include *The Tanala, a Hill Tribe of Madagascar*, 1933, *The Study of Man*, 1936, *The Cultural Background of Personality*, 1945. He edited *The Science of Man in the World Crisis*, 1945, and *The Rest of the World*, 1949.

Gardner Murphy is Professor and Chairman of the Department of Psychology at the College of the City of New York. Previously he was for many years a member of the Psychology Department at Columbia University. He was formerly President of the American Psychological Association. He is co-author of *Experimental Social Psychology*, 1938, editor of *Human Nature and Enduring Peace*, 1945, and author of *Historical Introduction to Modern Psychology*, 1929 and 1949, and of *Personality*, 1947.

Henry A. Murray is Professor in the Department of Social Relations at Harvard University; for many years he was Director of the Harvard Psychological Clinic. During World War II he headed the assessment center of the Office of Strategic Services and was later awarded the Legion of Merit. He is the author of *Explorations in Personality*, 1937, and co-author of *Assessment of Men*, 1948, and *Personality in Nature, Society and Culture*, 1948.

Harry Stack Sullivan (1893-1949) was a practicing psychiatrist and founder of the William Alanson White Institute of Psychiatry. He served, just before the recent war, as psychiatric consultant to the director of the selective service system. He was editor of *Psychiatry* and author of *Conceptions of Modern Psychiatry*, 1947. He died in Paris on January 15, 1949, while attending an executive council meeting of the World Mental Health Foundation which he helped to establish.

THE EDITORS

S. Stansfeld Sargent is Associate Professor of Psychology at Barnard College, Columbia University. He is the author of *Basic Teachings of the Great Psychologists*, 1944, and of a forthcoming textbook in Social Psychology.

Marian W. Smith, of the Anthropology Department of Columbia University, is now on a field trip to India. She has done field work among American Indians and Sikhs in the Pacific Northwest. Editor and former President of the American Ethnological Society, she is author of the *Puyallup-Nisqually*, 1940, and edited *Indians of the Urban Northwest*, 1949.